LANDING IN THE RIGHT PLACE

Building Family, Career & Community in Fort Wayne

Mac Parker

Copyright © 2020 Maclyn Parker

All rights reserved

No part of this book may be reproduced, or stored in a retrieval system, or transmitted in any form or by any means, electronic, mechanical, photocopying, recording, or otherwise, without express written permission of the publisher.

ISBN-13: 9798648228757

Cover design by: Art Painter
Cover photo by: Mollie Shutt
Author photo by: Neal Bruns
Printed in the United States of America

To my wife Pat and my daughters Pamela, Carole, and Kristi who have made the greater part of this journey with me.

CONTENTS

Title Page
Copyright
Dedication
Prologue
MOMENTOUS TIMES 1
BASKETBALL CRAZY 31
PICKING UP SOME POLISH 47
THE GREAT ADVENTURE 65
LAW & MARRIAGE 86
U.S. NAVY 106
WITHIN AN EYELASH 135
RETURN TO INDIANA 150
ON OUR OWN 185
FLINT & WALLING 199
THE INBALCO CASE 210
BRANCHING OUT 220
COCKROACH BASKETBALL 236
BIG BUMPS IN THE ROAD 257
STILL MOVIN' ALONG 272
INTO OUR NINETIES 282
Epilogue 305
About The Author 311

PROLOGUE

This book started out as a few short write-ups beginning in 2003. When I reminisced about some of the events of my life or places our family had visited, I began to put these ideas down on paper, thinking that grandchildren might take an interest in them down the road. When I had accumulated a number of pages of notes, I was encouraged to put them into a book, primarily for the family to read. Growing up during the Depression and World War II probably left the greatest impressions on my life, although as I struggle through the Coronavirus pandemic, this will certainly run a close second. The Great Depression was an austere time when everyone was faced with just putting food on the table, and the early years of World War II were particularly depressing. A betting person would not have put his money on the Allies, with the Nazis at the Gates of Moscow and the Japanese unstoppable in the South Pacific. Like most people, finding the Right Place to settle down to live is a function of knowing what you are looking for coupled with a great deal of good fortune.

I would like to thank my daughter, Carole Parker for editing and helping me publish my accumulation of notes. Without her able assistance, this book would not have been completed. Also, I would like to thank my very capable assistant over the years, Brenda Richardson, who provided typing and administrative support for this book.

MOMENTOUS TIMES
1929-1943

Without question, the two most momentous events of the 20th Century were the Great Depression and World War II. The Depression lasted over ten years and created disastrous economic conditions throughout the world. World War II lasted for six years, and millions of lives were lost and countries were destroyed.

I grew up during these tumultuous times. For many of these years, I had a morning newspaper route and eagerly read the daily paper, so not only was I a daily observer of these globe changing times, but a direct participant — albeit a small one.

Mooreland is a small farming community located in Henry County, Indiana, about ten miles from New Castle, the county seat. During the 1930s the population was between 400 and 500; in 2018, it was 357. In the 1930s, it had three streets, Broad Street and two side streets, two general stores, a drug store, two filling stations, a restaurant, a garage, and a funeral home but not much else. The town served as a small center of commerce for people living within a few miles of town. U.S. Highway 36 runs adjacent to Mooreland, but other than that there are no main highways. Many of the roads near town were gravel. One railroad went through the town, but it has long since been abandoned.

My grandfather on my mother's side, Enoch "Neve" G. Bouslog, came to Mooreland shortly after he was married in 1900. He was born ten miles west of Mooreland in another small town, Sulfur Springs, where he was a teacher before moving to Mooreland. My grandmother, Mary "Molly" L. Bouslog, was born in Millville, Indiana, an even smaller town about five miles south of Mooreland. They came to Mooreland and bought an existing general store on the corner of Broad and Charles Streets. The store — known simply as E.G. Bouslog's General Store — was owned by my grandfather until just before his death in 1943. My entire family life was centered around this store in my early years. My grandfather, grandmother, mother, and father all worked in the store. We lived approximately one-half block from the store. My grandparents lived in one house and we lived in a smaller adjacent house.

My father's family lived in Danville, Indiana, located about 40 miles west of Indianapolis, or approximately 100 miles from Mooreland. The Parker family was a very large family with nine surviving children (one died in childbirth); my Grandfather Herbert Parker was a veterinarian. Grandmother Ethyl Parker's maiden name was Dooley, and she grew up in a small community near Danville. She was a descendant of Aaron T. Dooley, who was captured and held for a long period in a Confederate prison in Charlotte, Virginia during the Civil War. My Grandmother Bouslog's father was also in the Civil War. Her maiden name was Hatfield and she used to tell the story of how her father was paid by another man to take his place as a draftee. He was injured in the war and had problems from the wounds for the rest of his life.

Neve Bouslog, my grandfather came to Mooreland as the result of decisions made by his great-grandfather, John Bouslog (my great, great, great grandfather), who was born in 1756, in Alsace, Lorraine, which over the years alternated between being a part of Germany and a province of France. John Bouslog was in the Army of one of the German principalities at the time. After a bad war experience, he came home on furlough and announced to his father that he was not returning to the Army and he did not want his two younger brothers to be forced to suffer the same experience he had in the service. The three brothers left for Hamburg where they either stowed away or bought passage for their trip to America. Once in New York, they decided one would go north, another would go west, and another would go south. They planned to return to New York after one year and decide which part of the country was best suited for their settlement. The two brothers that went north and west returned. The one that went south never returned and was never heard from again. The remaining two brothers and their families decided to move to Pennsylvania. From Pennsylvania, they ultimately came to Indiana in 1832.

John Bouslog lived to be 99 years old, and his wife to 97, both passing in 1855. Their graves are in the Harvey Cemetery, north of New Castle, and I have visited the cemetery and seen the gravestones. John Bouslog was Neve Bouslog's great-grandfather, David Bouslog was his grandfather, and his father was Abraham Wesley Bouslog, who married Amanda Peckinpaugh, my great grandmother. I have one photograph of Amanda, a very stern and no-nonsense lady, holding a rifle and standing with her many children. She had eight children by Abraham Wesley Bouslog, and after he died, another three children by Henry Veach.

John Bouslog and his brother, David, were the original ancestors of a great number of Bouslogs who lived in and around New Castle and Henry County, Indiana, and as a child, we would go to Bouslog reunions and I would see many cousins. The Hatfields were a much smaller family. My grandmother Molly Bouslog had a twin sister, Sally Marshall, and at least one brother, Tom.

Thus, my growing up in Mooreland, Indiana was the result of the original decision by John Bouslog to leave the Army and come to America, his subsequent decision to come to Indiana, and my Grandfather Bouslog's decision to leave teaching after he was married and become a store proprietor in Mooreland.

While the store seemed a huge place to a small boy, as I look back, it was really a small two-story building built sometime before the turn of the century. The floor had buckled on the 2nd floor and there were a number of places where there were big bulges and waves. The downstairs was probably no larger than 5,000 square feet but was advertised as "The Big Store that made Mooreland famous." At the back of the store was a storeroom and the meat and butcher counter. Along one side of the store were canned goods and all types of groceries. On the other side was hardware, dresses, shoes, shotgun shells, and almost everything imaginable. My father was the butcher. My mother did most of the purchasing. My grandmother in her 60s and my grandfather in his 70s, both worked at the store. In addition, we hired other people to help, particularly on Saturdays, which was the busiest shopping day of the week.

Saturday afternoon and evening at the store were not only a good time to shop, but a major social event for the whole community in the 1930s. People would come to town, mostly in overalls, some driving a team of horses and wagon, and others in cars. The wives would spend time shopping and socializing, and the husbands would go to the drug store or hardware store to play checkers or horseshoes and chew tobacco. There was no bar in town as this was very shortly after prohibition and almost no one drank. After they shopped, the women would sit behind the stove in the store and chat and gossip. Only when the fire burned out and they got cold would the women fetch their husbands from the drug store, filling station or hardware store and go home.

The store had no toilet facilities, only an outhouse. As a matter of fact, many of the homes in Mooreland did not have indoor plumbing at the time, and a privy in the back alley was very common. While we had indoor plumbing as did my grandparents' home in Mooreland; in Danville, where Grandmother Parker raised nine kids, they did not have indoor plumbing until the 1940s.

Operating the store during the Depression was a real struggle, as it was for any business. While there was competition from one other store in town, the real concern was that a great number of people had no job and those that were employed worked for very small wages. One farmer who lived outside of town would hire extra help at various times during the year. He would come to the store in a truck and meet the assembled men during the early morning. The men were paid one dollar per day or a dollar and a dime if they brought their own tools. This wage was for an entire day's work, but they did receive lunch.

This was also the time of the Works Progress Administration (WPA), the Public Works Administration (PWA), and many other agencies recently established by the Roosevelt Administration. An addition was built on Mooreland School during the middle '30s by the WPA — mostly to provide employment. It also was a time when people were hungry and desperate. Our store was robbed on several occasions. Once a man with a gun came into the store early in the morning and asked my grandparents to empty the cash register. My grandfather kept a gun in a drawer and while emptying the cash register, he started to go for the gun. My grandmother screamed and said, "For God's sake, NO, just give him the money." My grandfather handed him the money and he left. After that, the store was broken into a few times at night, and goods were stolen. My father slept in the store for a number of weeks with a shotgun.

Occasionally I would stay with my grandparents overnight. I would get up very early in the morning with my grandfather who would carry the cash to start the day's sales along with two pistols in a little leather bag with handles on it. At age five or six, it was a big deal for me to be able to carry the bag as we trudged to the store at an early hour.

A fellow who worked at the local garage had taught me to say the word "jackass," and much to my parents' chagrin I would sit on the counter at the store when people came in and say, "Hello, you old jackass." Grandfather Bouslog, a fairly humorless German in his 70s was less than pleased about this. Also, when I was five or six, if I used bad words, the standard procedure was to take me to the sink and wash out my mouth with soap — very distasteful, especially if one of the stronger soaps like Lifebuoy or Lava were used.

Only a few people in Mooreland had a college education. My mother, Lucille Bouslog Parker, completed two years of college, and my grandfather Neve Bouslog, a teacher, had graduated from college. Neve had gone to Central Normal College, located in Danville. When it came time for my mother to go to college, he wanted her to go to the same school. This is where she met my father, Crawford Parker, whose family lived there. She finished two years of college and he had completed one year of college when they were married in 1926. They both quit college and returned to Mooreland to work in the Bouslog General Store.

My mother had a very creative and innovative mind. She was one of the first people in the community to use a movie camera — beginning with black and white film and later moving to color. She organized a ladies club called the Cable Club that still exists in Mooreland. She was the prime organizer of many parties. She bought encyclopedias and other books for me as a child. She was also way ahead of her time as far as diets go. She ground our breakfast cereal from raw wheat. We normally had carrots and celery to snack on, never candy from the store.

She taught me elocution at an early age. With her help, I would memorize a number of poems and little stories and she would take me to various ladies clubs where I would wear my short pants and show off like a little prig. Later, she would take me to New Castle where she enrolled me in a tap-dancing class. I was not very graceful, and this did not last long. I also learned some words of wisdom from my mother, for example on how to apologize: "Never explain more than necessary; your friends don't need it, and those who are not your friends won't believe it anyway."

My father worked at the store as a butcher, but his real love was politics. His family were all Republicans and he became a Republican precinct committeeman. My grandfather Bouslog was a staunch Democrat and a big supporter of FDR, who my father disliked. For this reason, my father and grandfather never discussed politics. Perhaps it is fortunate that my grandfather died before my father was very far along in his political career.

My Grandfather Bouslog, as previously indicated, was 70 when I was born, and as one of the few people in Mooreland with a college education, he had an extensive library and loved to read. As a boy, I spent a great deal of time going through his library. The books that interested me the most were the adventure books: Theodore Roosevelt's *African Game*

Trails, an illustrated book about his safaris, another about *The Sinking of the Titanic* written just nine months after the actual event, and still another about *The Discovery of the North Pole* and other great polar expeditions. I still own quite a few of these books.

Grandfather Bouslog had a good head for business. The store supplied the livelihoods for both of our families and in addition, he had bought three or four small houses in Mooreland for investment purposes. He rented these out at low cost to our relatives and others. My grandfather taught me to play checkers, and he would help me with small projects, like building a birdhouse. Basically, however, he was not good at dealing with children — due in part perhaps to his great difficulty in hearing. A series of hearing aids did not appear to help.

Grandmother Molly Bouslog was a dear lady and much of my early life was spent with her because my mother worked full time at the store. Grandmother would prepare Sunday dinner and also many of the meals which we ate at her house. She loved to garden and work in the yard and my early interest in these activities was because of her. I would spend a lot of time with her working in the yard, planting flowers, and her vegetable garden, mowing and doing other projects. In the back of the house, she kept a chicken coup where I would go and collect eggs in the morning and then usually on Saturday afternoon, with a long wire, I would catch a chicken by the leg and she would wring its neck and cook the chicken for Sunday dinner. Grandmother and Grandfather Bouslog were a very integral part of my childhood. Living next door and being an only child, I really had four parents. Being an only child was not unusual during the Depression. Many families were small and some of my classmates were "only" children. I asked my mother why I didn't have brothers or sisters. She responded, "We are having enough trouble just feeding one." My mother was also an only child, although the Family Bible shows an earlier child was born in 1901 but died at birth.

As noted earlier, my mother did her best to give me some culture with elocution and tap-dancing lessons. Later, I had lessons on a French horn and ultimately on drums. Drums appeared to be my best possibility for learning music. But one day, tired of the noise of my practicing, my mother went to my father and complained that either the drums would go or she would go. That was the end of my musical experience — probably a good thing for the family — and the world.

Sports and outdoor activities such as hunting were more to my liking. Basketball in Indiana is the king of sports, and every small town had its own team and undying rivalries with other small towns and always against the county seat city. Mooreland was fortunate to have a very good team during most of my growing up years and the players, particularly during the season, were treated like princes. The whole town would turn out for the game on Friday night. After the game, there were usually chili suppers or social hours at someone's home. The players would arrive to loud cheers, particularly if they had won that night, but also if they had not.

As a young boy, I was very much into basketball. Like many of my friends, we had a hoop and backboard over our garage. I would shovel snow off the driveway in the winter so we could play outside — not too bad if you wore gloves and kept moving.

Our family attended the Mooreland First Christian Church. However, the high school basketball coach taught Sunday School at a little Quaker church in town. I started attending the Quaker church on my own just to be in his class. Needless to say, I made the team.

Other sports were not nearly as important as basketball. There was no football in Mooreland, but baseball was very big during the summer. Mooreland had an independent team with many of the men in their 20s or 30s playing on the team. Each Sunday afternoon during the summer, baseball was a big event, with most of the town turning out for the game in which our team would play independent teams from other small towns. My early experience with chewing tobacco was the result of playing on this team at age 15 or 16 as a substitute trying hard to fit in with the older guys. I went out in the field with a chew of tobacco in my mouth and after one or two innings I was so dizzy they had to take me out. This was my first and last experience with chewing tobacco.

I began track, particularly pole vaulting, at an early age. We would use a bamboo pole, make rough wooden standards to hold the bar up, and dig a hole in the ground to plant the pole; we would then land on the bare ground as there were no landing pads.

Ping pong was another favorite sport. My mother bought a ping pong table when I was seven or eight and converted a sun porch into a ping pong room. There we hosted tournaments with our family, the neighborhood kids, and others in the community. Everyone played ping pong, especially in the winter months. Subsequently, I became a fairly accomplished player and at age 13-14 played for the local town championship against an older boy. While I lost the match, I remember this annual community-wide event being a big deal every November. After all the early matches were played, the championship match was held in the local gym and included a potluck meal, called the Rabbit Supper. Originally, the men would bring only rabbits that they had shot for the supper, but later it was rabbit along with chicken, meats, and other special plates.

As a small community, you knew everyone in town, and everyone knew you. You knew where everybody lived, where they worked, if they had a job, how many children they had, and their entire family history. To a very great extent, the kids pretty well had the run of the town. I am reminded of Hillary Clinton's book about how it takes a village to raise a child. Everyone in Mooreland was a part of the village raising its children, and there were both good examples and bad examples. We had our share of mentally challenged people. We had veterans of World War I who still bore the results of their injuries, both physically and mentally, then called "shell shock" now better known as PTSD. The town banker was rumored to have had a series of liaisons with young boys. While this was sometimes whispered about, people generally dismissed it and went about the demanding business of trying to keep food on the table.

One of my very horrible memories as an eight-year-old concerns a man from Muncie who was murdered and his car ran off a high bank into a local gravel pit. A farmer happened to see the sun reflected off the rear window in the water as he worked in a field nearby and reported it. They brought in a tow truck and pulled the truck out of the water and sure enough there was August Glass - I remember his name to this day - who had been shot in the head and had his eyes, ears, and extremities all nibbled away by the fish. This gave me nightmares for quite a few weeks. I didn't think that the murder was ever solved, but my daughter found a 1938 clipping from the Muncie Star reporting some sort of love triangle mystery involving the rivalry for the attentions of one "blond Miss Dickenson". Both she and her boyfriend were ultimately freed because of a lack of evidence.

There was a robbery of the local bank located next door to grandmother and grandfather's house; the State Police came and one carried a Tommy gun, which was a relatively new machine gun at the time. This was during the time of Al Capone, the G men and Prohibition Agent Elliot Ness, and it created a local stir. Other than these few occurrences, Mooreland was a pretty sleepy small town.

However, there is a recent book about Mooreland in the 1950s. I couldn't believe that there would be enough interest in this tiny town for an entire book. A woman named Haven Kimmel (a pen name) spent her early years in Mooreland more than a decade after our family left and wrote a book about some of the small-town characters. Kimmel aptly described Mooreland as a town "with three churches but no taverns... bordered at the north end by a cemetery and at the south by a funeral home."

Many of the people in her book, *A Girl Named Zippy — Growing Up Small in Mooreland, Indiana,* are people that I knew very well. The book was on the New York Times bestseller list for quite a few months. When Kimmel lived in Mooreland, her house was right across the street from our house. When I was eight or nine, this house was occupied by the Harter family. Ed Harter was a year older and he and I would remain friends through high school. We both moved to New Castle in the middle of the basketball season — but that's a later story. The one thing I remember about the Harter house was that one of the rooms had all the furniture removed and was set up as a boxing ring. Ed got boxing gloves for Christmas one year. He was a year older than me and also considerably bigger. He used to whale the tar out of me and the rest of the neighborhood kids as well. I would invariably come home with a bloody nose — to the point that my mother refused to let me go over to their house.

In addition to sports, one of my early hobbies was building model airplanes. I would usually have a card table set up either in my room or elsewhere in the house in which I had an airplane under construction. The smell of banana oil glue would permeate the entire house.

I was always on the lookout for a way to earn money, and another project I took on was raising fishing worms to sell for bait. After a rain, there were certain yards in town that were thick with big nightcrawlers, a big fishing worm about eight to ten inches long. They lived in holes in the dirt and would come out after a rain. I would take a flashlight and when I found one outside the hole, I would put my thumb on the hole so it couldn't get back in. Then I would then pick them up and take them home in a can. I had a "bait pit" in the backyard next to the alley. This was a 12-inch deep hole in the ground, lined with screen wire so the worms couldn't escape and filled with soft dirt. I kept them here, feeding them coffee grounds, until I got an order that someone wanted a full can for fishing. Then I would dig the worms out with a trowel. The sale price was 25 big nightcrawlers for a dime.

At age 11 or 12, I acquired the morning paper route for the Muncie Star. I would go with my grandfather or sometimes on my own down to the store at 4:30 or 5:00 in the morning where I would work on my model airplanes until the bread man came in from Muncie bringing with him the morning papers. I would then get on my bicycle and ride throughout town delivering the newspaper. It would usually take me about an hour. During the winter, I rode my bicycle in the dark along the icy streets and sidewalks. One of the places I used to be deathly afraid of was the local funeral home, which had a blue neon sign out front. On a snowy dark morning, this only exaggerated the eerie feeling of knowing that corpses were inside and that they generally belonged to people I knew. I would ride fast and furious by the place, tossing the paper and hopefully landing it somewhere in the vicinity of the porch.

Passing newspapers during the early years of the war was a very sobering experience for a 12-year-old. I can remember exactly where I was when news of the attack on Pearl Harbor came — home listening to the radio. I immediately found my folks and grandparents to tell them. The subsequent year was a dire time for America, with the Philippines, Singapore, and many other places in Southeast Asia falling to the Japanese invasion. The first thing I would do every morning was open the paper and read the headlines, which were usually about the loss of another city or country, or the sinking of a major ship or tankers being torpedoed off the East Coast. During the first year of the war, the news was really depressing. I remember clearly when the Doolittle Raid on Tokyo took place. As I delivered the papers, I recall people looking at the headlines in amazement and saying they didn't believe it was true. I remember telling them that I didn't believe it either, because from my model airplanes I knew enough about American aircraft to know we didn't have any that were capable of going from our bases to bomb Tokyo. As it turned out, of course, I was both right and wrong; the planes had come from a carrier located within 500-600 miles of Japan. If you were a betting person, during the early years of World War II, you would not have bet on us!

Hunting and dogs were also a big part of my early life. My grandfather had been an avid hunter during his early days and while he was too old to go now, my father took me hunting at an early age. My job was to go with the dogs through the brush and scare out the game while my father and the other hunters stood on the high ground to shoot. In retrospect, it was a rather dangerous job and I was lucky not to be accidentally shot. My grandfather was also a great lover of dogs and when I was a boy, we had a succession of dogs. One was a beautiful English setter named Joe. Another dog named Vicki, a cross between a blue tick and another type of hound, was my constant companion for five or six years. After school, Vicki and I would walk along the railroad tracks outside of town usually in the snow looking for rabbits. On a good day, we would come home with a rabbit or two that I would dress (clean and skin) and then sell. Dressed rabbits sold for a quarter, and we had to leave a foot on so that the buyer would know that it wasn't a cat.

One of my favorite places to hunt was in the back of the Mooreland Cemetery. Rabbits would stay around the cemetery in order to feed off the tall grass, and I could take my dog and rely on getting a rabbit or two. I have visited this cemetery often since then, as this is where Grandfather and Grandmother Bouslog and both of my parents are buried. It is a nice little cemetery and well maintained.

At age 12, I also had a trap line out in the country along with a friend. We would normally tend the trap line together, but sometimes I would go alone. We usually left at 5:00 in the morning bringing our dogs and walking about a mile and a half out of town in the dark to see if we had any muskrats or rabbits or whatever else we caught in the traps. After that, I would come home, get on my bicycle and run the paper route, so by 8:30 when I went to school, I had both tended the trap line and run the paper route. At the time, it didn't seem like a big deal, it was just my morning routine.

We also went snipe hunting. A "snipe" is a mythical animal that can only be caught by running them into a gunny sack with a bright flashlight late at night. A group of older boys would take a younger one "snipe hunting," giving the young boy a gunny sack and a flashlight and stationing him at a specific location out in the fields or woods. He would be instructed to hold the sack open and wait while the older boys would branch out and drive the snipe his way and into the sack. After making appropriate noises in the beginning to assure the younger boy they were out there, the older boys would proceed to go home — leaving the young boy, so to speak, "holding the bag." After a while, the boy would finally realize he'd been "had" and would trundle home.

From the age of six or seven on, I was always expected to do chores. Carrying buckets of coal for the big stove in the living room was one of my early jobs. We needed four to five buckets to keep the stove going overnight. I would time this work with listening to Little Orphan Annie, the Lone Ranger, Jack Armstrong, and other favorite radio programs; During commercials, I could run out to the coal bin in the garage, shovel a full pail of coal, and haul the bucket back into the house before the radio program resumed.

During the summer when I was about eight or nine, I made arrangements with several families to mow yards. Most I mowed for a quarter, but one especially large yard paid 50 cents. Mowing was done with a push mower and when the grass was high, this was a hard afternoon's work. I also worked for a hybrid seed corn dealer in Mooreland. After school, we would take a team of horses and a wagon and shuck corn, then haul it in, run it through a sheller, and bag it. Corn shucking skills were a big deal. There were local, state and national corn shucking contests. But once the mechanical corn pickers arrived, this all passed into history.

I had a small savings account at the local bank and I was always saving money to buy something. I can remember buying my first bicycle as well as my first shotgun, a small 410, which I still own.

In the middle of World War II, when I was 14, I went to work during the summers with my cousin Ralph Harvey who owned a farm about five miles from Mooreland. I lived with the Harveys all summer for three years and worked on their farm. Farming during the war was difficult because there was so little help available; any warm body, even young kids, were pressed into use. There was a big demand for crops, but a serious shortage of equipment and gasoline. Farmers, however, were able to get additional gas rations for the tractors. At age 14, I got a license to drive a truck, but the license was not valid for automobiles and I was restricted to driving a large grain truck on the farm.

The Harveys had a large apple orchard. My job was to spray the orchard for various pests and diseases in the spring. One of the sprays was a lime-sulfur spray which came out entirely yellow. We had an old horse-drawn sprayer with a Briggs & Stratton engine on the back. I would get up early in the morning, hitch Old Kate, our oldest plow horse, to the sprayer, drive through the woods back to the orchard, fill the sprayer with water from the windmill, mix in bags of lime sulfur and begin to spray. On windy days, the lime sulfur would blow back toward me and by the end of the day, I was completely yellow, as was Kate and the sprayer. I would go to the house, take a bath, and remove the lime sulfur spray off me. Normally, I would also hose down Kate but sometimes Kate was left standing in the field and people would drive by and marvel at seeing a "yellow horse".

For two summers we had a full orchard of apples with no one to pick them. Ralph, who was a State Representative at the time, made arrangements with Fort Benjamin Harrison to have German prisoners come to the orchard and pick. About 15 or 20 prisoners arrived one day, bringing tents and camping out in the orchard. Three or four guards came with them and for the next two weeks, the prisoners picked the apples. By and large, they were good-humored and laughed a lot; they also worked hard. I'm sure they found this work more interesting and enjoyable than sitting in a cell. Ralph kept in contact with some of these prisoners for many years and when he became a Congressman after the war, he even visited one or two of them in Germany.

Ralph was a great storyteller, and could always be counted on for a good tale. One story I remember was about a relative he called "Uncle Billy." It seemed Uncle Billy's wife died at the very same time as the husband of a lady living down the street. After two to three years, the lady and Uncle Billy moved into one house. People in town began to talk and Ralph decided to confront Uncle Billy: "Uncle Billy, do you know you're living in adultery?" Uncle Billy shot right back, "Ralph, that's a damn lie, I'm living right here in Sulphur Springs where I've always lived."

During the three summers I spent on the Harvey farm, I learned many types of farm jobs: how to drive a team of horses and a tractor and how to work in a haymaking ring in which 30 men would all join together to make hay at one farm and then move on to a new farm the next day. The Harveys also grew hybrid seed corn, which had to be detasseled every August. We would hire crews from New Castle, and I would serve as "straw boss" for these "city kids". This generally involved breaking up a few fights before the summer was over . . . a bloody nose and black eyes were not uncommon.

Our swimming holes during the summer were usually the local creeks. The only real pool was in New Castle. Occasionally, we would get together a carload of kids and go to New Castle to swim in the pool, but after the polio scare in the late '30s, my parents ruled this out. I had one experience of jumping into a stream and hitting a piece of wire which went into my foot and broke off at about two inches long. I was first taken to the hospital in New Castle and then to Muncie, where they cut open the top of my foot to remove the wire. I was on crutches for about a month after that. They also used a sulfa drug (new on the market) to prevent infection since the wire was rusty. I had no ill effects, but I still have about a four-inch scar on the top of my left foot where they removed the wire.

Mooreland had a volunteer fire department and the fire station was out the back door of our store. Because we were the closest, my father usually drove the fire engine. Normally, a fire would be called in on the telephone, and the telephone operator had a button in her office that she would punch for the fire siren, which would be the signal for all the volunteers to head to the station. My father was usually the first one there, and the fire station key was behind a piece of glass in a little box near the door. There was usually a small wrench or hammer to break the glass and get the key. One time my father ran to the station and the wrench or hammer was not there so he used his hand to break the glass and badly cut his hand. I remember going to the fire and seeing my father with blood all over his shirt. My mother was beside herself, thinking he had been injured in the fire.

Only a few people in town had telephones, but we had one at the store — a wall telephone with a crank on the side — that everyone would come in to use. There was a central telephone station and the operator that manned it knew everyone in town. If you called and she rang and somebody wasn't home, many times she could tell you exactly where they were.

Although Prohibition went out in the early '30s — there was no place in Mooreland where you could buy alcoholic beverages. Our store did not handle beer or wine, and the nearest tavern was in New Castle. As people in business, and in a small town just a few years after Prohibition, everyone was very careful about drinking. Neither my parents or grandparents kept liquor in the house — except later I discovered my grandfather, an old German, would occasionally keep a case of Berghoff beer (bottled in Fort Wayne) hidden in his basement. However, my folks were part of a bridge club that would meet monthly at one of the homes. One year the bridge club had a New Year's Eve party, with quite extensive drinking, lots of silly hats and songs — really pretty tame by today's standards. My mother took along her movie camera and filmed the entire event. She thought she had the film well hidden, but I found it and showed it to all the neighborhood kids, who immediately told their folks. I can't remember exactly how I was punished, but I recall it was not lightly!

Although conditions were really tough during the Depression, one of the things I now understand and am grateful for is the number of relatives that we were able to help because of our store. Four or five of my father's brothers and sisters came from Danville to live with us during the summer, or sometimes during the whole year while they worked at the store or did other jobs in Mooreland. My Grandfather Bouslog had a sister who was married to a doctor in Muncie and I remember visiting when I was a very young boy at their very sumptuous house in Muncie. However, the doctor died, the family funds ran out, and Grandfather's sister came to live with us in Mooreland. My Grandmother Bouslog's brother lost his home in New Castle and he too came to live in Mooreland where grandfather helped him to buy a small place and remodel it into a restaurant. These were all things I never thought very much about at the time; I didn't even connect them to the economic impacts of the Depression until later. It was just something everybody did.

The Bouslog store was one of the few places that gave credit during those years. The credit was not very extensive, maybe $25.00 or $30.00 was the max, but at that time this might buy three or four weeks of groceries. When the store was ultimately sold in late 1942, there were thousands of dollars outstanding on the credit accounts. My mother told me later that during the war when everyone was working again, that almost to the last dollar these accounts were all paid, often with nice letters indicating that grandfather or my mother or father had extended credit to them during 1937 or 1938 when times were really tough and that they had never forgotten it, and they wanted to repay with thanks. Forty years later at my father's funeral several old-timers thanked me as well.

During this period the wholesale grocery truck would come from Fort Wayne, and the driver would sit on the street and wait until he was paid in cash before he would unload the goods. Some days we didn't have enough cash available and my mother would get on her bicycle and ride around town collecting a dollar or two here and there in order to have enough money to pay the driver to unload.

In 1940 just before the War, Mooreland decided they needed new incentives to bring people into town to shop, so the Mooreland Free Fair was organized. My father was in charge of obtaining concessions. For many weeks before the

Mooreland fair, my father and I would go to all of the fairs in the surrounding area and book people to do concessions, sideshows and rides for the Mooreland fair. This was a big deal for me, getting to go to all the fairs. The Mooreland Free Fair was a big event and continues to this day; a lot of people return to Mooreland for the event each year and often make it a homecoming or family reunion day.

Before the war, in 1939, my grandfather and grandmother decided that they wanted to take a trip to the West Coast while they were still able to travel. My grandparents, my mother, a relative from New Castle named Elmo Wood, and I, left in our car for California. My father stayed home to manage the store. It was a great trip for a ten-year-old. We went to Taos, New Mexico, to see my grandmother's twin sister, Sally, whose husband, Horace Marshall, was the President of a small university there. We drove on to San Diego, Long Beach, and San Francisco. During the time in Long Beach, we went aboard the battleship Oklahoma which was later heavily damaged at Pearl Harbor. On the way back through the deserts of Nevada, we had a tire blow and the car spun out and rolled over at 70 or 80 miles an hour. I was the only person not injured. My grandmother and grandfather were both thrown out of the vehicle and had internal injuries, but later recovered. Elmo Wood was also injured. My mother's arm was broken in three places and she had difficulty with this arm for the rest of her life. The car was a total wreck.

I climbed out of the car up to the highway and after a long while was able to flag down a car and a truck that took all of us to the little town of Lovelock, Nevada. I went to the town office and sent my father a telegram saying something like: "had bad wreck, send money" which, of course, alarmed him to no end. Without a car, we returned to Mooreland via Chicago on the "Super Chief", an outstanding and well-known train at the time. After the accident my mother made numerous trips to Ball Hospital in Muncie, and at least two or three trips to the Mayo Clinic to try to get more usage out of the arm, but unfortunately, she never got more than about 50 or 60 percent flexibility after the accident.

One of my mother's trips to Mayo Clinic for her broken arm was the occasion for a story about my grandfather Bouslog that I will never forget. Will Parker, my father's brother, was living with us at the time and Will drove my parents to Muncie to catch the train to go to Mayo. On the way back, I asked Will to drive me close to my trap line since I hadn't been able to check on it that morning. Unfortunately, this was spring and the farm lane that we took was firm at the beginning but later became very muddy. After we were down the lane about half a mile, we had the car, owned by my grandfather, stuck in the mud, and I mean really stuck! I walked into town to get help. This was on a Sunday. Very shortly, half the town of Mooreland either drove or walked to the farm lane to see Neve Bouslog's Buick stuck in the mud.

We tried all kinds of ideas to free the car. A tractor was not able to get it out. The first team of horses we tried was totally inadequate. People talked about leaving the car until summer, or dismantling it and taking it out in pieces. Finally, someone suggested we bring in a team of horses that had won a horse pulling contest at the Mooreland Free Fair that year, and sure enough, this team was able to get the car out. It was 7:00 in the evening by the time we got the car unstuck and returned home. It was probably 25 degrees outside, but my grandfather got out the hose and made Will and I wash all the mud off of that car. Neither Will or I have ever forgotten that adventure.

Halloween is always a big event in small towns and Moorland was no exception. While the acts were not "wholly" destructive, soaping of windows, pushing over privies, disassembling buggies, and assembling them again on top of barns, were standard fare. The local Town Marshall would usually deputize town people to try and stop the pranks but usually to little avail.

Christmas, of course, was another big event. We would decorate the store with colored lights and stock all types of Christmas gifts for sale. I can remember our first Christmas tree had real candles on it which we lit on Christmas Eve for a short period of time. Working with the volunteer fire department made us keenly aware of the risk of doing this.

Sometimes, we would drive to Danville and spend Thanksgiving with my father's family. They lived in a small home on South Cross Street. Somehow all of our family seemed to be able to stay in this house, usually sleeping on the floor with pillows or doubled up in the various beds. Of my father's nine brothers and sisters, all but one went to college — mostly, by working their way through Central Normal College located in Danville, although Will Parker went to DePauw University in Greencastle, Indiana on the GI Bill. Other than one sister who did not attend college, my father had the least college education of any of his family, but was able to do quite well through perseverance and hard work.

Wayne and Lora Lough came to Mooreland in 1937 or 1938 to take over the drug store. Their daughter Luan was an only child and a few years younger than myself. Later after Wayne died in 1960 and my mother died in 1965, my father married Lora Lough and they had a good marriage until his death in 1986. Lora survived until almost 100, passing in 2007 in Fort Collins, Colorado where she lived near her daughter Luan. She was laid to rest in Mooreland cemetery next to her first husband Wayne, and not far from my parent's grave.

Grandmother would prepare "Sunday dinner" for our family at about 1:00 in the afternoon. This usually consisted of chicken, sometimes beef or ham, sweet potatoes, mashed potatoes, green beans, jello, and usually a couple of pies and cakes. After we finished the meal, my grandmother would look at my grandfather and ask him whether he had enough. He would invariably push back from the table, start to get up, and say, "Well, it will do until we get someplace where we can eat right."

Often, the young women who worked at our store would also live at our house. Their wages were about $5.00 a week, including room and board. One time when Will Parker was living with us, he and I decided to play a prank on the young lady living with us at the time, whose room was upstairs right across the hall from Will's and my room. We got a mannequin head from the store and tied a flashlight on it. We opened the door to her room and had this head on a fishing pole and dangled it over her bed. Then we proceeded to wake her. She awoke with a start, took one swing at the mannequin, knocked it off the fishing pole, and screamed. She never forgave Will and me for that trick.

Because my father's birthday was in September, my parents belonged to a group of 10 or 12 families who got together each year to celebrate September birthdays. Another person in this group was a fellow named Fred White who worked in a plant in Muncie. Later, during the war, Fred was in charge of the U.S. Rubber Plant in Fort Wayne, a major defense plant. Fred was also a basketball referee and would sometimes referee DePauw games. I ran into Fred many times at games and we never acted as if we knew each other, but I got more breaks, more free throws and more good calls from Fred than any other referee and no one had any idea that our relationship went back to Mooreland many years earlier.

Mooreland's link to the outside world was by train. A train originating every morning in Indianapolis, would come through New Castle and then through Mooreland. It would stop, drop off mail, packages, and other freight then head east to Ohio, and come back through Mooreland about 4:00 in the afternoon before returning back to Indianapolis. This train, nicknamed the "Doodlebug" would carry both passengers and freight and was our primary link to the outside world, in addition to cars, of course. As soon as the Doodlebug arrived at 9:30 in the morning, mail was unloaded and delivered to the post office where it was sorted by the postmistress. Beginning about 11:00, people would wander into the post office to check their mail. You could normally run into most people in town during the hour from 11:00 to noon when they came to the post office to get their mail.

Mooreland School had perhaps 100 to 125 pupils in all grades, one through twelve. My class had 12 kids. For a rural school, it was probably satisfactory but with a limited budget and only a small number of pupils, many courses were not available. Only after transferring to New Castle was I able to study subjects like chemistry, advanced algebra, Latin, etc. Later, Mooreland School merged with four other schools in the 1950s to form what is now called Blue River Township School. With just 400 students, Blue River is still a small high school, but it consolidated four small-town schools that existed in that region during the '30s.

My father was Lieutenant Governor at the time school consolidation took place, and he would later tell me that the biggest opposition to consolidation was because every small town had its own basketball team and people couldn't bear the idea of losing their individual teams even though it meant attending a much better school. School consolidation took a long time to complete, but eventually the 14 or 15 small schools in Henry County were consolidated into three school districts.

Growing up in Mooreland, I was more focused on sports and hunting than on girls — but I do recall one or two romantic interests. At age 8-9, I thought a girl in my class named June Houser was quite okay. I was too bashful to hardly even speak to her, but I found out that she had a birthday coming up. With my mother's help, I decided to get her a small umbrella as a gift. My mother wrapped it, but told me I had to give it to her myself. I was much too bashful for that, so I waited until she and another little girl were playing in her garage, and I rode by on my bicycle and pitched the umbrella in the door. June's mother told my mother how I had made the birthday "delivery"; my mother thought it was hilarious and told the rest of the family. I didn't live that story down for many years!

During the middle of the war, gas was rationed so tightly that it was very difficult to drive anywhere. The normal allocation was three gallons per week. To get more you had to show that your business was essential to the war effort. I had a friend, Bill Bales, who was a little older than me — he was 16 and I was 14 — who lived on a farm and had access to gas for his tractors. Bill's folks had a '37 Chevy, which they let Bill drive. Every Saturday night during the summer, there was a small band at the outdoor pavilion in Memorial Park in New Castle. This was where all the young teens went to meet and dance. To get inside the pavilion, you had to buy a 10¢ ticket for each dance.

During this time, I bought a tweed suit with a green stripe in it — a heavy wool job. I also had green suspenders and a green tie with red and yellow dice emblazoned on the fabric, really a garish looking outfit and way too hot for summer. Bill saw this outfit and thought it looked great, so he bought exactly the same one. We thought we were really a big deal, with our foxy outfits, Bill's '37 Chevy and tractor gas. But the New Castle girls just laughed and called us a "couple of rubes from Mooreland"!

My father was elected County Clerk in November, 1942, and took office in January, 1943. Some months after that, my parents bought a home in New Castle, the county seat, but I stayed with my grandmother in Mooreland after my grandfather's death to keep her company and to play basketball. I was on the Mooreland team and we had a good team. But by the middle of my sophomore year, I came to realize the importance of getting a broader education that was not available in the mostly rural district of Mooreland and moved to New Castle. Ed Harter's father took a new job in New Castle, and so he moved as well. At the time both Ed and I were starters on the Mooreland team. Because a number of the older New Castle players were drafted into service, we were both able to make the transition from the Mooreland team to the New Castle team and became starters shortly after transferring. New Castle is in the North Central Conference and played larger high schools including Central of Fort Wayne, Anderson, Muncie, and other basketball powerhouses. However, at the time of the sectional the team we played in the second round was our old team from Mooreland. This was a very traumatic experience for Ed and me because we had grown up in Mooreland and the people who attended the game were our neighbors just a short time ago. When we came through the crowd to get to the floor, a number of people spit at us and called us all kinds of terrible names. Basketball means that much in Indiana, and lo and behold, our former Mooreland team beat New Castle that night — a small David beating the Goliath county seat town. This was an experience that has stayed with me all these years.

Mooreland in 2019 is very much as it was when I lived there. Many of the houses that existed when I was a boy are still there, and only a few new houses have been built. There are almost no businesses still in town, perhaps a store or two and one filling station. Times have not been easy on small Indiana towns and Mooreland is no exception. The old Bouslog store is still standing but was vacant for many years and then converted into an apartment. The house where I was born and grew up has been torn down. My grandmother and grandfather's house is still standing. The drug store owned by Wayne and Lora Lough still exists but almost all the other businesses are gone. A few of the friends I had in high school still live around Mooreland but not many.

As I look back on it, Mooreland was a good place to be "from". People there had a good sense of community. While times were tough during the Depression, people helped each other through the worst. Despite a few instances in the 1930s when times were really tough with break-ins at the store to steal food, there were almost no burglaries, assaults, rapes, or other violent crimes while growing up in Mooreland. No one locked their doors.

Almost everyone was hard-working. Some of the men worked in factories in either New Castle or Muncie, but most were farmers working small family farms. A life of farming, hunting, and other outdoor activities was the norm. There was only one African-American family in town. The father worked at the Chrysler plant in New Castle, and rode to work with other Mooreland men. The family attended a Seventh Day Adventist Church in New Castle instead of a local church. The kids went to our school and the boys were on the track team. One of the girls worked at our store and I often played with one of the boys. While they may tell a different story, no one seemed to pay much attention to the color of their skin — they were just another family trying to get along during the Depression. As I recall their home, it was nicer than many other homes in town.

Looking back at both my parents and grandparents, I was surrounded by some good role models growing up. They were thrifty and hard-working, as was most everyone during these times. More than that, they were "do-ers." This was especially true of my mother, who was usually the first to come up with a new idea, or a better way of doing something. She bought encyclopedias and encouraged me to look things up; she bought Richard Halliburton books on adventure travel for me to read, and without being pushy she encouraged me to develop a curiosity about many things. All the family worked and by some sort of osmosis, I developed a work ethic myself. I never thought of work as something to be dreaded; if there was something to do, you went ahead and just did it. As an only child, I never felt like I was pampered or privileged. As to toys or other material things, I had about the same as other kids I knew — and none of us had very much. To get a new baseball glove or a bicycle was a big deal that you and your parents planned and saved for. Grownups did not pay as much attention to kids as they do now. Parents, even the best, did not reserve "family time" or spend special time with the kids, although we certainly spent plenty of hours both working and playing together. We were expected to fit into whatever activities the grown-ups were doing, and in effect, be seen and not heard.

My father was the ultimate "do-er." With one year of college, he came within an eyelash of being governor. Frankly, he was cheated out of it — but that's another story. If he had been elected, he would have been the first governor elected in Indiana in the 20th Century without a college degree, and quite possibly the last.

In addition to learning a work ethic, another good thing about growing up in a small town is that kids were given a great deal of freedom to explore and learn about all kinds of things on your own. I could roam all over town by myself, watch the blacksmith shoe a horse — he was also the local bootlegger — and see him slip a bottle to a customer now and then. I could go barefoot all summer and never put on shoes except for church on Sunday. I could go to a farm and ride the wagon when the men made hay. I could ride my bicycle out to a stream to swim or fish. I could hunt rabbits with my dog.

I could hang around the drugstore in the evening and learn about sex from the older boys, who would talk about which young ladies did not pull down their blinds at night when they undressed. I could play baseball or shoot baskets, or go ice skating on the pond in winter. All of these things and many more I did without being on a "field trip" or any adult planning — and generally without any adults present at all. The only requirement was to be home in time for supper.

I also developed a sense of responsibility. Early on I learned it was my responsibility to feed the dog — or the dog went hungry. Later, when I mowed yards, I learned to sharpen and oil the mower. Working in the store I learned how to meet customers, operate the cash register, make change, and understand that the "the customer was always right". Later when I worked on the Harvey farm, I learned to go to the field, round up the horse team, get them into the barn, put on their harness, and work them all day. At the end of the day, I took off the harness, fed the horses, and turned them out for the night. I learned to repair equipment, change a flat tire, gas up the truck and the tractor, and how to drive on the highway. From athletics, I learned teamwork and how to take direction from a team leader. And later when I was older, I learned how to give direction so that people would listen.

I am sure kids learn some of these same skills and ethics today working at McDonald's or lifeguarding at the local pool. But it is likely in high school whereas my generation learned these lessons at age ten or younger. It is also probably not possible for kids to have the same kind of freedom today — even in small towns — as the world is so much more complicated. All in all, though, a small town was a good place to grow up, especially during the Depression and the War. I learned a whole lot about a whole lot of different things. Some of the stuff I learned I never used again — but some would prove useful down the road. I don't think that there was any question that my folks planned for me to go to college, as both had gone but did not finish. Where the money would come from was the question. My interest in sports-particularly basketball-helped solve that problem.

BASKETBALL CRAZY

1944-1947

Before television, basketball was the primary winter entertainment in Indiana. Every high school had a team, and in March every team — 740 in all — played in one tournament that took place over four weekends. All of the arenas where the games took place were sold out, and almost every conversation during March began or ended with high school basketball. For the two and a half years from 1944 through 1947, my life was consumed by sports with basketball by far taking the greatest bandwidth.

After my father was elected County Clerk, my folks moved to New Castle, the county seat, in 1943. I stayed in

Mooreland with my Grandmother for a short time. But by the middle of my sophomore year, I came to realize the importance of getting a broader education that was not available in the mostly rural district of Mooreland.

Moving, of course, meant leaving behind all of the friends that I knew and into an entirely new environment where I knew no one. While I continued with sports, it meant giving up other important parts of my life including dogs, hunting, and working in the store. As the County Clerk, my father already knew a number of people in New Castle and my mother had begun to establish a new circle of friends as well. The house we lived in at 1124 Bundy Court was very small, with only one bathroom on the second floor and three small bedrooms. My father paid Ed Arnold's parents $7,500 for it in 1942. The house was certainly nothing elaborate and this price was about average for a small house in a good neighborhood.

Our house was next door to the home of Joseph and Lena Shapiro. Their son Mort, a year older than I was, became a lifelong friend and later operated "Shapiro's" a renowned restaurant and delicatessen in Indianapolis. I was fortunate to be able to make an immediate transition from the Mooreland basketball team to the New Castle team, and this opened many avenues for socializing and friendship.

I also enrolled in a drama class, with Horace Burr as the teacher. I don't recall what motivated me to do this, but I was immediately cast in two or three plays. One role required me to kiss Ed Arnold's sister, who was a senior. I was too bashful to attempt to kiss her during rehearsal and there were bets as to whether I would actually do so when the time came for the performance. In the end, I did kiss her, but only after a few not so subtle hints from Mr. Burr that my grade would be very adversely affected if I did not.

New Castle High School was a considerable change from

Mooreland where there were only 12 students in my class. The high school had over 1,000 students, and my class was 240. Even more significant to me, New Castle is in the North Central Athletic Conference, which has won more basketball championships than any other conference in the state. The conference was made up mostly of high schools from mid-sized cities in the state — Logansport, Richmond, New Castle, Anderson, Muncie and Lafayette. In addition, it included Central High of Fort Wayne and Arsenal Tech of Indianapolis, which at this time was the largest school in the state with almost 5,000 students. The competition in basketball and other sports was the best in the state, and our closest rivals — Richmond, Anderson and Muncie — were tough adversaries in every sport. Years later, New Castle High School produced Kent Benson who played center on the Indiana team that won the NCAA National Championship in 1967, and Steve Alford who played on the Indiana team that won the NCAA Championship in 1987. Both were also outstanding players at New Castle High School. While Indianapolis and other locations were considered, the Indiana Basketball Hall of Fame was eventually built in New Castle in 1962 — a town that best captured the essence of "Hoosier Hysteria".

Socially, I hung out with friends at the YMCA Teen Canteen and the Presbyterian Church basement. We formed a group called "The Big Five" which included Jay Gray, Bob Keesling, Mort Shapiro, Russell Coors, and myself. Four of us were on the basketball team and other teams and Mort was the student manager and statistician for many of these teams. Mort also owned a pre-war Buick convertible, which was our primary mode of transportation. Very few kids in high school had a car and "The Big Five" stood out not only because we were on the teams, but because we had wheels.

While we may have been envied for our wheels, Mort's car had a great number of problems. During the war, it was almost impossible to get tires and you were forced to recap or retread any tires you had. Driving to Anderson one night, Mort slammed on his breaks at a red light and had two tires blow out.

Mort's attentiveness to traffic signals was learned the hard way. Before the convertible Mort had a little Cushman scooter. On one occasion, Mort was riding the scooter with Bob Keesling on the back. When they came to a stoplight, Bob says to Mort, "Go on through, there is nobody looking." And this is exactly the line that the police officer reported to the judge in court just a few weeks later.

I worked a variety of jobs every summer and at Shapiro's delicatessen during the winter. For two summers as an "Ice Man", I drove a truck and had an ice route which included one of the older sections of New Castle. At this time, many people did not have electric refrigerators but had an icebox. They would buy ice from the truck perhaps two times a week to keep their ice boxes cold. If they needed ice, they placed a sign in their window indicating the amount they wanted that day, either 25, 50, or 100 pounds. Generally, no one was home when I delivered because the people would be at work. The back door would be open and I would carry the ice in and stack it in the ice compartment of the icebox after removing and replacing the milk, butter, and other items around the new block of ice. I was 15 and proud to own a special permit to drive the ice truck for Consumer's Ice and Fuel. I still have my original Social Security card I filed to get the job.

As an "ice man" — or really an "ice boy" I had some interesting experiences. Sometimes women would come to the door skimpily dressed and make provocative remarks while I loaded the ice in the refrigerator. Other times I had to tiptoe through houses carrying ice on my shoulder and pass by bedrooms where even my 15-year-old self knew that sleeping was not the only thing going on. One customer that I grew to hate was a guy who wanted a 150-pound block delivered every week, because one large block lasted longer than two smaller chunks. I will never forget hauling 150 pounds on my shoulder down his very narrow staircase into his basement.

My other summer job was working in the County Surveyor's office where I surveyed ditches to determine the amount of excavation needed for a clean-out. This generally involved cutting through high weeds staking a line and shooting the elevations. I started this job as the" cutter" or the man with the machete cutting through the weeds. Luckily, I'm not allergic to ragweed, but I would generally end up suffering from poison ivy for much of the summer. Later, I graduated to staking the line, then rodman, and ultimately to running the surveying instrument. On rainy days, when the survey crew couldn't work, I hung around in the courthouse and watched trials, a factor that interested me in going to law school.

But sports were the predominant factor in my life during high school. With above-average ability and a good work ethic, I was able to play five sports in high school and actually dabbled in a sixth — boxing. When I graduated, I was the only person to ever earn letters in five sports at New Castle.

Basketball was the most important and gave me the greatest visibility. As a sophomore, I was able to break into the starting five almost immediately after moving from Mooreland, in part due to the fact that a number of seniors on the team were drafted into service and the coaches had to fill in with underclassmen. My opening game was against Central of Fort Wayne in the second half of the 1943-44 season. I was assigned to guard Murray Mendall Jr., a leading scorer and the son of Murray Mendenhall, Sr., Central High School's coach. Needless to say, Murray ran rings around me. My compatriot on the basketball team was Ed Harter, who also moved to New Castle from Mooreland. That sophomore year our team was rather mediocre and we had tough games against Anderson, Muncie, and other North Central Conference powers, not to mention the earlier mentioned spitting episode against Mooreland during sectionals.

In my junior year, we had a very excellent team, although we were quite small. Harter at 6'3" was the tallest. At 5'11" Bob Keesling and I were the top rebounders, not because we had any height or particular ability, but we worked hard at getting into position and had a good sense of where the ball might land off the backboard. At one time our team was ranked third in the state and we even defeated the eventual state champion, Anderson, on their home floor in the last game of the season.

One of the big disappointments in my life, however, was when we played Muncie Central in the Regional. We had beaten Muncie twice that year and a number of sportswriters had us picked to win the State. However, Muncie Central beat us in triple overtime. At that time, triple-overtime was a "sudden death" and the first team to score wins. Muncie got the tip from the center jump and scored right away. Hence our hopes of going to the State Championship were dashed.

In my senior year, I dislocated my shoulder playing football but was able to recover in time for the basketball season. Then I was involved in a minor traffic accident in which I suffered a greenstick fracture of my leg and so was out for the early part of the season. I eventually returned and helped the team win a number of games, but again we ran into our old nemesis — Mooreland — in the Sectional. I had the indignity of being home in bed with the flu and unable to play. Mooreland won again. The two losses to Mooreland, together with the loss to Muncie Central in the Regional were the low points of my high school years.

I had never played football before moving to New Castle, but in my junior year I tried out and made the Junior Varsity team. Interestingly enough, some of the guys that I had fights with years earlier at Ralph Harvey's farm when we all worked together on a corn de-tasseling crew were also on the football team and gave me a pretty hard time in the beginning. Absolutely, the worst aspect of football is the twice-daily workouts during the hot days of August when you are trying to get in shape after the summer off. At that time, it was believed that drinking water was detrimental to building strength and so Coach John Janzanuk would post either Mort Shapiro or another manager by the water fountain to make sure that no one had a drink of water either before or during practice. Combined with our heavy pads and uniforms and days of 100-degree heat, the net result was that we would sweat profusely and nearly pass out during our practice sessions. The "no water" rule was a common practice at the time and it's a wonder more people didn't die of heatstroke.

Coach Janzaruk was a good coach but also a real character and larger than life in our eyes. He took the entire football team to Chicago for two summers where we watched the College-Pro All-Star Game at Soldiers Field. This was before there was a Super Bowl and it was the biggest game of the year. Going to Chicago with the team and hanging out in the bars as a sixteen or seventeen-year-old was a big deal at the time.

Coach Janzaruk was also a great one for practical jokes. If you goofed off in practice, he might have the student manager slip some analgesic balm ("red hot") in your jockstrap hanging in the locker. This treatment really burned after becoming a little sweaty. The Coach also worked at Shapiro's at the same time I did. Sometimes he would slip vinegar into your Coke or sneak an egg into your overcoat pocket. Later, when you retrieved your coat to go home, he would give you a big hug, breaking the egg of course.

But perhaps my favorite Coach Janzaruk story came years later after he had left New Castle and moved to LaPorte. It was a joke that nearly did him in. In addition to coaching football, Janzaruk had an evening job at a warehouse where he decided to pull one of his usual pranks on the night watchman. The watchman would switch the lights on and off as he made his rounds. In one warehouse the light switch was situated on top of a board and required running your hand along the board to locate the switch. One night the Coach put a mousetrap on the board and as the watchman ran his hand along the board to find the light switch, his finger was caught in the mousetrap. I heard Coach retell this story a few times — each one more colorful — but the ending is always the same: the watchman attempts to track down Coach with a shotgun, but fortunately Coach heard about the watchman with the shotgun and left town!

In my senior year, I graduated to the first string in football and was a starter, playing both half-back on offense and safety on defense. In the opening game against Crispus Attucks High School in Indianapolis, I was fortunate enough to score two of the three touchdowns, one a 90-yard punt return. In the second game at Seymour High School, I returned to the huddle after being tackled and couldn't move my arm. Coach moved me to the side of the field and was prepared to snap my dislocated shoulder back into place and send me back into the game. Fortunately for me, my Father raced out of the stands and told Coach he didn't think that was a good idea. Father drove me to the hospital where a doctor relocated my shoulder. I was out for the rest of the football season and part of the basketball season too.

In the spring of my junior year, I played two sports: track and baseball, and that summer I also played American Legion baseball. This team was mostly high school students but also involved some older men, including Carl Erskine at Anderson High School, who would go on to become a Hall of Famer after many years of pitching for the Los Angeles Dodgers.

After Erskine graduated, the next year we won our local region in American Legion ball, our prize was to play the Indiana Reformatory at Pendleton, now the Pendleton Correctional Facility, a maximum state prison housing adult males over 22 years old. Our team of mostly 16, 17, and 18-year-olds entered through numerous gates and electric bolted doors behind the big walls at Pendleton, and then we were strip-searched. Next, we warmed up at the ball diamond inside the walls with the Reformatory team of mostly older men, while some four or five hundred prisoners stood behind a chicken wire fence and rooted against their own team, resentful of their special privileges.

The pitcher, who was 6'5" or 6'6", had played minor league baseball. The coach and third baseman, a man of about 40, had played five years with the Cincinnati Reds. The Reformatory team scored a number of early runs and we were having difficulty even getting a man on base. Finally, we learned that the big pitcher was weak as a fielder and so we got two or three runs off his errors by bunting. One of their players hit a home run over the wall and we all enjoyed a light-hearted moment as all the prisoners jumped up and down and enthusiastically offered to retrieve the ball.

After the game, we showered in the prison and each of us was assigned a "trusty", an inmate granted special privileges as a trustworthy person generally because they are close to being released and don't want to mess it up. As I came out of the shower, my trusty handed me a towel and brought me my clean clothes. Then we were served a meal afterward, with my trusty standing behind me to refill my water glass or bring more food.

The other sport I participated in both my junior and senior years was track. In track, I pole vaulted, broad jumped, and was on the relay team. Pole vaulting was my best skill and, at that time, it was performed with a bamboo pole. The pole would occasionally break, which was generally a bad experience as you would either fall back on the track or the boards surrounding the sandpit.

One of the big meets we had each year was the Kokomo Relays. In my leg of the half-mile relay, after I had previously consumed a bowl or two of chili, I had a lot of gas. I remember passing a couple of guys and as I am going by them, I am putt-putting along just like I was propelled by my own jet engine.

In my senior year, I again played two sports in the spring, but shifted from baseball to golf in addition to track. I had never been on a golf course before we moved to New Castle, but my father got me a few lessons with the pro at the local country club and I was able to master some of the fundamentals.

I also tried my hand at boxing for a short time. While I was in good shape from basketball, I was not prepared for how tired your arms get in boxing. Two rounds were generally more than enough to wear me out, but I do recall one personal grudge match that went quite a few more rounds. Jay Gray and I were part of the same social group, had a love/hate relationship, and found ourselves at odds over various matters. One day a coach suggested we put on the gloves and fight it out in the ring. Jay was a year older, a bit bigger, but the match went to a draw, perhaps because I wanted it more. After that, Jay and I got along much better.

High school, of course, involved girls. We normally socialized with the girls at the YMCA teen canteen. We also met girls after church, where a number of us sang in the Presbyterian Church choir. We would meet up at the drug store after church and sit in someone's car with the heater turned up high. This ensured that the windows steamed up and no one walking by might see us sitting in the car and necking. What we called "necking" was really pretty tame — seldom more than kissing. It was a different time and girls would quickly put you in your place if you were inclined to try anything else.

I remember at least three of the girls I dated. Jeanne

Long was a senior. I dated her when I was a sophomore and I'm sure the only reason this was possible was because many of the boys in the senior class had been drafted into service. In fact, when one senior boy came home from service a year later, I was out. Another girl was Dorothy Raines. Dorothy was a nice looking gal who ultimately went to Hanover College in Indiana. Another girl I dated did come back to reunions — but that's a later story.

At some point during my junior year, the Shapiros moved from the house next door to a large estate at the edge of town. The original owner of the estate, a gentleman named Macy Teetor who was one of the owners of the Perfect Circle piston ring company, had built this beautiful Spanish stucco home he called "Casa Manana" on five manicured acres of grounds and gardens, gorgeous furnishings, an expensive built-in Page organ, and a retractable awning in the atrium. It was one of the most outstanding homes in the whole city and the Shapiros paid a $50,000 purchase price, by far the largest price paid for a home in New Castle at that time.

The Casa Manana became the second home for the Big Five and we hung out there as much as we could. Mort's mother, Lena, was always bringing home all kinds of food from Shapiro's Delicatessen and we did our best to put away substantial portions of it. For wheels, I was sometimes able to drive my parent's 1939 four-door, Chrysler Imperial, on a Friday or Saturday night, a car my mother had inherited from my grandfather. Unfortunately, the car got very poor mileage — probably not more than 12 miles to the gallon — and with gas rationing, our use of the car had to be very limited. My father used to complain that every time I returned the car to the garage, it was almost out of gas. Once, I ran the gauge so close to empty that when my father backed the car out of the garage the next morning, the car did not even make it out of the driveway. On the plus side, it was built of heavy steel and my two or three fender benders left barely a few scratches on this tank, although they did cause damage to the other cars.

One time, on a lark, I drove the entire cast of a drama class play to a cemetery in the big old Chrysler. One of the girls became quite hysterical upon seeing an open grave that was being prepared for burial the next day. We got her back in the car and I drove her directly home. Still sobbing, all she could say to her father was that she had been with me ... in the car ... in the cemetery. Her father immediately called the police. By the time I had finished driving the rest of the cast home and arrived at my own house, there was a police car in the driveway along with my father and mother. Neither the police or my parents or the girl's father knew what had actually happened and began to speculate that perhaps the girl had been assaulted or raped. But eventually, with the help of others in the car, I was able to get the story straightened out.

In my senior year, I tried out for another class play called *The Fighting Littles* which was a story about teenagers, dating, growing up, etc. I got the male lead role of Ham Ellers. Interestingly, this same year Pat was the female lead in her class play in Bloom Township High School in Chicago Heights. The play had a different name — *A Date with Judy* — but very similar themes.

This of course was the time of bobby sox and poodle skirts and proms. Prom was always a big deal. We would rent a tux, buy a gardenia for our date, and try to scrounge some wheels. After our senior year prom, we went to Westlake on the west side of Indianapolis, a dancing pavilion where big bands played. Driving to Indianapolis was always a big deal; you not only had to find wheels, but enough gas to get you there and home. None of us drank, so at least drinking and driving and drugs were never an issue.

I somehow ended up in the top ten academically in my senior class and was invited to sit on stage with the principal at a graduation convocation. The best course I had that year was English Comp with Helen Rogers. We were required to do many themes and lots of writing, very helpful for freshman English in college just a year later. I was also thankful for a freshman Latin course — unavailable at Mooreland — that helped me in the study of law years later. I remember learning the Latin version of Jingle Bells and being called the "old geezer" by the young freshman in the class.

I learned a lot at New Castle High School but discovered very early in my first year at DePauw that my educational experience was not really comparable to that of the Indianapolis or Fort Wayne high schools.

As County Clerk, my father knew everyone in the courthouse. He later became Republican County Chairman, and had contacts throughout Henry County. In my junior year, when we had a very outstanding basketball team and he was running for reelection, he would come to the games. If we won or I played particularly well that night, he would stand at the door and heartedly greet everyone on the way out after the game. But if we lost or I played poorly, he would sneak out the back door and be home before me.

My father's post as Republican County Chairman was a mixed blessing. Each County Chairmen throughout the State was entitled to a license plate with a star on it. His license plate was the only star in Henry County. While the county was very strongly Republican, the City of New Castle was primarily Democrats and many of the police force were appointed by Democrat mayors. The star plate got a lot of attention, forcing me to be extra careful when driving around. If I parked with a date at "lovers' lane" the police would invariably come by and move me along. Once I made the mistake of providing a false name, requiring a great deal of explaining the following Monday morning in my Dad's office.

While I was too young to serve in World War II, in my senior year I joined the Indiana National Guard. My intention was to get a higher rating if I was drafted and join the Army Officer Candidate School (OCS) a program established to provide commissioned officers for the war effort. I attended weekly drills at the Armory and went to Camp Atterbury in southern Indiana for maneuvers on several occasions. Later in college, during the Korean War, students were deferred if you passed examinations each year and kept your grades above a C. But if your grades lagged below, the school was required to notify the draft board, and you were drafted.

On this basis, I was deferred until I finished law school. The draft board notified me each year that I was at the top of their list to be drafted. Finally, when I finished Law School, they sent me a notice to report for induction. I sent the notice back saying "Sorry guys, I just joined the Navy." When I left the Naval Reserve later in the 1960s, my active duty Navy time, plus my time in the Reserve, plus my National Guard service totaled to 12 ½ years total military service. I seriously considered signing up for another term in the Reserve in order to qualify for 20 years and a pension, but I had just started my law practice and the Navy Reserve was calling up people with experience similar to mine in the Navy.

New Castle High School has a unique reunion for alumni, inviting back all classes every five years, thus allowing you to see people in classes both ahead and behind you as well your own year. I returned for three reunions and we always had a very good turnout for the Class of 1947. At my 50th high school reunion, I was struck by the number of people still smoking and the large weight gain of those in my high school class. I was particularly surprised when chatting at my 50th high school reunion with a lady who I had briefly dated in high school when she suddenly asked, "Would you mind if I take my teeth out?" I stumbled, "Yes, I guess I don't mind." She proceeded to take her teeth out, hold them in her hand and continue our conversation. In a few minutes, I made an excuse to go to the bar, get a drink, and of course never returned.

At this same reunion, I chatted and introduced myself to a gentleman who seemed familiar but I couldn't recall his name. He says, "I remember you, Mac. I was in 8th grade when you made good grades and played on all the teams. You were my high school hero." He then introduces himself as Robert Allen, who was not only the principal speaker and honoree for the reunion, but Chairman of the Board and CEO of AT&T at the time. Needless to say, I was totally embarrassed.

Over the years New Castle has remained much the same as when I lived there in the '40s. The population is about the same at 17,000. The Chrysler plant, which was the backbone of employment, is now closed. While once a manufacturing center for steel, automobiles, caskets, scales, bricks, and more, getting new industries into town has been very difficult. One reason is that during the '50s at the Perfect Circle Piston Ring plant there were a number of violent labor disputes. After this, many employers avoided New Castle. When my father was Lt. Governor, which at the time included serving as Chairman of the Indiana Department of Commerce, he made a number of attempts to bring new industry into New Castle, but with limited success.

Like many small towns across the country, downtown New Castle is but a shadow of what it used to be, with one shopping center remaining on the edge of town. The high school I attended is now a middle school and a new high school, Chrysler High School, replaces it. CHS has a school gym that is not only the largest in the U.S., but indeed in the world, seating almost 10,000 people. As a matter of fact, of the ten largest high school gyms in the world, six are located in Indiana and most of these are in the North Central Conference where basketball games still sell out on Friday night.

Overall, my high school experience in New Castle was a positive one. The two losses to Mooreland and the loss to Muncie Central in basketball were life-long heartbreaks. And as I would later discover, I didn't spend as much time studying as I should have. But I gained a broader horizon and a better education in New Castle than if I had stayed in Mooreland. Like Mooreland, New Castle had a lot of hard-working people, but the social strata was more complex and many people had a college education. In New Castle, my family was by no means among those who had an old family business or deep pockets, but my father's position in politics and my mother's ability to get along in almost all social circles eased our transition into this city and helped me make friends.

Later, my parents would move to Indianapolis as did Mort Shapiro. Bob Keesling became an oral surgeon in Cincinnati. Ed Arnold moved to Washington, D.C., and had a great career in the V.A. Nate Roth became a doctor in Pasadena, Califronia, where his son, David Lee Roth, became a world-renowned rock star. Nearly everyone I knew moved away from New Castle but the lessons I learned there have stayed with me for many years. I learned a great deal in playing sports which helped me in many phases of my life thereafter, including keeping myself in reasonable if not good bodily shape.

PICKING UP SOME POLISH

1947-1951

Moving to a sophisticated college campus like DePauw University for a boy who was only two and a half years out of Mooreland was a substantial cultural shock. DePauw, in Greencastle, Indiana, not only draws students from all over the country, but draws heavily from the very wealthy suburbs in St. Louis, Indianapolis and Chicago. Many of my DePauw classmates had gone to private schools or to very outstanding public high schools. Also, when I enrolled in September, 1947 almost all of my freshmen class came straight from high school, but most of the male upperclassmen were returning veterans. Some of these men had attended DePauw during the war in a Navy Officers' Program, and returned to DePauw to finish their degree.

There were really four highlights to my three years at DePauw. I say three instead of four because I spent one year overseas on a scholarship, a story for a later chapter. The first and most important event was meeting Patricia Opie from Chicago Heights, Illinois. Our romance and marriage would eventually lead to most of the good things that happened subsequently in my life.

The second was to pledge and be an active member of the Beta Theta Pi fraternity. I learned more in my freshman year in this fraternity than in any other single period of my life, especially from the returning war veterans.

The third was athletics. I was fortunate to have made a decision to attend a small university where I was able to participate and play. I was also fortunate that DePauw had some excellent players at this time because of the returning veterans from the Navy Officers Program, as well as a top athletic schedule for a small university.

The final important factor was being able to spend a year abroad at University College, Southampton, a division of the University of London at the time. At the same time, Pat spent her junior year in Sweden. This had a profound effect on both of us and we matured very significantly that year. Pat's folks were able to visit her once, in Paris, but I was gone for the whole year with no visits, only correspondence with my folks and friends.

For a short period after the war, there was a complete demobilization of U.S. forces, but when the Cold War started heating up, the draft was resumed. While I was too young to be drafted for World War II in high school, the draft resumed while I was in college. The Selective Service instigated a procedure where they looked at college grades; in addition, persons eligible for the draft took a written examination to be able to continue their education with the intent that they would be drafted after they completed college. This began in my sophomore year at DePauw, and I was able to finish DePauw under this program. I was also able to complete law school on the same basis. For part of this time, I was also in the National Guard and attended weekly drills and two weeks of training camp in the summer.

A neighbor of ours in New Castle, a nationally known cartoonist named Dick Turner, suggested I consider DePauw. My other choices were Purdue, Princeton, and Tulane. I applied to Princeton and surprisingly was accepted; I still have the acceptance letter. I don't recall filling out the final paperwork for either Tulane or Purdue. I was interested in Tulane primarily because of basketball. A former coach in Logansport, Indiana named Cliff Wells, was at Tulane, and after a tryout in Anderson, Indiana, he offered me a basketball scholarship. I also applied for and received a Rector scholarship at DePauw which paid for all of my tuition. The Rector scholarship paid one-half of the tuition freshman year, three-quarters of the tuition sophomore year, and all of the tuition in the junior and senior years. Furthermore, in the final year, it covered all of the tuition paid in the freshman and sophomore years. The tuition at that time was $1,400 per semester, and our bill for room and board in the fraternity was $75.00 per month.

At the request of Dick Turner, the Phi Delta Theta house invited me to attend a spring rush weekend. I was fixed up with a young lady named Bambi Campbell, who was one of the best-looking sophomores on campus and really way too sophisticated for me. After our date, I went back to the Phi Delt house and a group of us sang songs around the piano. The singing eventually degenerated into dirty songs and somehow, I knew more than anyone else. I really thought I was a big hit. But I was never invited back to the Phi Delta Theta house.

Sometime after this experience, my uncle Will Parker found out that I was interested in DePauw. Like many other upperclassmen, Will was a returning veteran and came back to DePauw to finish on the GI bill. He was a member of Beta Theta Pi, and he and his wife, Lois, lived in the Johnson House, a housing unit for married service families. I visited DePauw for a second time on a spring rush weekend and stayed at the Beta House. Before the weekend was over, I was subjected to "the hot box" a mostly friendly session in which two or three of the older fraternity members would ask a ton of questions, talk up the benefits of membership, and hopefully ask you to pledge. After several sessions, I pledged Beta in the spring rush of 1947, along with three or four other recruits. It was the oldest fraternity on campus, dating back over 100 years.

Later during the fall rush, the balance of our pledge class of 16 was complete. It quickly became apparent to me that I was running in pretty fast company. Our class included four valedictorians from top midwestern high schools, including a number from Fort Wayne. Bob Koenig was the valedictorian or runner-up from North Side High School. Jack Fishering and Steve Ayers were also from Fort Wayne. Like being in the Army or Navy, we lived together for three years; it was much like going through boot camp; we shared many good and adverse times and learned a lot about each other and the world.

The Beta house was close to campus but an old house, formerly a doctor's residence, and totally inadequate to house 60 men. We were cramped in very small rooms. A saving grace was being able to use the dining room for a study hall at night. All of the freshmen and even many upperclassmen slept on a back porch converted into a sleeping dorm. Because of the numbers, many insisted that the windows were left wide open all night and it was not unusual to have snow on your bed when you awoke in the morning. I was very happy to eventually secure an electric blanket to keep somewhat warm at night.

With the exception of the freshmen class the rest of the

house were all returning veterans. Some had seen action in Europe, others in the Pacific, and all were a number of years older than us freshmen. Our pledge trainer was an ex-Marine. Every Monday night we had "line up". All of the freshmen pledges would line up in the living room facing the big stairway where the pledge trainer would stand eight to ten steps up. He would call each of us forward by name and review our transgressions for the past week: being late for study table, failing to properly address or show respect for one of the active members or their girlfriends, failing to know the names of each of the men in the house, not keeping your room clean, etc. The entire house stood around and watched this ordeal for the better part of an hour each Monday night. Every small fault from failing to tie your tie properly to lack of table manners was paraded out before your peers and we were each properly chewed out and awarded demerit points and chores to work off. While many DePauw fraternities used a paddle to correct pledges, this was not a practice in our house. But we were subjected to a punishment called "dead horsey" often several times a day for even small infractions; An active member would order you to lay on your back and pump your legs like a bicycle until they okayed you to quit.

Pledges were also expected to promptly be at the study table every night from 7:00 to 10:00. As older returning veterans, many of the active members were extremely serious about making up for lost time, getting an education and graduating with a degree. Many DePauw upperclassmen in our house ended up as Phi Beta Kappas and as a result, we had many good role models to guide us with studies.

We worked hard and played hard. No drinking was tolerated in the house, yet there was plenty of partying on the weekends at the Legion or elsewhere by the veterans. In addition to various initiation rites, pledges were required to complete a number of "projects". Either alone or in pairs, we were taken far out into the countryside and left to our own devices to return to Greencastle. Generally, pledges were left on a lonely country road where they would walk back to a main road and then hopefully be able to hitchhike back to campus. The greatest threat in completing this project was outrunning or outsmarting farmers' dogs at night.

All freshman pledges were required to wear green beanies and it was common practice to steal beanies from other fraternity's pledges and display them as trophies. This was generally in good fun, but sometimes led to other pranks and even fights. The Beta House had a particularly keen rivalry with the Sigma Chi House, which was located just around the corner from ours. Across from the Sigma Chi House was Meharry Hall, which had a high bell tower, with a bell that rang automatically to signal the start and end of classes. The bell had been donated to the University by the Sigma Chi's.

When the Sigma Chi bell rang at night, everyone knew it was because someone had hiked up to the third floor and crawled into the bottom of the bell tower to pull the rope. The Sigma Chi pledges would immediately stream from their House to hopefully catch the malefactor. They would bring him (or her which was sometimes the case) back to the Sigma Chi house and shave their heads. It was a big sport to try to ring the Sigma Chi bell and escape punishment!

During our sophomore year, a real flap developed when some Purdue students came to DePauw and rang the Sigma Chi bell. When the Sigma Chi pledges came out to apprehend them, a group of Purdue men lying in the bushes ambushed the pledges and a big fight ensued. But the Purdue men were outnumbered and the Sigma Chi's were able to capture a few and drag them back to their house where they shaved their heads, shaved all the hair off their legs, and painted argyle socks on their feet.

But the feeling of revenge was short-lived. The very next night a large caravan of cars headed down from Purdue to

Greencastle — about an hour and a half drive — with the intention of starting a big fight with the Sigma Chi's. The Sigma Chi's got word that the Purdue group was on the way and enlisted our house plus other nearby fraternities to assist in what was going to be a free-for-all brawl. We all laid in the bushes surrounding Meharry Hall primed for an epic fight with the Boilermakers from Purdue. Thankfully, the State Police also got word of the impending battle and stopped the 20-car caravan of Purdue men outside Greencastle, and the big fight never happened.

All of the fraternity houses had a house mother who was responsible for maintaining decorum and proper manners. Ours was Nanny Brooks, a wonderful lady of perhaps 70. When we had fraternity dances in our house, the young ladies would use the bathroom in Nanny's quarters. One night, unbeknownst to the girls, we planted a microphone in Nanny's bathroom so we could listen to the girls' private conversations while in the bathroom. I might add that this led to the breakup of a number of romances.

Our longtime master of maintenance and everything else that needed fixing in the house was Oscar Chapman. Oscar worked with the Beta house for almost 40 years, through the War and a succession of graduating classes. Oscar was an institution and when we returned for reunions, he was always the first person we wanted to see.

For one semester, I lived in a room next to a guy named Burley Colbrum, an Army veteran from St. Louis who also served as the President of the house. Burley had a head for business and later started a successful restaurant in St. Louis. I learned a small bit of business wisdom from Burley. House members would often come to his room to complain about a variety of problems from the small budget for food, to tiny rooms and difficulty paying house bills, etc. Burley would tell each one of them, "Alright, I'll take care of it. I'll take care of it." One day, I say, to Burley, "You know, I hear you tell all these people that you are going to take care of their problems, but you never actually do anything about their concerns. Burley shrugs his shoulders and replies: "If you don't do anything about most problems, 90 percent of them will go away anyway." The question that has lingered with me all these days is how to figure out which ten percent won't.

By the end of our freshman year, the pledges were grateful to learn that our entire 16-member pledge class made grades and were initiated into the Beta house. Less surprising is that from this class emerged a good number of doctors, lawyers, and successful businessmen. I was pleased to have been selected as the outstanding freshman pledge and received what was called the "Worth Merit Badge", a bejeweled Beta pin that I was permitted to wear during my sophomore year. While my grades were certainly adequate, by no means did I have the best grades in our class and I credit receiving the Merit Badge to my involvement in basketball and track. This was one of many times in my life that involvement in athletics was a deciding factor.

My final year in the Beta house was my senior year after returning from studying in England my junior year. I ended up rooming with my high school pal from New Castle, Bob Keesling, in the "crow's nest which was a small room on the top floor near the staircase. I returned from England with a number of affectations such as using the word "bawth" instead of "bath", drinking tea and smoking a pipe. But thankfully Keesling quickly cured me of such British mannerisms, by mimicking my behavior while doubling over in laughter.

I also returned from England with a small BSA motorcycle which I left at home in the garage when I returned to DePauw. About a month into my senior year, I got a call from my Mother, "Mac, come home and sell this damn cycle! Your Father has been trying to ride it. He's fallen off and nearly killed himself." I went home the following weekend and sold the cycle.

Pat was a pledge of Kappa Alpha Theta. DePauw is the Alpha Chapter of Kappa Alpha Theta, where the sorority was founded. They had a beautiful house at the other end of the campus, and Pat was part of a large pledge class of very attractive girls. They made a pretty picture with their poodle skirts and bobby sox. I met Pat at a football rally. She was a drum majorette, leading the band. When I first saw her, I leaned over to Jim Cory, one of my pledge brothers, and exclaimed: "Look at those legs — who is that?!" Jim replied, "I know her," and later introduced us. I was immediately smitten, although it took us a few years of dating other people before we formed a steady relationship.

During the war, DePauw served as a Navy officer's training school and a number of good athletes came through this program. After the war, officers often returned to DePauw where we had a number of good basketball players and an excellent schedule. We opened Indiana University's basketball season every year and Butler, Ball State, and Wabash were our biggest in-state rivals. In addition, we played many great out-of-state teams including Penn State, University of Iowa, University of Chicago, Washington of St. Louis, and others. There were no NCAA divisions at this time and colleges were all in one national ranking. I don't think we ever made the top 25, but IU and Butler did regularly. Our best player was Red Gardner, who went directly from DePauw to the Lakers, located in Minneapolis at the time. He played with the Lakers for a number of years.

I felt very lucky to make the JV team my freshman year as there were many returning good upper-class players from the previous year. And I was pleased to be promoted to the varsity team after leading the scoring in three or four JV games. I spent the rest of the year on varsity and even managed to start in a few games. As a freshman, I particularly remember going to Penn State. Penn State won, but we were in the game, and just getting there was an adventure. We took a Greyhound bus to Indianapolis where we caught the train to Pennsylvania and then took another bus to State College. Going home I recall riding in the back of the bus and listening to the veterans talk about their war experiences in Europe or the Pacific, while John Stauffer, another freshman, and I worked on our freshman Spanish.

Bill Garrett was the first African American in the Big Ten and a great basketball player at IU. Under Branch McCracken as coach, Indiana was a "fast-break" team and they usually outran everyone they played. Garrett would sometimes rebound, then was fast enough to be the point man on the break at the other end of the floor. I don't think DePauw won any of the three games I played at IU, but we were never totally blown out either.

Butler and Ball State were a different matter. We would beat Ball State on a regular basis and Butler on occasion. In my sophomore year, Butler had an outstanding team, ranked 11th nationally. Tony Hinkle was the athletic director and also coached football, basketball, and track. On this great team was a top scorer named Buckshot O'Brien, and a top guard named Jimmy Doyle. Jimmy and I always played head to head and it was always a real battle. On my best night, I got 18 off him, and held him to 10. Jimmy ended up as an All-American honorable mention. I was second in scoring overall that year, even leading the team in some games. Our record was a credible 12-7.

But while many of the games blur together, I have many distinct memories of our team my sophomore year, and especially our coach, Hal Hickman. When we played in St. Louis, we started to check into our hotel until the clerk looked at Russ Freeland, an African American and one of our best players and said: "I've got your rooms all ready and I've made arrangements for Mr. Freeland at a very nice hotel just down the road." Coach Hickman immediately stepped forward and said, "Do I understand that Mr. Freeland can't stay here with the rest of our team?" The clerk replied, "That's correct." Coach then said, "Then book us all at the hotel down the road." The clerk did and we left. There were no arguments, no push back, it was just the right thing to do. I have always very much respected Coach for making that decision with no hesitation and I'm not sure many others would have done the same thing. After all, it was 1948, 16 years before the Civil Rights Act became law and racial segregation and the Green Book still designated where black travelers stayed on the road. Nevertheless, neither the Coach nor our team was going to put up with discrimination against one of our players even if this was the norm in St. Louis.

After spending my junior year in England and not playing basketball for a year, I couldn't decide whether to play my senior year. In my first few weeks back, I still labored under the delusion that I was a worldly intelligentsia and above mundane things like basketball. The new coach, Jay McCreary, talked with me and I finally came out. I had terrible shin splints for the first month, a fact that I had completely forgotten until attending the 40th reunion of our '50-'51 team. Coach McCreary walked straight up to me and said, "Hi Mac. Remember those bad shin splints you had?" Jay McCreary moved from DePauw to Muncie Central High School where he served as a coach when small-town Milan beat Muncie Central in the final game of the State Tournament, a game made famous by the movie *Hoosiers.*

Our team my senior year was 14-3, with losses to IU, Iowa, and a heartbreaker to Wabash at the end of the season. We had two wins over both Butler and Ball State and ended up ranked 58th in the country, which was a pretty big deal in the time before NCAA class basketball. Our center and leading scorer was Lee Hamilton, who would go on to represent the 9th district of Indiana in Congress for 34 years and later served as vice-chairman of the 9/11 commission. Our team was not big, but we worked well together. There were no slackers on the floor or academically. A photo of our team in the Indianapolis Star that year touted the GPA of our top eight players as a 3.4; two went on to become doctors and two to be lawyers.

The Iowa game was quite interesting that year. We were coming off a loss at IU and we opened Iowa's season. They had an outstanding team, with an All-American center, 6'11" Chuck Darling. I guarded a 6'9" forward named Calsbeck. On defense, I would occasionally get shifted to Darling. I came to his shoulder in height. My instructions from the coach were to immediately foul Darling whenever he got the ball.

With about ten minutes left in the game, our coach sent in Don Markle, a pure shooter, but not as strong otherwise. Markle dropped in three shots and suddenly we were down two or three with five minutes to go. As we stood in a huddle at timeout, Markle pleaded: "Give me the ball, guys, give me the ball — I'm hot." On the next play, as Markle drove for the basket, one of Iowa's big men, also a football player, hit Markle hard. We dug him out about four rows up in the stands and he limped off the floor. That was the end of our run at Iowa. The final score was Iowa 74, DePauw 67.

In track, I limited myself to pole vaulting. I started with a bamboo pole and later switched to a metal pole and was vaulting about 11.5 to 12 feet. This was good enough for most small college meets. In my senior year, I won the Little State Meet (all small colleges in Indiana) which qualified me to go on to the Big State Meet, which also included IU, Purdue, and Notre Dame where I placed either fourth or fifth. The meet was at Notre Dame, in South Bend, and I attended with Dave Shepherd, another teammate from DePauw who also qualified. We traveled by commercial bus from Greencastle to Indianapolis to South Bend and each leg I passed my vaulting pole through a window to lay on the floor of the bus.

Much of the social life at DePauw involved fraternity and sorority parties and dances. Some of these were formal. The University would have two or three all campus dances each year usually at the gymnasium. Less formal were the "blanket parties" at either Robe-Ann Park or Handy's Pasture, a cow pasture at the edge of town, an often-messy affair when blankets ended up on cow pies. Most common was meeting a date or friends for 'pop' and hamburgers at the Double Decker or the Duck and then going out for a movie at the Von Castle or the "ArmPit", a local theater whose real name escapes me but we called it that because it smelled so bad.

Two events stand out from the end of my sophomore year that are interrelated and ultimately were life-changing. In addition to considering Princeton, Tulane and Purdue my senior year in high school I also considered the U.S. Military Academy at West Point. I was not accepted that year but applied again in my sophomore year at DePauw and was successful. I accepted the appointment and traveled to Fort Knox, Kentucky that spring where I took the required physical. The physical included not only a medical examination but also required passing a number of strength and endurance tests such as running a mile and a 100-yard dash within certain time limits, lifting weights, and doing a certain number of push-ups. One requirement involved doing backhand chin-ups on a bar. Because I had been a pole vaulter and had done chin-ups as part of an exercise program for a long time, I broke their chin-up record by a substantial number. I recall that the Sargent administering the test stared at me in disbelief.

I passed the physical and confirmed my plan to go to West Point. However, a few days later I ran into Pat while walking across campus. She told me she was giving strong consideration to going to Stockholm for her junior year and had applied for a scholarship. She told me that there was also a scholarship available to study in England and suggested that I might want to consider applying. Studying abroad at this time was fairly unusual, with only two or three students going from DePauw each year.

I did apply, was accepted, and ended up turning down the West Point appointment and instead went to England. I often wondered where I might have ended up if I had gone to West Point. By the time I would have finished my training, the Korean War would have been over, but I would have still been in the Army when Vietnam rolled around in the '60s.

Another milestone of my sophomore year was not quite so pleasant. While Pat and I had been dating, we both continued to date other people. I dated a Theta pledge from Indianapolis named Martha Curry. Martha and her sister, Helen, were both models at the L.S. Ayres department store in Indianapolis and very attractive young ladies. Martha was having trouble with freshman English and I pulled out one of my freshman English themes from the previous year to give her some suggestions. She got desperate for time and ended up copying a portion of my paper and turning it in as her own work. Unfortunately, she had the same professor I had the year before who remembered my theme, found it in his files, and saw that she had plagiarized part of my work. We were both called up in front of the Disciplinary Commission. I recall wearing my letter sweater with a big "D" to the hearing room even though it was a frightfully warm day and the room was small and hot. I ended up getting a reprimand and she lost credit for the second semester of her freshman English course and had to take it over again.

During the summers while at DePauw, I worked at home in New Castle, either at the Chrysler factory on the shock absorber line or on a surveying crew for the County Surveyor. The foreman of the shock absorber line had a potent mixture of employees to contend with, including 300 to 400 high school and college kids as well as 100 to 150 old-timers in his department — all trying to turn out shock absorbers for Dodges and Plymouths. My shift was 6:30 in the morning until 2:30 in the afternoon. As soon as I got home from work, I would take a shower and immediately head to the golf course and play until dark. Then I would scrounge a car with friends and "buzz" the drive-ins, hoping to find a party or meet some girls. I eventually got home by midnight — sometimes later — and then got up at 5:30 the following morning to dress, catch the bus, and start my factory shift at 6:30. After two or three weeks of this lifestyle, my father made the observation that I probably wouldn't survive the summer. Somehow, I did.

During my sophomore summer I also visited Pat at her home in Chicago Heights. Her folks belonged to Olympia Fields Country Club, which was in the magnificent position of having four 18-hole golf courses. When I returned to DePauw that Fall, I commented to my fraternity brothers that when I saw these four 18-hole golf courses I knew it was true love. Pat has never liked this story for some reason.

Another time while visiting Pat in Chicago Heights I was out with another fraternity brother from "Da Heights" named Wilbur Cielke. We were riding home late one evening with a friend of Wilbur's named Jimmy Zerante, who had been a local high school legend as a football player. We pulled up to a stoplight about midnight and the car in front didn't move as soon as Jimmy thought it should and so he laid on the horn. Immediately all four doors of the car opened and four large African-American men jumped out ready for a fight. Jimmy said to Wilbur and me, "I'll take care of this." Jimmy was only 5'9", but about three feet wide. Jimmy got out of the car and walked toward the guys. They all recognized him immediately and exclaimed "Oh, Jimmy, what a great player you were, you're da man, and so on." They all shook hands and got back in the car. All the while, Wilbur and I crouched under the dashboard.

Yet another time visiting Pat, my good friend Mort Shapiro came along and we went to Chicago's Soldier Field to see the College All-Star Game. This was the end of the season attraction before the Super Bowl where the best college players played the best pro players. Through Pat's Dad, I booked a room for Mort and me at the Edgewater Beach, a posh resort that stood on the lakefront for nearly half a century. But when we walked up to the registration desk, the clerk pointed at Mort and said, "Mr. Shapiro will not be able to stay at this hotel." We picked up our bags and immediately left. This was 1949 in Chicago. Mort, who traveled quite a bit, had run into this before but this was my first experience with discrimination against Jewish people. I was greatly embarrassed because I had made the reservation, but in the end, there was nothing I could do about it.

In addition to athletics, I was involved in three other activities in my senior year: speech, debate, and politics. I entered a campus-wide speech contest and made it to the final three where we gave our speeches in Meharry Hall to faculty and about 400 to 500 students. My speech was on Communism, a hot subject at the time. The fellow who won was an Army veteran who gave a riveting presentation about the horrors of being one of the first to enter Buchenwald at the end of the war.

I also participated in a number of debate tournaments and especially recall one meet at Purdue on the topic of "The Future of the World is not Culture but Agriculture."

Finally, I served as the Campaign Chairman for a bright guy named Jack Anderson in his run for DePauw student body president. Jack and I made the rounds, speaking at all the living units, running a nighttime rally, and a big parade. Alas, we came up short. Jack went on to Harvard Law and had a very successful career with one of the big Chicago law firms, ending up as the Chairman of the Joyce Foundation, a sizable national foundation.

Because of our year abroad, Pat and I were not eligible to become members of Phi Beta Kappa; otherwise, I think that both of us would have qualified. Our overseas classes did qualify for graduation credit, but not for Phi Beta Kappa. As a senior, I received the Scholar-Athlete Award, which is awarded to the person in each class who best combines scholastic and athletic performance. This is one of the awards that I was most pleased about because it was not limited to athletics. I have always believed that participation in sports can assist academic achievement. In sports, you learn discipline and hard work, teamwork, responsibility, and also, humility. All of these are important not only to academic achievement, but in life. Sports help develop character and teach how to deal with both success and adversity. Many of the good things that have come my way were either directly or indirectly due to participation in sports. Many years later, I was very pleased to be selected to join the DePauw Athletic Hall of Fame for my participation in basketball and track.

After Pat and I returned from our year overseas, we dated almost exclusively. I gave her my fraternity pin and this was a symbol of "going steady". I don't think we dated other people from then on — at least not to my knowledge.

The ties of a small college like DePauw is illustrated by the fact that Pat and her sorority sisters have kept a pledge class letter going for 70 years. Each sister writes a letter twice a year that is copied and sent to the entire group. The reunions are always very well attended; at our 50th reunion over 200 of our class of 384 returned which is quite substantial considering the people we had also lost.

At our 10th reunion, I recall trading news and gossip and jokes at a cocktail party. One fellow points to an attractive woman standing some distance away and begins to reminisce at length about her lively sex life on campus a decade ago, jumping into bed with this guy and that guy. As he continues to elaborate, another guy chimes in and asks, "I wonder what she's doing now?" A third guy standing next to me replies with the straightest face in the world, "Well, I'll tell you what she's doing now, I married her." Everyone looks down at the floor for an awkward moment and then excuses themselves to get a drink or go to the bathroom and the group quietly dissipates.

As it turned out, DePauw was probably a wise choice for me. I would have been fortunate to make the bench playing ball at either Purdue or Tulane. I got to be a slightly bigger fish in a smaller pond and the fraternity house helped me polish some of my rough edges growing up in rural Mooreland. Pat and I built friendships that have lasted over many years. DePauw had and continues to have a good academic reputation which I'm sure was helpful in my getting into law school. And most importantly, this was where I met Pat.

I can't help but wonder how things might have been different had I chosen to go south or east to school or to West Point. Perhaps, things would have turned out okay, but I think the odds are good that I made the best choices — both as to college and my lifetime partner.

THE GREAT ADVENTURE
1949-1950

Reviewing one past year of my life leaves me exhausted. Even as a 20-year-old with a vast amount of energy and out looking for adventure, I'm astounded by how much got packed into this brief period of time.

I elected to turn down an appointment to the U.S. Military Academy and instead take a scholarship to University College, Southampton, located in Southampton, England, a division of the University of London at that time. It is now Southampton University. This meant leaving my life at DePauw, which had become fairly structured and predictable, and going into a totally different environment. It meant leaving behind not only my friends and classmates at the DePauw campus, but the athletic teams - track and basketball - where I was very involved.

DePauw, in 1949, had only three or four students studying abroad and no one else went to England that year. I knew almost no one in England and was away for a year. My only contact with friends and family was limited to letter correspondence. Long-distance telephone calls were very expensive, and I can remember only one or two calls with my parents at most.

However, immediately after the War, there was a great deal of good feeling about Americans, and people were very willing to help when they found out that you were a "Yank". The Marshall Plan also created a lot of goodwill. On the other hand, the Cold War was just beginning to heat up, and was a very potent political force in Europe, and in England, Churchill had been voted out of office and Clement Atlee and the Labor Party were voted in.

I traveled from New York to Southampton on the original S.S. Queen Elizabeth and my tourist class fare was $165. The ship sailed directly into Southampton, a major seaport on the south coast of England. Southampton had suffered extensive damage to the whole port region from bombing during the War.

One very good thing happened shortly after I arrived - the British pound was devalued from $4.00 to $2.40 to the dollar. This meant that my U.S. dollars went considerably further than anticipated.

At the end of World War II, Britain was on its knees economically. There was tremendous damage from the German bombing and the war debt was gigantic. In certain respects, Britain emerged from the war in worse shape than Germany. The Chancellor of the Exchequer, Sir Stafford Cripps, became known for his Austerity Plan in which everybody tightened their belt and tried to make the best out of dire economic circumstances. Almost everything was rationed and one of my first tasks was to go to the local office and get a ration book. Sugar, tea, shoes, meat, and almost everything else was rationed.

I had the name of only one acquaintance before I arrived — Marjorie Harbor. She was a schoolteacher who lived in the south end of London. Before the War, she had taught in New Castle and had kept up a correspondence with friends we had in common. I went to visit her shortly after I arrived in London, and she was a really good friend to me, especially during the first few months when I knew no one else. Her home was not damaged by the bombing, but many of the houses on her block had been damaged or totally obliterated.

Most of my classes took place at Southampton, although I did have some lectures in London at the London School of Economics. I lived in a residence hall, about a 20-minute walk from the University. I had a scholarship that paid for my residence hall and tuition, and I paid for any additional expenses on my own.

The residence hall was a brick building built around a quadrangle with a commons or dining area in one wing. At each entryway, there were four rooms on the first floor and four rooms on the second floor. We had a small kitchen and a communal bathroom that we shared for our entryway.

To get from the residence hall to the campus we normally walked, but at some point, I purchased a bicycle and rode it. We had to attend all classes wearing a black gown, which was the academic uniform. One of the photos I have is of me riding the bicycle with the black gown streaming out back. We also had to wear a gown to the dining hall in the evening for dinner.

Overall the food was bad even for a college dormitory. Because of rationing, meat was very hard to obtain and very expensive. Sometimes for dinner we had whale meat, which was not bad, especially if served in a thick gravy. We also had Australian rabbit with legs sometimes 10" long and so tough you could hardly chew it.

We were required to eat dinner in the residence hall. This was a formal procedure where we all stood in gowns at our assigned tables and waited for faculty members who lived in the residence hall to come in. They would file in and stand at the high table. Next, Reverend Herbert Livesy, a Vicar of the Church of England and "master" of our residence hall, would come in. After a moment of silence, the Vicar would say a prayer in Latin and we would all be seated. We were required to sit for a reasonable period of time before we could excuse ourselves. Many times after dinner, we would either go back to our room and attempt to cook something edible in our little kitchen, or we would go out to a pub for fish and chips.

One of my friends, Peter South, was married and his wife, who lived in the north of England. would send him goose eggs, carefully wrapped in thick excelsior. Sometimes, she sent as many as a dozen in a box. My folks had sent me a case of Spam from home. So, Peter and I would go back after dinner and cook up Spam and goose eggs. That was a traditional dinner for us, then sometimes we would go to the pub for a beer afterward.

It was a custom, also, for the Vicar to invite some of the students living in the residence hall to his private quarters for a "drop of port" before dinner. In the beginning, this was an honor to have the Vicar taking a personal interest. Later it became apparent that the Vicar would start with his port before guests arrived and by the time dinner was served, he was well into his cups. One now-famous evening we went through our normal custom of all standing in place in our gowns waiting for the faculty and the Vicar to file in. The Vicar finally came in and stood for the moment of silence before giving his prayer in Latin. After a minute or two, it became apparent that the Vicar could not remember the prayer and he finally said, "Boys, I can't remember the damn prayer, please sit down". The place went into immediate uproar.

As I was the only American in the residence hall and indeed the entire University at this time, my nickname was "the Yank". But I did become friends with one Brit living in the residence hall who had lived in the U.S. — Alan Cheshire. Because of the bombing in England, Alan was one of a great number of British children who had been sent to the U.S. to live during the War. Alan had spent two or three years living with a family in Boston where he went to high school. He was the only person who had any personal knowledge of the U. S. Alan and I spent a great deal of time together. Alan suffered from epileptic seizures and I eventually learned how to support him. This was before Dilantin and other drugs which are now able to control such seizures. We would be out in the evening at a pub or maybe even just sitting in the room after dinner and Alan would have a seizure. The first time or two this happened, I was fearful for his life and didn't know what to do. But over time, I learned to get him on the floor and hold him so he couldn't thrash around and hurt himself. I would loosen his tie and make sure that he could breathe. After perhaps five minutes the seizure would pass, and Alan would return to a semblance of normality, although it would usually leave him very exhausted. If we were out, I would help him walk home.

Another friend was Tony Sutton. Tony was from London and had grown up in a tough working-class neighborhood. However, Tony was very enterprising and he ended up immigrating to Los Angeles in the late 1950s. The last I heard of him, he had a very successful business career there; unfortunately, I lost track of him. However, daughter Carole found him on the internet. He became a Fellow at the Hoover Institute at Stanford and was the author of over 20 books, many dealing with the Cold War and the Soviet Union. He became very well-known as a political activist before that was popular.

Another friend was Alistair. I can't remember his last name, but he was very much into parapsychology and hypnotism. I spent a great deal of time with Alistair and we took many trips to London where we attended meetings of the British Parapsychology Society. Alistair would hypnotize me, Tony, and some of our other friends. This was my first exposure to hypnotism and autosuggestion. I was not a very good subject, perhaps because of my lack of concentration!

Cess Ascoff, another friend, was an ex-RAF pilot. Cess was the only person I knew who had a car — a small two-seat MG. Later, Cess would introduce me to a young lady, and, along with his girlfriend, we would squeeze four of us into his two-seater car and go for rides in the countryside, generally on Sunday afternoons.

Another friend, Peter South, who received the goose eggs from his wife, was an ex-RAF pilot and had five German planes to his credit. Peter gave me flying lessons, which I will discuss later.

Two other friends, I remember distinctly, although unfortunately not their names. One was an officer in the Polish Navy during the War who had seen considerable action aboard a British destroyer in the North Sea. The other was a Jewish boy from Holland who somehow managed to survive Buchenwald. There were other friends from playing rugby and classes, but these are the ones who left the strongest impressions. Since leaving England in 1950, I have only seen Cess Ascoff again. In the 1980s we were in London and went to Fleet, a small town outside of London, where Cess and his wife lived. He was retired at this time, mostly teaching folk dancing, but had enjoyed a long and interesting career as one of the designers of the Concorde. Unfortunately, I lost track of all the other friends I had in England.

The courses I took at the University were mostly political science and political theory. However, I did have one course in English Law. In general, the students were more advanced and studied longer hours than university students did in the U.S. Course work is handled differently than in the U.S. Students are expected to attend classes and take notes, but there are no interim exams. The only exam was at the end of the fourth year and then the students took one comprehensive examination to determine whether they received a degree. The exam not only determined the degree, it determined the grade of the degree. The highest grade is an "upper first". To get an upper first from Oxford or Cambridge is a very distinctive achievement. After an upper first, it is a "second" and then a "pass". If a student is not successful in passing the comprehensive examination then they can take it again in another year, possibly more than once. But if they do not pass the examination, they do not receive a degree.

Although there were no interim examinations, there were plenty of papers to prepare and course work to complete. The professors expected us to participate in class discussions. There were also no course textbooks but we were given a long list of books to read.

In my Political Theory class, I was expected to read not only John Locke and Hobbs but also Hegel, Marx, Engels, and many others — not abstracts, but the original works. I might be asked to give my interpretation of a particular writer and his views, or what a particular writer would think about the current political situation, where he would stand, and why. I found all of this very challenging, and spent considerable time reading either in the library or my room. Often, I would be asked to postulate on how a particular writer's view or a current topic might be perceived from an "American point of view". I kept most of my notes in a notebook, which I still have.

In addition to my political theory classes, I took a course in British Law from a local Barrister who came to the University one afternoon each week. He also invited us to the Assizes in Winchester where he was defending a murder case. It was very interesting to see how a British capital trial was conducted. The defendant had to stand almost the whole time in a "dock" facing the judges, and the courtroom. While I do not remember the details of the case, my Barrister teacher lost, and his client was convicted.

Most of my professors were very liberal, bordering on either Socialist or even further left, and I was not immune from some of this indoctrination. Many of my letters home to my parents exhibited my newfound liberal opinions and positions. I am sure my father — being the good Republican that he was — began to question his decision to let me study in England.

The late 1940s was also a period of testing atomic and hydrogen weapons both in the U.S. and Russia. A prevailing mood among my University friends was great doubt as to whether any of us would reach our 25th birthday because of the very distinct probability of a war between the U.S. and the Soviet Union.

I did write home a few non-political letters discussing my daily routines at the University and describing general life, customs and culture in England. My father passed these letters along to our cousin Congressman Ralph Harvey, who passed them along to several newspapers, including the New Castle and Indianapolis papers, where they were published.

One of the first things I did in England was to try to find a basketball team to join. The nearest team was in London some 70 miles away and it was not practical to travel that far by train just to play basketball. I next decided to try my hand at soccer, but quickly discovered that, unlike my British friends who grew up kicking a soccer ball, my foot coordination was not that good. Even after various lessons from friends, I had little luck learning to play soccer.

Rugby was a different matter. Having played football in high school, I discovered that rugby had many familiar aspects. The ball is larger and the rules are somewhat different, but there are a lot of similarities. I was not great at kicking on the run, but I could pass the ball, which my teammates had never tried. I was able to gain a spot on the rugby team and ended up "winning my colors" which is equivalent to earning a letter in sports in the U.S.

Rugby games took place rain or shine and it seemed like we always played in the mud. Before the game was half over, we were often covered with mud. Once I went down in a muddy field and got up thinking I had a hand full of mud. Instead, my finger was broken and bent over to the side. Another finger was jammed. I had the British Health Service take care of both of those fingers, but they are both still a little crooked today.

For a rugby match, we would go to another university on a bus. While we didn't have cheerleaders there was always a group of young ladies who went along to watch the match and serve tea at halftime. They would bring a table and teapot out onto the field and we would stand around and have tea with the opposing players. I always found the halftime custom of drinking tea with my opponents strange after trying to beat each other's brains out on the field. Then sometimes after the match we would go out with the opposing players to a pub or enjoy a keg of beer together on the bus. It was all quite civilized.

I took all of my clothes to England in a big old trunk and kept it in my room. There was almost no room for hanging clothes, with only one very small closet. Because of the economic Austerity Program, most of the students had only one sport coat, one suit, and a couple of sweaters. This was usually the extent of their wardrobe.

I also represented the University in track meets although the University didn't technically have a track team. As a pole vaulter, I went to various meets including the all-United Kingdom games held at Wembley Stadium in London — still a world-renowned arena. Pole-vaulting was almost an unknown sport in Europe at the time and a crowd would gather whenever I practiced or vaulted in a meet.

My social life was not extensive, but my friend Cess Ascott was dating a young lady at the French Legation in Southampton. She had a friend, Lauren McDougall, who had been in the WAAF (women's RAF) during the War. Her job was in an air raid plotting unit where they traced incoming German raids on a big table. Cess and his young lady and Lauren and I double-dated a number of times using Cess' MG and squeezing all four of us into the two seats. Lauren lived alone with her mother as her father had died many years earlier. I kept up a correspondence with Lauren for a short time after returning to the U.S. when she went to live at her uncle's rubber plantation in Malaysia. One of my letters to Malaysia was returned a year or two later with a note that Lauren had been killed during a Communist uprising where insurgents took over the Uncle's plantation.

I also wrote articles for the University campus newspaper. There was a lot of discussion at this time about education and segregation in the United States and I wrote three or four articles on this topic. I also was on the debate team and made two or three trips to London and Oxford and other universities for debates. I got involved with the National Union of Students, which I found out later was a Communist-front organization. I went to the NUS conference in Cardiff, Wales, where there were many resolutions condemning the U. S. and supporting Soviet Union positions in the Cold War.

At some point, I decided that my bicycle was insufficient and I needed faster "wheels" to get around. I scraped together some money and bought a pre-war BSA motorcycle for about

$90. This cycle had been used all during the War by the RAF and had god-only-knows how many miles on it. It was in bad repair, but I was able to use one of the University's machine shops to do repair work. While I was not very competent, I always found people willing to help "the Yank." With this motorcycle, I not only took trips to the Isle of Wight, a scenic and well-known tourist area which lies just off Southampton, but I also traveled through the New Forest where I visited John Everett Clayton's parents. John was married to my Aunt Martha and his parents lived in a beautiful thatched hut in the New Forest. I spent a beautiful spring day riding through the forest and enjoying afternoon tea at their house before riding back to Southampton.

On July 4th it was traditional for the American Embassy to hold a Fourth of July party and invite all visiting Americans. The daughter of the American Ambassador was a very good friend of Princess Margaret so she attended the party and we were all able to meet and chat with her. She was perhaps 20 or 21 at the time and had a very engaging personality.

With Alistair, I often took trips into London to go to the British Parapsychology Society. We heard lectures on hypnotism and extra-sensory perception. We listened to a number of stories about poltergeists. Once Alistar and I were assigned by the Society to a London veterans' hospital where we spent the night watching for a ghost who was supposedly frequenting a hallway. Another time we spent the better part of the evening at a bombed-out building looking for a "lady in brown" who purportedly had been killed when the building was destroyed. Traveling with a group by motorcycle, we went to Stonehenge just outside of Winchester in the early dawn of Summers Solstice which was when the ghosts of the druids supposedly returned each year. We wandered freely among the ancient stones searching for ghosts as Stonehenge was not closed to the public at that time.

If the motorcycle and parapsychology adventures weren't enough, I also decided to take flying lessons. My friend Peter South, an ex-Spitfire pilot, said that if I would agree to rent a plane, he would give me lessons. We decided on a Tiger Moth, an open cockpit, twin-seat biplane, and the primary trainer used by RAF during WWII. Of course, after flying a Spitfire and with five German planes to his credit, this was mere child's play for Peter.

On the first trip out, after various spins and maneuvers, we tried a loop. Just as we got to the top of the loop and were hanging upside down, Peter stalled the plane and we lost centrifugal force. Suddenly, I felt myself coming out of the open cockpit. My whole life flashed before my eyes. I had a parachute but no instructions on how to use it. A split second later, I stopped. All I did was fall to the end of my straps - only a couple of inches. Of course, Peter knew this would happen and once we landed, he laughed uproariously. I am reminded of an old saying that only me and the laundry man knew how scared I was that day.

I did, however, learn to fly the Tiger Moth. We simulated stalls and spins and I eventually even learned to land the plane. One day Peter decided I was ready to solo. We had just flown over a terrible aircraft accident not far from the small field where we were doing practice landings and we were now sitting on the end of the runway. Peter jumped out and exclaimed, "This is your day to solo!" I replied, "What, after seeing that accident? I'll cream this thing." "Nope, you are ready to go," he assured me. And so off I went.

I subsequently completed four or five hours of solo time and still have my logbook. But that was the last of my flying lessons. Many years later while traveling in New Zealand, we stopped at a small airfield in the countryside where they offered exhibition rides in a Tiger Moth. Unfortunately, the pilot was not there that day as I would have liked to go up in one again. With the open cockpit, you feel just like the Red Baron.

In addition to the day and weekend trips, the real highlight of my stay in England were the trips I took between terms. Under the British university system, we got four weeks off at Christmas and another four weeks for Spring break. The British students utilized this time to study, read, write papers, and generally catch up on academic work that they didn't have time to do during the regular term. I on the other hand utilized this time to take trips.

The first trip was Christmas 1949 to Stockholm to see Pat. On my way, I went to London to shop for a Christmas present for her. I bought a fur jacket that cost about $50. I thought it was the greatest thing going, but when I gave it to her, she wasn't all that excited. I am not sure what type of fur it was. It may have been rabbit, or even something less valuable.

Anyway, I took the ferry from London to Malmo, Sweden, and then traveled by train to Stockholm. Pat arranged accommodations for me in a girl's dormitory. Most of the girls had gone home for the holidays, but a few were still there. They all wore long underwear, which they washed and hung in the bathroom. I will say that none of them were bought at Victoria's Secret.

Pat had taken an exchange scholarship and lived in Stockholm with the Lilliekreutz family. The Lilliekreutz's son, Bengt, studied at DePauw at this same time, with financial support from Pat's parents. The first semester Pat attended the University of Stockholm and the second semester she moved to a small town north of Stockholm to study at the University of Uppsala. Before starting the exchange program, Pat took a crash course in Swedish at the Berlitz school in Chicago since all of her classes would be in Swedish. The Lilliekreutz family was in the export business and they were reasonably well-to-do. Mr. Lilliekreutz had the title of

"Baron" and traced his family back over ten generations. We ate formal dinners in their dining room surrounded by paintings of his many ancestors.

The Lilliekreutz family had plans to spend Christmas at a lake cottage they owned about 60 or 70 miles out of Stockholm and took Pat with them. Pat made arrangements for me to spend Christmas with a family in Stockholm. One of the interesting things we had to eat was called "lutefisk", which is a fish boiled in a lye solution. This is a traditional Swedish Christmas dish and very bitter to the taste. How I got more than one or two bites down I will never know. After Christmas, I took the train to the Lilliekreutz cottage and spent two or three days there. We went elk hunting and tramped around the woods for an entire day but unfortunately got no elk.

I returned to Stockholm and took a train to Hamburg, Germany, and then across Germany to Munich and then to Bad Tolz in Bavaria. Hamburg was not damaged as badly as Dresden, which was completely obliterated by one of the British "1,000 plane raids", but it was still damaged extensively, particularly in the area of the railroad yards. This was four years after the war ended, but the damage was so great that it would take years to rebuild.

During the train ride across Germany, I saw devastation everywhere from the Allied raids, and Munich, of course, was badly damaged. There was a U. S. Army divisional headquarters in Bad Tolz and my uncle Earl Bywaters, married to my father's sister, Helen Parker, was stationed there. Earl was a small plane pilot that did artillery spotting and other duties. I spent New Year's Eve with them at an Officer's Club on the base. The following day we went skiing at Mt. Zugspitze in Bavaria. It was a beautiful sunny day and the ski resort area was absolutely gorgeous.

After visiting with them for three or four days, I took the Orient Express from Munich to Paris and then on to London.

The Orient Express, made famous by Agatha Christie's novel "Murder on the Orient Express", was a luxury train before the war but in 1949 it was not terribly opulent. This was a good thing because I did not have an opulent budget. In fact, my entire four-week trip from Southampton to London to Stockholm and then across Germany and France and then back to London was all done on a very minimal budget at student rates.

During the winter months, I purchased the beat-up BSA motorcycle. For Spring break, a British friend Seymour and I planned to ride double on the motorcycle through France and into Spain, then over to the French Riviera, back to Paris, and then back across the channel to London. This was our very ambitious plan for a beat-up old cycle that had seen many thousands of miles as a "messenger cycle" for the RAF.

The first part of the trip went well. We took the ferry across to Dieppe, and then started south through France. We would stay at little pensions or inns or whatever we could find for each night. Neither of us spoke French. My friend Seymour spoke German while I spoke "some" Spanish. We found that if we really got stuck understanding French, Seymour could speak in German. The French, after years of occupation, generally knew or understood German, but refused to speak the language until actually forced to do so.

Numerous times we traveled in the rain. We bought two old RAF flying suits that were fairly warm and somewhat rainproof, but we usually ended up soaked down to our underwear.

Outside of Bordeaux in the south of France, just as we were leaving a little village, a young lady ran out in the road and stopped us yelling "hospital, hospital, hospital!" We thought perhaps someone was hurt so we turned down a side road to see what we could do to help. Immediately, three or four guys jumped out, grabbed us, and took our wallets. Luckily, we kept our passports, identification, and most of our money in money belts so they didn't get much money with just the wallets. They let us have our cycle back and we moved on. But we were a lot more careful about getting off the main roads after that.

Spain, after the Spanish Revolution in the 1930s was under the dictatorship of Francisco Franco. We had difficulty even getting visas to go to Spain. Traveling on the roads, we were stopped every 15 or 20 miles by the Guardia Civile, the Spanish National Police, who would check our passports. They controlled all traffic on the highways and people could not pass from one district to another without proper credentials. With American and British passports, we were a real anomaly. The Guardia Civile did not know what to do with our credentials so they just let us through!

We spent a day in Burgos, a beautiful city that had been Franco's headquarters during the Civil War. Then on the way from Burgos to Madrid, our cycle broke down outside of a small village late in the afternoon. There was no inn or place to stay in this village. Finally, some of the villagers took us to one of the leading citizens and he agreed to keep us overnight. The wife went out behind the house and pulled a rabbit out of a cage, twisted its head off, skinned it and cooked it over an open fire for dinner that evening. They had a young daughter in her late teens and she had heard many American songs on the radio. She was very happy to join us in singing a few American songs in English.

The next day we scratched around for some means of getting into Madrid where we hoped to repair our cycle. Finally, we located a truck with mostly junk aboard that was going to Madrid. We got an old door and pushed the cycle up the door onto the back of the truck and onto the load of junk. We rode in the front with the driver into Madrid. We didn't know where to go but since Seymor was British we decided to go to the British Embassy. The Embassy is a very imposing building with a beautiful fence and Marine guards on every gate. We stopped in front of the Embassy with our junk truck and got out to unload the cycle. Very quickly Marine guards hustled us around to the back of the Embassy. They weren't about to let us unload from a junk truck at the front of the British Embassy.

We finally found a repair shop and got our cycle repaired. After sightseeing in Madrid for two or three days, we set off for Barcelona. In Barcelona, we stayed at a little pension where we met two young ladies who we invited to go to a bullfight. Because there were almost no restrooms at the bullfight, men urinated everywhere on the streets after the fight. I carefully guided my date back and forth across the street to avoid having someone urinate on us as we left the bullring and returned home to the pension.

From Barcelona, we traveled across the high desert into Zaragosa and from there across the Pyrenees into France and up to Lyon. In Lyon, Seymour and I stayed with a young lady (and her husband) who had worked in the Washington office of my cousin, Congressman Ralph Harvey. They were both studying at the University of Lyon at the time. We spent a day or two with them and then started out for Paris. A few miles out of Lyon, our cycle gave up again and this time it was beyond repair. They wouldn't let me sell the cycle in France, or even give it away. I had to ship it back to England, so I put it on a train back to London. The shipping costs took almost all of the small amount of money we had left so we had no means of getting to Paris. We decided that our only option was to hitchhike.

Our first ride was a tanker carrying wine up from the south of France into Paris. The driver would stop every two or three hours, take out a big can, go around to the back of the tanker, turn on the spigot and fill the can with wine, with much more spilling on the ground. We passed the can around and drank for three days while he drove towards Paris One night the driver stopped overnight in a small town and he stayed at an inn. We didn't have any money so we stopped a policeman and asked him if there was any place we could stay. The only place that he knew of was the jail. So Seymour and I spent a night in jail at Villafranca, France.

A day or two later in Paris, I met up with Pat and her folks who had come to visit from the U.S. They were among the first passengers of the Lockheed Constellations which just started making transatlantic flights and this was the first pressurized-cabin civil airliner series to go into widespread use. Because meat was so expensive and nearly unavailable at that time in Europe, Pat's father, Earle, decided to bring steaks packed in dry ice on the plane with him. We took the steaks to one of the nicest restaurants on the Champs-Elysees and handed them to the waiter to send to the chef to prepare for dinner. Before handing over the steaks Earle took out his pocket knife and notched the bones in a certain way so that he would recognize the steaks when they returned. He had brought steaks all the way from the U.S. and he didn't want anyone substituting something inferior and keeping his steaks for themselves!

Upon returning to England, I repaired the cycle and immediately sold it. I learned that I could buy a new motorcycle without a purchase tax if I agreed to take the cycle out of the country with me. This represented a very substantial savings and made a brand-new cycle no more than $250. Somehow, I scrounged up this amount of money and bought a new small 125cc BSA which I planned to use in the summer to travel to the north of England and Scotland.

Upon completion of the Spring term at the University, I headed north on my new cycle. I had agreed to participate in three athletic events on this trip; one was a track meet in the European Games in New Castle, England, to represent Great

Britain in the pole-vault. Because there were very few pole-vaulters at the time, I ended up tying with another vaulter from France for first place. I had my vaulting pole shipped by rail from Southampton to New Castle for this event. Later I shipped the pole to Luss, a small village on the banks of Loch Lomond, where I was asked to give a pole-vaulting exhibition during their Highland Games. I also had my golf clubs shipped to St. Andrews, where I had been invited to play in the All British Universities Match. This was a two-day golf tournament. On the first day I was one of the leaders, shooting a 77. However, the second day I did not play well and fell out of contention.

When roaming on your own on a motorcycle you meet a lot of interesting people. At Luss, I met an innkeeper's daughter and we went for a picnic on a beautiful island on Loch Lomond. We spent some time touring together on the Isle of Skye. However, when I got to St. Andrews, I found that the innkeeper's daughter had followed me there and attended my golf tournament. I had some difficulty explaining to her that this was not the romance of the century.

The Isle of Skye is a very picturesque place, with the Cuillin Mountains which seem to come straight out of the sea. I also toured the lake country of northern Great Britain and went across the moors in Yorkshire. This was a rather scary situation, although perhaps mostly in my head. I came across the moors late in the afternoon just as it was getting dark and the fog was rolling in. There was no traffic and all I could think of was the Sherlock Holmes tale, *The Hound of the Baskervilles*. The moors are a very desolate area anytime but especially so when night comes on.

One night in a pub I met an engineer who invited me to go visit his friends outside the village who were gypsies. We went to where the colorful gypsy wagons and horses were parked and spent the evening there. One woman, a friend of the engineer, told us she was very unhappy with her husband and so she sometimes changed him into a cat. Sure enough, you would either see the husband or you would see the cat, but you would never see them both at the same time.

Traveling on your own, particularly as a Yank in Britain was relatively easy — there was a lot of goodwill left over from WWII. On the other hand, traveling by yourself over a long period can be pretty lonely and I was glad to get back to London.

I had one last trip planned and this was to go behind the Iron Curtain into Prague, Czechoslovakia for an International Union of Students Conference. At this point, I was aware that the IUS was pretty much a Communist-front organization. Still, I decided that this could be a very interesting trip and I made plans to ride my motorcycle across France and Germany and into Czechoslovakia. However, the Czech Embassy would not give me a visa. I went to the Embassy many times, but they kept putting me off. I think the only people they finally permitted to go behind the Iron Curtain were those they could confirm to be Communist card-carrying members. Later, when I had to get a security clearance for Navy Intelligence, I was glad I hadn't gotten into Czechoslovakia because this would have led to a lot of embarrassing questions if this visa had showed up on my passport.

Since I was not able to attend the conference in Czechoslovakia, I decided to take a course in French offered at the University of Pointier near Bordeaux. I took my cycle and went across the Channel and down to Pointier for this course. I don't recall much about the course and didn't learn much French, but I do remember a big celebration at the end of the course which began at 11:00 in the morning and lasted until 4:00 in the afternoon. A different wine was served with each of ten different courses from appetizers to dessert and even after-dinner drinks. There was one other American in the course and after the grand celebration, we accompanied two Swedish girls to the beach. I have only two recollections of this evening: the Swedish girls were able to get undressed and put on their swimsuits under their clothes in the most miraculous way, and throwing up red wine makes it appear as though you are bleeding to death.

Pat and I originally had made plans to go back to the U.S. on the same ship but we were having one of our periodic spats and she decided to go back on the S.S. Queen Elizabeth. My passage was already paid for on the French Line, a small ship named the DeGrasse. Pat did agree to take my trunk back as a part of her luggage. As for my own luggage, I had disassembled the BSA motorcycle, packed it in a sea trunk and shipped it home to Indiana. Pat says that when she got back to NY and unloaded the luggage there was a woman's slip packed into the top of my trunk. Neither one of us can explain how it got there.

The DeGrasse was a small ship and pitched and rolled a lot on the way home. I remember being seasick for a good part of the trip. My friend from New Castle, Indiana, Mort Shapiro, met me in NY and we drove home together. I bored Mort with all of my stories and undoubtedly annoyed him with many British affectations in my speech. When we got home, I'm sure he was very glad to unload and be rid of me.

Pat spent the summer as part of a Swedish Folk dancing group touring Europe and she and another girl also hitchhiked partway across France and Germany. But that is her story to tell. We both took hundreds of photos of our great adventures that year. Unfortunately, all of our photos were stolen along with many other things when our car was broken into in San Francisco a few years later. As a result, we have very few photos of our trips and our friends in Sweden and England. But we do have many good memories.

LAW & MARRIAGE
1951-1954

The University of Michigan Law School is an absolutely impressive place. Most other academic buildings at Michigan and other college campuses pale by comparison. It is a stone quadrangle encompassing a whole city block with student dormitories on two sides, a dining hall and common room along a portion of a third side and classrooms and a large law library down the fourth side.

William W. Cook was a University of Michigan lawyer who made his fortune in the early years of International Telephone and Telegraph. He left many millions of dollars to the University to build a new law school in the late '20s. The Law School was designed to be an exact copy of Magdalene College, Cambridge, complete with heavy stone gargoyles, stone buttresses, slate roof, and even pull-chain toilets. The corridors of the law school have many stained-glass windows and no expense was spared. The interior of the dining hall is modeled after a Cambridge commons area with wood-paneled walls and a 70-foot high ceiling. The law library is even more impressive — a huge building with stained-glass windows, paneled walls, and a ceiling 80 feet high. The Law School is situated in the center of the University of Michigan campus with the Student Union Building across the street.

My first impression upon seeing the Law Quadrangle for the first time is that I had been transported to one of the Cambridge or Oxford University colleges. It has become even more impressive since I graduated as they have added an extensive addition to the library, which is basically underground. The addition was built on a parking lot adjacent to the library and is five or six stories underground with a glass skylight that illuminates the entire underground portion of the library with nothing visible above ground except grass. The Law School has received many national architectural awards for this design. A second addition to the law library and the classroom area was then added. While built almost 100 years ago, the Law School Quadrangle is timeless and I doubt that there is a more impressive physical plant for a law school anywhere.

The UM Law School also has a larger enrollment than most law schools with 1100-1200 students. It is considered a "national" law school, drawing students from all over the country and the world. The other national law schools are Harvard, Yale, Chicago, and Stanford.

In my last year of DePauw, I considered going to either law school or graduate school. I applied to three places — Harvard and Michigan Law Schools and Princeton Graduate School. Fortunately, I was accepted for admission to all three. In the end, I decided on Michigan because it was the first to come through with a scholarship, it was a well-known top law school, and perhaps most importantly, Ann Arbor was a lot closer to Pat in Chicago than being in the east at Harvard or Princeton.

After graduating from DePauw in June of 1951, I entered the Law School in September of 1951. I was fortunate to have a scholarship during the three years which paid all of my tuition. In the first year, I lived in the Lawyers' Club, which was in the quadrangle, and my roommate was Ray Payne, a friend from DePauw.

After World War II, there was a tremendous number of students eager to go to law school and the school admitted a very large class with the admonition that only a portion of the students would actually graduate. One professor would tell his students to look at the person on the right and the person on the left because next year one of you will not be here. In recent years, the Law School has become much more selective in admissions and relies less on weeding people out to reduce class size. Our class admitted 400 students my first year but the attrition was significant with only 218 graduating.

While the transition from high school to college had been difficult and required considerably more studying, it was nothing like the transition to law school. The first year of law school is reputed to be one of the most difficult of all disciplines and my experience was no different. The material is all new. The "case method" that is used requires a great deal of concentration. The legal concepts are not easy to master and the competition is fierce. Further, only one first-year course had an exam at the end of the first semester; All of the other courses held just one exam at the end of the year. In other words, your final grade and whether you passed or failed boiled down to one 4-hour examination at the end of the year. This was the case for an eight-credit class on "Property" as well as a six-credit class on "Contracts". As you can imagine, there was considerable pressure on students before these end of the year examinations. The pressure was somewhat relieved by the opportunity to take one hour "preliminary examinations" which did not count, but gave you an opportunity to see how the exams were written and graded and to get feedback from professors.

My curriculum was typical for a first-year, including courses on Property, Contracts, Torts, Civil Procedure, and Criminal Law. The textbooks are wholly cases from federal or state law reports, selected because they emphasize certain points in the course being taught. It is up to the student to read the cases assigned, each of which may be 15 or 20 pages long, prepare notes on the important aspects of the case, how the court reached its decision, how any dissenting judges reached their decision, and how the law of this case may relate to earlier and subsequent cases.

The standard procedure was for the professor to call on a student to recite the salient points of a case, describing how the judge or judges reached their decision and how the case related to the important rules of law the professor was attempting to illustrate. Obviously, if you have not read the case or were unprepared, the professor moved along to another person, but you were marked in that professor's eyes as a laggard. Every night and weekend were devoted to studying. If we had football and basketball tickets, we either did not attend the game or would try and catch just the last half.

Diversion mostly consisted of hitting the bars on Friday or Saturday night to ease the pressure including team "chug-a-lug" games at the Pretzel Bell, the Old German, or one of the other nearby pubs. A team was made up of four men, each with a tall glass of beer in front of them. Upon a signal, the first man on the team would down his glass of beer as quickly as possible, and when the glass hit the table empty the next man would begin drinking and so on down the line to the fourth or "Anchorman". During my second year of law school, we had Bill Brown from DePauw as the anchorman on our team. Bill was 6'5" and weighed almost 400 pounds. He had the ability to open his mouth and take down a large glass of beer with one swallow. When Bill was on our team, we made mincemeat of the teams from the Dental School and Medical School. Who would have thought that Bill would later become an outstanding state judge in California, appointed by then-Governor Ronald Reagan!

The Pretzel Bell was also the scene of a potentially embarrassing fiasco for me. Swabens, another pub where our chug-a-lug team hung out, had the men's john at the back of the main room. In the Pretzel Bell, it was downstairs, and the women's john was at the back of the room. Late one evening after a few chug-a-lug contests, and with the Pretzel Bell filled with people, I excuse myself to go to the john. Thinking I am in Swabens, I go into the john at the back of the room. Luckily, it is empty, but I find no urinal — instead, I see odd looking dispensing machines on the wall. All at once it dawns on me, I am in the women's john. Gathering whatever wits I had left, I carefully opened the door and walked out backward. As I passed a large table of men and women, I heard one woman exclaim, "Did that guy just come out of the women's john?" A guy sitting there said, "No, I think he just walked up to the door and then walked away." My walking backward trick had worked!

The other diversion was writing letters to Pat, who was in Chicago Heights working for Northern Illinois Public Service. She was able to visit once or twice during the year when we had dances. In addition, Granger Cook, who was dating Joan Talent from Evanston, and I would manage to hitchhike to Coldwater, Michigan, where Pat and Joan would drive in from Chicago. Neither Granger nor I had a car, but we had an elaborate plan for hitchhiking to Coldwater. The night before we would make a number of signs and stash them in our suitcase with the big "M" on the side. In the morning we would take a bus to the west edge of Ann Arbor. From there, we would put out our signs. The signs would say "100 feet to two terrific guys", "50 feet to Granger and Mac, don't pass us by", and "Here we are, Mac and Granger, great conversationalists". Whenever someone would stop, we would run back, collect our signs and get in. We learned to be rather picky and accept only rides that took us all the way to our destination after several bad experiences of being dumped out in the countryside by short rides. Many people, however, just smiled or laughed and drove on by. But overall, we found this a very effective and fun way to get a ride.

Our two separate romances with Pat and Joan became more serious and Joan and Granger became engaged Christmas 1951, as did Pat and I. I can't remember exactly what I said, but I do remember proposing to her and also talking to Pat's father, Earle, for permission to marry his lovely daughter. I'm sure that Earle had more than a few qualms about my proposal. I had very little money, no car, and while I was in law school my financial prospects for the future were dubious at best. What small amount of money I had managed to save I spent quickly at the very prestigious jewelry store, Peacock's, in downtown Chicago. Here I took Pat shopping for an engagement ring and looking back, it was one of my better investments. Okay, it was my best investment!

First-year professors are the key to whether you stay in law school or not and I will never forget one of mine, Marcus Plant, who was a professor of torts and very well known throughout the academic community. He was also the University of Michigan's representative to the Big Ten and received a lot of PR in this capacity. In tort law, there is a doctrine known as "Last Clear Chance" which roughly means that if you see a person who has gotten himself into a position of danger and you have an opportunity to avoid the accident but don't avail yourself of this "last clear chance" to do so, then you can be also be held liable. Marcus Plant illustrated this doctrine by talking about a friend of his who was an engineer on the railroad. He said to his friend that, "If you look out ahead and see a car stalled on the tracks with a man and his wife and four kids in the car, you are required to try to stop your train in order to avoid the accident because you have the last clear chance to do so." Prof. Plant said the engineer thought about this for a minute and then said, "Well, I will tell you what I would do. I would jam my throttle wide open in order to hit that car going as fast as possible." The Professor then said, "Well, by God, then the railroad would be liable because you had the last clear chance to avoid the accident." The engineer replied, "Well, I would feel really bad for the family in that car, but if I have 400 people in my train and I hit that car slowly, I am going to derail my train and kill a lot more than six people." So much for the doctrine of Last Clear Chance!

During the summer of 1952, I lived in Chicago Heights. Pat and I planned a September wedding and we wanted to be together for the summer. I had a room in a house down the block from Pat's with a lady named Mrs. Elliott, and Pat and I and her folks were able to spend quite a lot of time together. I got a job with a new community development outside of Chicago Heights called Park Forest. The developer was American Community Builders. My first job was on the sewer cleanout crew. When the regular crew members found out that they had a new college boy you can imagine who got the dirtiest jobs—going down into manholes, filling buckets with sewage, etc. I was on the job just two weeks when I saw an opportunity to join one of the surveying crews, utilizing my previous experience with the Henry County Surveyor.

After only a few days surveying, however, I was given another job and then worked pretty much on my own. While no one described it this way, my job really turned out to be that of a paid informer. American Community Builders had a number of subcontractors on the job: one built houses, another put in sidewalks, another sewers, water mains, and streets. With all these separate subcontractors, there would occasionally be damage to a previous contractor's work. For example, someone running a bulldozer grading around the houses might back over a newly installed sidewalk and damage it. American Community Builders would then have to pay the sidewalk contractor to replace the sidewalk, but no one ever seemed to know who caused the damage. It was my job to find out.

I would take my jeep and drive around the project and set up my surveying instruments to appear to be surveying the roads. Along the way, I would nonchalantly ask questions about what bulldozer backed into this house, who damaged this sidewalk, etc. I would then write down the number of the equipment, the day the damage occurred and any other details I could determine and turn in my notes at the end of each week. At the end of the month, American Community Builders would backcharge the various contractors for the damage done by their operators. The contractors couldn't figure out for the life of them where American Community Builders was getting this information. Luckily, the summer was short and I left before my cover was blown. Otherwise, Chicago being a well-known town of mobsters and the contracting business being notorious for organized crime, I might have ended up back in the manhole — this time upside down.

Granger Cook and Joan Talent were married in August that summer in Evanston and I was part of the wedding party. Pat and I were married the next month on September 6, 1952, at the Presbyterian Church in Chicago Heights. Rev. John Winegarden officiated at the wedding. A reception was held after the wedding in the church basement and then a party afterward at the Opie's house. My best man was Bob Keesling, my friend from New Castle and DePauw. In the wedding also were Granger Cook from Law School, Bob Koenig and Bob Gibson from DePauw, and Pat's brother, Bob Opie.

On the night before the wedding, Bob took all of the guys in the wedding party to various bars and strip joints in Calumet City and I arrived home at 3:00 in the morning. One of the groomsmen woke me up about 7:00 am to inform me that they had no shoes for the wedding and that I needed to help him find some. I did eventually make it to my own wedding, but the net result was that I was so tired on our wedding night that Pat had to drive us both to the Edgewater Beach Hotel with me asleep in the back seat and "Just Married" signs still attached to the car.

After spending our honeymoon night at the Edgewater Beach, we left for Colorado the next day in a small Chevrolet coupe that Pat's folks had given us as a wedding present. While Pat's account differs, when I tell this story it took us four days to drive to Colorado but only two days to drive back. We toured parts of Rocky Mountain National Park and then spent three or four days in the Broadmoor Hotel in Colorado Springs.

After returning from our honeymoon, we went straight to Ann Arbor where we rented a part of an older home for $75.00 a month. This was our first apartment. The landlord's name was Mrs. Slocum and upstairs was a professor of literature named Professor Rhinehart, who was very unhappy to have anyone other than the very sedate Mrs. Slocum living downstairs. Pat got a job as a dietician at the Livonia School System outside of Detroit and was put in charge of buying all the food and preparing menus for the many schools in the district. At the tender age of 23, Pat oversaw a large group of cooks and other people who worked for her and this proved to be a very challenging job until she was able to get on top of it. I had a part-time job at Overbeck's Bookstore, and along with a scholarship for my tuition, both of us working, and minimal expenses, we actually saved money during the two years we spent in Ann Arbor.

In addition to Joan and Granger Cook, our other good friends Jim and Jan Buchanan were also married this same year. The Buchanans had set up in their backyard an archery range. Along with friends Dave and Sue Ray, we bought bows and big steel-headed arrows. We practiced shooting and planned a deer hunt in Northern Michigan. When the season opened in late October, the six of us headed north. We brought sleeping bags but no tent and spent two or three nights on the ground arising early in the morning to hide in blinds and wait for deer with our bows at the ready. Pat claimed she did not even have the will to shoot a deer if she got the opportunity.

However, after two or three days of being cold, eating food peppered with sand and arising before daybreak to head to the deer blind, Pat confessed that if she got the opportunity she would not only shoot a deer, but would beat one to death with her bow just to be able to return to civilization. One morning she took a small bottle of bourbon with her to the deer blind. After an hour or two, I crawled from my blind over to hers to see whether she had seen anything. I found her sitting there giggling and drunk as a skunk. We didn't bag any deer on this trip but Pat did manage to bag a small bottle of bourbon by herself sitting in the blind. Deer could have eaten her hat and she wouldn't have known it.

Other friends at law school were J.B. and Portia King from Indianapolis and Jim and Joan Nicholson. Jim Buchanan and Jim Nicholson were both Democrats and J.B. King and I were Republicans. Many days we would brown bag our lunch and eat in the downstairs lunchroom at the library. Invariably, this would develop into a political argument and we had many spirited debates over lunch. This was the time of Joe McCarthy and the Communist investigations and the following year were the Army/McCarthy hearings. Sometimes we would go home, eat lunch alone, and turn on the radio to listen to the soap operas. The next day at lunch we would then have running commentary on *The Romance of Helen Trent, One Man's Family*, and some of the other popular soap operas of the day.

In my first year, I joined one of the three legal fraternities, Phi Alpha Delta. In the second year, I was elected President, and this took some of my time. In the Spring, I also went to work for L. Hart Wright, a well-known professor of taxation. I did research work for him and had a particular interest in taxation. During an interview with the law school newspaper, I indicated that I was hoping to have a career in taxation and hoped to land a job with the IRS. For the good of myself and the country, it was a wise decision that I didn't pursue that career.

Sometime during my second year of Law School, I developed a terrible toothache from an impacted wisdom tooth. I learned that I could get it removed for free at the Dental School so I made an appointment. The professor in charge indicated that dental students would do work under his supervision. I did not feel comforted about this decision after hearing two students arguing about an examination. One of them had flunked the exam and the other was trying to explain to him where he had gone wrong. I hoped I might get the superior student but no such luck. The professor is called away for a few minutes and I am set up with the flunky student dentist to remove my wisdom tooth, attended by the superior student and a nurse. The student gets hold of my wisdom tooth with the extractor and begins to take it out. All at once the tooth collapses into many pieces and blood gushes everywhere. There are three doors in the room, one to each adjoining room and another to the hallway. The students and the nurse all scatter by different doors screaming for the professor. After a few minutes, the professor shows up, uses forceps to extract all of the broken tooth slivers, cleans up the blood, and stitches up my mouth, while the students stand wide-eyed and terrified. I had another wisdom tooth extracted that year. Needless to say, I went to the best dentist I could find in town and avoided the Dental School by a wide berth.

In the summer of 1953, Pat and I lived in New Castle, and

I worked for Mike Edwards, a local practicing attorney. I did research on an estate tax problem he had, and it was about the only work I did the entire month. In my spare time, I hung out around the courthouse and observed the lawyers. This was before it was customary to pay salaries to law students on summer jobs, and I was no exception.

Before the summer was over, Pat and I decided to take a trip to Mexico to see her friend Carmen Trevino in Monterrey and to visit Mexico City. We drove the little Chevrolet coupe to New Orleans and then on through Texas to Monterrey, Mexico. We had Carmen's address but couldn't find exactly the right street. We were driving very slowly down an avenue looking for side streets when Pat yelled "Turn!" Without looking, I turned into the side of an old school bus and crashed. No one was hurt but all the passengers exited out of the bus one by one walking across the hood of our car. Each one muttered in Spanish that the accident was our fault. Pretty soon a policeman came to take a report. Luckily, we had taken out Mexican insurance that morning in Texas. Also, fortunately, Carmen's home was on that very corner, her husband Raoul was taking a shower upstairs, looked out the bathroom window, saw the commotion, and immediately came down and helped us with the police.

Pat and I both had many years of Spanish but this was almost no help. We were asked to proceed to the police station accompanied by various officers. Raoul in the meantime called the insurance agent. While waiting in the police station, a big hassle took place between the insurance agent and the police officers. Finally, we are permitted to leave and go to the repair shop where they had taken our car. I asked Raoul what all the hassle was about with the police and he said the officer who was on the scene claimed that I tried to bribe him. I told Raoul that I certainly had not, and Raoul said, "no, you don't understand? What he really meant was that he was very unhappy you didn't try to bribe him. Then the insurance agent paid him and everything was fine.

After three days of staying with Carmen and her family while our car was being repaired, we set out for Mexico City. We drove 500 or 600 miles over very bad roads and through areas where people are now afraid to drive because of bandits, kidnapping, and other crimes. After two or three days of sightseeing in Mexico City, we went to Taxco, a small silver mining town. The town is really beautiful with bougainvillea of many colors all over the city and many wonderful examples of silver jewelry. On the way back, we met up with some friends of friends in Houston, Texas, and then returned to Ann Arbor for the final year of law school. For whatever reason, Mrs. Slocum's place was not available — probably because Prof. Rhinehart wanted us out — so we moved into a small duplex on South Ashley Street right next to the 7-Up factory. Pat resumed her job as a dietician for the Livonia School System and I continued working for Professor Wright doing tax research.

The Barristers' Society is an honorary for senior law students. Students are selected in their junior year and become members the following year. The purpose of the Society is to sponsor two annual Law School dances with the proceeds going to scholarships and to host Barristers parties. The Spring dance is known as the Crease Ball, although I do not know the origin of the name. It is a formal dance held at the Student Union or one of the other university ballrooms.

In order to publicize the Crease Ball, Granger Cook came up with the brilliant idea of renting an old horse and putting it in the beautiful courtyard in the interior of the Law School building. This courtyard can be seen through the windows but is inaccessible to everyone except gardeners and on rare occasions, the faculty. Granger somehow got a key to the courtyard door, rented this horse, and unloaded it on the south side of the Law School where he proceeded to walk it through the corridor of the Law School and into the beautiful courtyard. A sandwich board was draped over the horse with a big sign on each side: "You bet your ass I'm going to Crease Ball."

Granger Cook, Jim Buchanan, and I had Professor James for Corporate Law at 8:00 in the morning. The horse is busily grazing away on the courtyard grass when we arrive for class the next morning. Almost everyone at the Law School has come by to see the horse in the courtyard. Professor James begins class a little differently that morning, Addressing Jim Buchanan who was President of the Barristers, James formally states: "Mr. Buchanan, Dean Stason arrives at the Law School promptly at 8:20. When he finds out about the horse, the rear door of this classroom will open and the Dean's secretary will call you into his office." Professor James' prediction was only two or three minutes off. At 8:23, the rear door burst open and Dean Stason's secretary requested Mr. Buchanan's presence in the Dean's office. The horse was removed, we got great publicity for the Crease Ball, and best of all, no one was disciplined. This story has been greatly embellished over time and written up in many law school publications. It is usually referred to as "The Unicorn in the Garden" tale.

Granger was also the leader and perpetrator of another notorious prank our freshman year involving Don Steiner — aka Steiney — a friend of ours from Canton, Ohio. While we all liked Steiney, he was always a little too proper. When Steiney went home one weekend, Granger had three tons of old newspapers delivered to the Law School. We spent almost the entire weekend wadding up old newspapers and filling Steiner's room from floor to ceiling. By the time Steiner returned to school on Sunday afternoon, the whole Law School had been by to view Steiney's room and the Detroit Free Press even sent a reporter to take photos. When Steiner unlocked his door, he was greeted by a wall of wadded up newspaper. He couldn't get into the room. He couldn't even see his bed.

Inez Bosarth, the woman who managed the Lawyer's

Club, had a pretty good idea who the perpetrators were. She proceeded to do some detective work and found out for sure. We were called in and informed that the only way we could get off without severe discipline was to extract all the paper from Steiner's room, the sooner the better because it constituted a fire hazard. The following morning, we secured a big canvas which the maintenance crew used to rake leaves and unloaded all the paper in Steiner's room through the door and windows onto the canvas and then hauled it away to the dump.

These two pranks, both thought up by Granger, brought him infamy at the Law School and have survived over the years. They epitomize our class of 1954. Granger, who was a very well-known patent attorney in Chicago until his death in 2015, also played a major role in keeping our 30 or 40 members in touch over the last 7 decades. About every five years, Granger would send out a call for letters from each of us. We would mail him a letter with news of our lives. Granger would then consolidate the letters, make copies, and mail out to the entire group.

In the summer of 2000, some of our Law School class and wives visited Granger and Joan at their beautiful cottage overlooking a lake in southern Canada. All five couples piled into Granger's boat to go to a restaurant across the lake. While at the restaurant we ordered a pitcher of beer or two, but in general conducted ourselves as proper 70-year-olds. At another table sat a group of local police. On our way back across the lake, and within eyesight of Granger's cottage, a searchlight goes on and we are flagged down by these same policemen. They want to inspect the boat to see if we have the proper life preservers. Then they ask Granger, who was driving the boat, to take a breathalyzer test. The five of us University of Michigan lawyers huddle and decide this is not a good idea. Instead, we come up with the argument that Granger is not really in control of the boat, he is just the helmsman, and Jud Rogers, who because of a recent heart operation had not drunk anything, was really the "captain" and in control of the boat. This was not without some basis, because Jud had been in the bow of the boat with a light guiding Granger to keep in the channel. But the Canadian cops did not buy this story. Granger had his boat license suspended and had to return to Canada later for a trial, where unfortunately the Court agreed with the police.

One other significant event happened during my third year in Law School. Pat became pregnant. While daughter Pam wasn't born until September when I was away in the Navy, the early stages of Pat's pregnancy were not easy. During May and June, I was up late every night studying for both final exams at Law School and for the Michigan bar exam. Pat would get up early in the morning and have breakfast before heading to work at Livonia. I would be awakened by a stamping of feet and Pat throwing up into the sink or toilet from morning sickness.

In Michigan, you can take the bar exam before completing law school, and I planned to take the exam in June because I was going into the Navy before the next bar would be given. I stayed up late studying for the bar many nights, often smoking a pipe or cigars in order to stay awake. In one two-week period, I smoked a whole box of cigars and by the time the examination rolled around, I was about three-quarters sick from all these cigars. At some point during the bar examination, my eyes gave out and I was unable to finish one part of the exam. But I managed to pass the bar with the portions I did complete.

Because I went into the Navy before the next Indiana bar examination, I was later admitted by motion in Indiana and have never taken the bar in Indiana. However, the Michigan bar was reputed to be far more difficult than the Indiana bar and I have never felt bad about not taking the Indiana bar.

While I had received a student deferment from military

service during my last two years at DePauw and all through law school, at the end of law school my time was up; the Draft Board informed me that I was number one on their list. However, I avoided the draft by enlisting in a Navy Officer Candidate program. In this program, you went to Officer Candidate School in Newport, Rhode Island, and then served in the Navy for three years after OCS. If I had decided to go into the Navy Judge Advocate program, I would have done legal work and been commissioned as a Lieutenant Junior Grade immediately after OCS. However, I wanted to serve in Navy Air in some capacity. Because I wore glasses, I did not qualify for flight training, but I was eligible for Naval Air Intelligence and this was the program that I ultimately joined.

With my taxation job, Pat's full-time job, and our low living expenses, we were able to save money during these years. At the end of law school, we went looking for a new car and I was able to make an arrangement through a law school friend whose father was a Plymouth dealer in Texas to purchase a brand new 1954 Plymouth direct from the factory in Detroit. We got the car at just $50 over the dealer's cost for $1821. We kept this car all during the Navy and during the first year or two after we settled in Fort Wayne.

In 1954, Michigan only required a rear license plate, but Indiana required plates on both the front and back of the car. Since we were going to sell the little Chevrolet coupe, I had the bright idea of using one Indiana plate on the Chevrolet and putting the other plate on the new Plymouth until we were able to sell the Chevrolet. This worked well for a few months until we made the mistake of parking both cars close together in front of our house with the same license plate on both cars. The police picked Pat up and ran her down to the station where she had some tall explaining to do as to why we had two cars with the same license plate.

After working and studying long hours for three years,

Law School graduation was pretty anti-climactic. All the professional schools, along with the undergraduate university had one large graduation ceremony at the University of Michigan football stadium — the "Big House." On graduation day it rained. When I say it rained, I mean cats and dogs. People were all lined up to go into the stadium — hundreds and hundreds of people in their caps and downs — when the heavens opened up. Pat left the stadium and ran to the American Legion which was nearby to escape the rain. I stayed out for a little while. Finally, the President of the University went to the microphone and said, "Degrees are hereby confirmed on everyone whose names are listed in the program. Adjourned." That was the entire graduation speech and the end to my Law School career.

I have gone back to various Law School reunions, including the 25th, the 40th, and the 50th. At the 25th reunion, I ended up chatting with the photographer while we got ready to take our class picture. He casually asked me, "What group is this anyway?" And I replied, "It is the law school class of 1954." He thought for a minute and said, "Well, I knew you weren't doctors." I asked how he knew this. He didn't hesitate, but came right back with," Well, the wives aren't dressed well enough." After that, the hallmark for the evening was, "My you look nice, just like a doctor's wife."

At another law school reunion, I got re-acquainted with a friend and fellow pole vaulter Jerry Donnelly, who practiced law in Colorado Springs. At 65, he retired from law school and began volunteering at the Air Force Academy to coach their pole vaulters. He returned to pole vaulting himself and became one of the Master Track champions, vaulting 12-13 feet or about the same height that he and I were reaching in college. He told me that it took him two years to learn the new technique with fiberglass poles and that the sport is very different now because of the spring in these new poles. Jerry began traveling to Italy, Japan, and other far-flung locations to participate in track meets. He told me that he met one 80-

something gentleman from France that still pole vaults 11 feet.

While I had planned on entering OCS in Newport, Rhode Island in late August or early September, immediately after law school I got hired by Northern Trust to work in the Trust Department on a permanent basis. Pat and I got a small apartment in Chicago Heights and I took the Illinois Central into downtown Chicago every day. I started as a trainee, working the first week or two as a teller in the savings department in the main bank building on LaSalle Street. After that, I was placed in the Trust Department where I worked as an assistant to a vice-president who handled some of the large trusts for old Chicago families. Northern had many large old family trusts — the Donnellys of printing fortune, the Cudahys and Armours of meatpacking, and more. While I spent only two months there, it was interesting learning about these trusts and working with these monied families. Once I ran into my boss on the street during lunch hour and he stopped me and remarked, "Parker, Northern men wear hats." I immediately went out and bought a straw hat and was not without it thereafter.

My boss had one beneficiary in particular that greatly taxed his powers of patience. She was from one of the old Chicago families and lived in Paris. She received a trust distribution check every quarter but constantly spent money in anticipation of getting the check; often the check would not stretch far enough to pay for all the things that she purchased. Once the vice-president turned over to me certain files to handle while he flew to Paris — very unusual at this time — in order to deal with a particularly bad spending problem. The beneficiary had purchased about 200 pairs of shoes at a department store in Paris, which used up her trust fund distribution for several months ahead of time. My boss had to go to her apartment, corral all these shoes, and return them to the store.

Being part of a big bank like Northern was very interesting and I was a bit sorry I didn't return. They offered me an opportunity to come back after my Navy career, but I decided to go into practice instead. One reason I decided not to return stemmed from a lunch I had one day with my boss, a bank Vice President. He says, "Parker, did you grow up in Chicago?" No, I replied. "Did you go to Northwestern? "he asked again. No, I replied again. "Well," he concluded," you'll have a good career here in the Northern Trust Department, but it won't be great." I decided right then and there that I needed to find another Right Place to land.

It is interesting to see where my law school classmates ended up. Ted St. Antoine, one of the top men in my class, became a law professor at Michigan and later became Dean of the Law School. Dave Belin, an attorney in Des Moines, was on the Warren Commission that investigated Jack Kennedy's death. These two became fairly well known but there were many more highly successful men in the class of 1954. Incidentally, there were only two women in our law school class of 400. Now each class is over 50 percent women.

U.S. NAVY
1954-1958

I enlisted in the Navy for eight years and four months. Of this, 16 weeks was in the Officer Candidate School, three years on active duty and five years in the Reserve. This was a lengthy commitment, but looking back, not only do I not regret the time, but I consider it a very meaningful period in my life.

I arrived in Newport, Rhode Island in late August 1954 for Officer Candidate School with approximately 500 others. A great number of our class were not only college graduates but had advanced degrees in law, engineering and even a few with PhDs — vastly different from the normal Navy recruits We were given the usual physical exams, shots, and issued Navy seaman's clothing down to the 13-button blue dress pants. Our rating during Officer Candidate School (OCS) was

"Seaman 2d", or one rank above the lowest Seaman Recruit.

The 16 weeks in OCS are a mixture of regular Navy boot camp and academic training a student would get at the Naval Academy. Many of our courses were taught from Naval Academy books, compressing two or three semesters of courses taught at the Academy into one jammed course for us. I was familiar with the terms used in some of the coursework, such as the "Uniform Code of Military Justice", but others such as "Naval Engineering", "Fire Control", "Propulsion" and others were more attuned with the engineering students. As it worked out, we helped the engineers with military justice coursework, and they helped us with the courses focused on engineering.

We were formed into 30-man platoons and lived in barracks. We were in Charlie barracks and our platoon was called "Charlie 1". We were then formed into a battalion of the 500 men enrolled in the School. Everything we did was as a platoon: assembling in the morning and marching to breakfast, assembling after breakfast, and marching to class or drill practice where we did precision marching with or without rifles. We had no free time. As soon as courses were over for the day, we either drilled, cleaned the barracks, or both, and then assembled to march for dinner. Every night we had a study table and there was very little time to complete the piled-on coursework before lights out at 10:30. Many of us resorted to buying small flashlights and studying under the covers after lights out. It was demerits if we were caught doing this.

There was a strict honor code. Anyone caught cheating on examinations, no matter how slight, would be immediately dismissed. One of the class' top students was in our company. In the final exam in Navigation class, the problems were long and intricate and took a long time to work. This student had worked all the way through the last problem and was in the process of writing the answer when the instructor called time. He took an extra two or three seconds to put his pencil down and the instructor submitted this infraction to the Disciplinary Board. It was such a minor infraction and he was such a good student — an honors graduate of Amherst and Yale Law School — that we all thought that the Board would ignore it and he would graduate and be commissioned. No such luck. He was flunked out of OCS and spent two years in the Navy as an ordinary seaman. Another student was not commissioned even after graduating OCS when he went out on the town graduation night and got into a minor flap with the local police.

Going through boot camp with all of the surprise inspections and often superfluous requirements such as everything in the locker be folded in a certain way, shoes shined, uniform spotless, bed made precisely, and room, johns and barracks always absolutely clean is difficult at age 19 or 20, but at age 24 or 25 when many of us were graduates with advanced degrees, married, many with families, it often felt like a lot of chicken crap. Boot camp or OCS is one of those things that you are glad you went through in retrospect, but you never want to do it again. In addition to all the disciplinary details, we were routinely subjected to derision from the regular base crew, almost all of whom were ordinary seamen who had nothing but dislike for OCS students who in a few short months would become commissioned officers. When going through the mess line, a favorite trick of a base crewman serving food was to flip the little pad of butter into your gravy, splashing gravy onto your uniform. This "accident" meant that you had to miss the meal and return to the barracks to change your uniform before the next inspection.

Again, athletics helped me in surviving OCS. I am sure that the officers in charge of the program looked over resumes and chose athletes for leadership roles. Our Battalion Commander, which was the highest student position, was Dick Kazmeier. Dick had just graduated from Harvard Business School, after winning the Heisman trophy in 1951 from Princeton. I was selected as our Charlie One Platoon Commander and got some perks I otherwise would not have received. On the other hand, as Platoon Commander, I was held responsible for all the infractions of anyone in the platoon. Nonetheless, I was pleased to be selected for one of the five top positions of the Battalion out of the 500 enrolled.

It was customary for the fall semester OCS class to have a basketball team. I tried out, made the team, and was also selected as the player-coach. We played six games and our record was split even. We played the small colleges in the area, and also one game against a Coast Guard Base located nearby. The starting guard that I coached was Heisman winner Dick Kazmeier. I learned that Dick had actually gone to Princeton on a basketball scholarship, and that football was his secondary sport before college.

During my second or third week in OCS I got a call from Pat's folks that she was going into the hospital in Chicago Heights for Pam's birth. I went to the Chief Petty Officer in charge of our Company to request leave time to visit her. He informed me that in the Navy "I was essential when the keel was laid, but not when the ship was launched — Leave denied!" However, the very next weekend we had time off from Saturday noon until Sunday at 4:00 pm. I made the most of this opportunity, traveling to Providence by bus, then caught a plane to New York, and another plane to Chicago. Pat's dad Earle met me at the airport and drove me directly to the hospital where I visited Pat and met my new daughter, Pam. I drove them home from the hospital and then returned immediately back to the airport, where I caught the two planes and bus back to Newport, just barely making the 4:00 time on Sunday.

On graduation from OCS, we had to buy our Navy officer's uniforms, which consisted of one dress blue and two suntan outfits, together with shirts, shoes, and even a sword for ceremonial occasions. I still have both a Navy suntan outfit and my dress blues, which surprisingly still fit. At some point, the sword was lost.

From OCS, the officers designated to be in Naval Air were transferred either directly for flight training or to the Air Ground Officers' School in Jacksonville, Florida. Because of my vision, I did not qualify for flight training and so elected to go to Air Ground Officer's School, with an Air Intelligence designator.

Along with Dick Kazmeier and his wife (also named Pat), Pam and Pat and I arrived in Jacksonville, Florida, in the middle of the winter. We found a small apartment with one very small heater and learned that Jacksonville, although hot much of the year, gets very cold in the winter. Pam was four months old at the time and I don't think we have ever spent a period of time when we have been quite so cold.

After eight weeks of instruction on all aspects of Naval Air, we were transferred to the Naval Air Intelligence School in Washington, D.C. This was located at the Naval Observatory on Connecticut Avenue, which is also the home of the Vice President's mansion so we needed a lot of special security just to get in and out of the gates.

Trying to find an apartment in Washington, D.C., in the Spring of 1955 was very difficult. When we first arrived, we stayed in a small motel in Arlington. I would go to the Intelligence School every day, and Pat would stay in the motel and make phone calls looking for an apartment. Then when the Washington Post came out late in the afternoon, she would immediately pick up a copy and we would drive to new listings before anyone else could get there. It was very difficult to locate any housing in reasonable proximity to the Naval Observatory and when landlords saw we had a baby, we were persona non grata. Once we found one place we thought was suitable, and I told the landlord we would take it and he agreed. Then he walked me to my car and saw Pam in the back seat and said, "Oh, you have a baby?" And I said, "Why yes, we do". And he replied, "Well I'm sorry, we don't permit any babies."

After several similar occurrences, Pat and I had a story ready that we hoped might shame a landlord or agent into giving us the apartment. I said, "Will you hold the apartment for us? We are going to take the baby over to the Potomac and get rid of her and we will be right back." The landlord looked at us wide-eyed and said, "You are some kind of nuts. I'm calling the police." We assured him that we were just kidding but he didn't relent and we were back to square one on apartment hunting.

We finally were able to lease a place not far from the Washington Zoo. It was a basement apartment that three men had previously lived in and it was an absolute mess. We spent the first week cleaning and painting in order to make the place somewhat livable. While the apartment wasn't ideal, there were a few benefits; we met a lady who lived nearby, whose recently deceased husband had been an Army officer, and she was a good babysitter for us. We were surprised to later learn that she bought the entire building where our basement apartment was located. The other bit of luck was that the apartment was located close to the Washington zoo. We spent many happy hours walking Pam in her stroller around the grounds and seeing the animals.

At the Air Intelligence School, I learned the many duties of an Air Intelligence Officer. One aspect was to study aerial photographs — usually with a highly-skilled photo interpreter — and identify possible target areas for enemy bombing. Then, working with ordinance people, we were responsible for selecting the bombs, rockets and other munitions that would be used on a particular target, and for briefing the pilots on the best routes into the targets as well as identifying radar, anti-aircraft and enemy air aircraft stationed in the vicinity. Another aspect of our job was to teach aircraft and ship recognition to the pilots so that they could distinguish between friendly and enemy aircraft and ships.

Most of our courses were taught at the Naval Observatory, but occasionally we also had courses at the Naval Intelligence School, which was at another location in D.C. Here we learned means of interrogation and I found the psychological aspects to be quite interesting. I recall one particular lecture by a Naval interrogator whose job had been to interrogate German sub crews during World War II. He told us that when a German sub was damaged or disabled, the crew might be rescued by patrolling ships. Onboard the rescuing ship, the sub crew would be separated into officers and enlisted men. Specially armed sailors (or Marines if they were aboard) would pick out an enlisted German sub crew member and ask him tactical intelligence questions critical to the survival of the task force such as, "Are you operating with other subs? Are there other subs in the vicinity?". If the man refused to answer, they took him to the other side of the ship and you would hear a loud shot ring out and a large splashing noise in the water below.

After this occurred to the second or third enlisted man, the interrogators were able to find out the tactical information they sought. According to our lecturer, what actually happened was that the enlisted man was taken to the other side of the ship, a shot was fired into the air and a sack of potatoes was dumped overboard. However, knowing the number of people and ships lost to German subs in World War II, you wondered whether this was always the case.

The lecturer also described a strategic method of questioning used with the sub-officers, particularly the Captain. Once ashore, the sub Captain would be kept in a room by himself with no clothes whatsoever and a single light bulb which was on continuously. He would then be brought into the interrogator's office, a well-appointed, wood-paneled office with the interrogator behind a desk in a coat and tie and acting quite affable. The interrogator indicates to the Captain, normally a high-ranking German officer, that they have his dossier and proceeds to ask him questions about his family, his home town, his neighbors, etc. Interrogation might last for an hour one time or only 15 minutes the next. The Captain would be brought in at odd times, sometimes late at night, other times early in the morning. Sometimes two or three days would elapse before he was brought in for questioning and other times, he would be called in two or three times in one day. These meetings with the interrogator would be the only contact whatsoever with anyone.

One day the interrogator might ask him, "Do you smoke?" And the Captain would say, "Oh yes, I smoke." The interrogator would give him a cigarette but no match. And so when the Captain comes in for the next meeting, he still has this cigarette but of course no match to light it. The interrogator then says, "Why haven't you smoked your cigarette?", and the Captain would reply, "No match." The interrogator would then proceed to light his cigarette.

One day after they had been meeting for perhaps two weeks, with the Captain sitting there without a stitch on for all these meetings, the interrogator says, "I notice that you are not wearing a shirt." And the Captain would say, "No I don't have a shirt." When the Captain returns to his cell, he finds a shirt on his bed. This back and forth game might continue for some weeks and the lecturer indicated that the day the Captain got a pair of pants is the day he began to truthfully answer critical questions.

After four months in Washington, I was assigned to the West Coast. We left D.C. and went to Chicago, putting everything in our little Plymouth. I then drove across the country with three other officers who were also transferred to the West Coast, and Pat flew in later. We stopped in Las Vegas — where shows and dinner were completely free if you gambled — and then drove on to San Francisco to pick up our final orders for reassignment. I parked the car in front of the Federal Building in San Francisco, where it was broken into in broad daylight and many things were stolen. The most valuable thing we lost was all of the photos from our wedding, honeymoon, baby pictures of Pam, and all of the slides that Pat and I had taken while students in Sweden and England. This was a great loss for us and we made many trips to the San Francisco Police Department to try to locate the slides and photos but without success.

My orders were to VF-194, a squadron based at Moffett Field, near Palo Alto, California, and about 30 miles south of San Francisco. Moffett Field was an interesting duty station. Although much of the region was orchards (primarily walnut) and farming, this area would later become known as Silicon Valley. Across 101 was Stanford, and Ames Laboratory was located at Moffett, the advanced jet propulsion lab for NASA, as well as many other buildings for aircraft research and development. Also, at Moffett were huge former blimp hangars, when the base had been utilized as a blimp and zeppelin base. Our squadron was based in Hangar One, one of the largest buildings in the world at almost 1,000 feet long, 350 feet high, and 400 feet wide, with big clamshell doors that shut at each end. Hangar One was large enough for two or three fully inflated blimps. In fact, the hangar was so huge that occasionally clouds would form inside the hangar and we would get slight rain or heavy dew because of the atmospheric changes. I caught a segment on the Discovery Channel recently on the largest buildings in the world and Hangar One at Moffett was featured prominently. Also, because Moffett Field was situated close to one of the San Andreas fault lines, we would get a lot of earthquake tremors. The whole giant hangar would shake and things would fall off your desk. Pat and I returned to Moffett a number of years ago and Hangar One is still being utilized, partially for the Air National Guard and in part as a Navy Air Museum.

Twelve officers were assigned to VF-194, including ten pilots, a maintenance officer, and myself. Our commanding officer was Commander Jeep Streeper, a Naval Reservist who decided to stay in and make a career of it. About 2 years previously, he had been reassigned temporarily to the Air Force, where he flew a C-154 in and out of Berlin in the Berlin Airlift. During the time I was in the squadron and before we deployed, Jeep Streeper had a wedding reception where all of the officers in the squadron stood with crossed swords outside the hall for he and his bride to walk through.

On a previous deployment to the Far East, VF-194 had been stationed aboard a carrier in the South China Sea at the time the French Army was surrounded by the Viet Cong at Dien Bien Phu. An operations plan had been worked out to drop a small tactical atomic weapon on the Viet Cong in order to help the French Army break out. Copies of this plan were in the top-secret safe that I inherited as Intelligence Officer for VF-194. This op plan had been worked out by the Carrier Task Force Staff, sent up the chain of command through Pacific Fleet HQ and to the Joint Chiefs of Staff, and then to President Eisenhower, who vetoed the plan. The French ultimately surrendered at Dien Bien Phu and were taken prisoner by the Viet Cong. This planned use of the first atomic weapons after Nagasaki never saw the light of day thanks to Eisenhower, but I was amazed that it had gotten as far as his desk. Only many, many years later was this made public.

Our squadron was a part of Carrier Air Group 9, with the rest of our air group based at NAS Alameda, across the bay from San Francisco. We would be ashore for about nine months during a training cycle before deploying again to the Far East.

With Pat and Pam still in Chicago, I looked for an apartment, and finally was able to find a suitable place, but it was unfurnished. I saw an advertisement for one of these high-pressure warehouse furniture places that offered three rooms of furniture for $399 and I thought this was really a great deal. However, I hesitated and decided I should clear this idea with Pat before signing up. When Pat arrived with Pam and I told her about all of our clothes and photos being stolen, and then showed her the unfurnished apartment, and the "good furniture deal" for $399, she sat down and cried. She had a new baby, had just flown all the way from Chicago, and the last thing she wanted was a lot of cheap crappy furniture that we would lug around the rest of my Navy career. In the end, we were able to get the landlord to provide furniture and we took the apartment.

Almost all of our friends were officers from our squadron or others we met at the base. The senior officers in our squadron were all World War II veterans, and most had seen combat. One story that "stuck" with me was from one of the veterans who had flown anti-sub patrol out of Guantanamo Bay, Cuba in a single-engine aircraft. The patrol was six to seven hours long and he had extra fuel tanks for the mission. He had been out drinking the night before and was suffering from diarrhea. There was no way he could stop the patrol or turn back, so he claimed he loosen his shoulder straps, took down his flight suit, and utilized a brown paper bag that he had brought with sandwiches to handle his bowel movement. While still on patrol, he said the smell was so terrible that he threw the sack over the side. When he returned from the mission, his flight crew chief pointed out that most of the excrement had streamed down the side of the aircraft and on the tail section.

Since my job was to brief pilots on targeting, Claude Leving, one of the senior pilots, decided I should get some flight time to get a pilot's perspective on approaching target areas. We signed out a TV-2, which was the Navy version of the Lockheed F80 "Shooting Star", one of the first combat jets and now used by the Navy and the Air Force for training. We made a number of runs by going out to sea 30 or 40 miles, then flying 100 feet over the ocean at 400-500 mph, then going through passes in the mountains — because this was how our planes would have to penetrate the enemy coastline if they were on a mission. We then did low-level flights ("flat hatting") across the valleys, keeping the plane below radar level and ascertaining what landmarks would be discernible from a navigational standpoint. This training helped me considerably in target planning because I gained an appreciation of what pilots go through with a plane moving at 400 mph across unknown terrain. My one and a half hours in the F-80 was duly logged in my pilot's flight logbook from my Tiger Moth days in England.

Late in 1955, we went to sea aboard the USS Oriskany. The Oriskany was completed as World War II wound down. It was an Essex class carrier, 800 plus feet long, and approximately 43,000 tons. (Incidentally, the Titanic was also 43,000 tons.) With the Air Group aboard, we had 2700 personnel, and about 85 aircraft. Our planes were F2H McDonnell Douglas Banshees that our squadron flew, F9F Grumman Cougars, AD-5 Douglas Skyraiders, A3D Skywarrior, which was the heavy attack aircraft for nuclear weapons, and a small detachment from a helicopter squadron with two helicopters. We went to Hawaii and spent two weeks there doing Operational Readiness Inspection, where staff from Pacific Fleet HQ comes aboard and inspects the ship for all aspects of combat readiness. The aircraft do practice bombing and rocket runs on one of the target islands, and the ship is put through a great number of tests and readiness criteria. This usually takes about two weeks. After this was over, we were usually allowed two or three days of liberty in Hawaii before deploying to the Far

East.

With the Korean War just concluded, negotiations on a peace treaty were still very tense and only a cease-fire existed. Also, since the Chinese had entered the Korean War, relations with the Chinese were turbulent, to say the least. In addition, the Cold War with the Soviet Union was very much in process. For these reasons, the Navy's Seventh Fleet, based out of Yokosuka, Japan, had seven carriers ready for action. Of these, four were always at sea, located from the south coast of China clear to the north off Vladivostok and the northern Russian ports. The mission of these carriers was to incapacitate enemy airfields in the event of hostilities within a 100-mile range of the coast. The carriers rotated duty stations and also rotated liberty time in and out of Yokosuka and the other ports in Japan, Hong Kong, and the Philippines. While on duty, our carrier would be assigned a certain number of airfield targets within the range of that particular duty station. Most of the airfields were to be incapacitated by the use of small three to five kiloton atomic weapons. My job was to accumulate all information possible about each one of these airfields, utilizing old maps for the surrounding terrain and recent photos taken either by our photo planes or by Air Force planes. From our own patrol aircraft, we had information about enemy radar and anti-aircraft or missile sites. A proposed route would then be planned to the target and avoiding these hazards.

Generally, an aircraft on its way to a planned target would descend to 50 to 100 feet over the ocean within 100 miles of the coastline so that it would fly under the radar screen. Likewise, when it is over land, it would fly at very low altitude so that the radar could pick up ground clutter. In making a bombing run, a pilot would see various points of identification when approaching the target. At a certain designated point, usually called the IP or Initial Point, the pilot would release the bomb by one of two methods: either pulling the nose of the aircraft up and releasing the bomb so that the bomb would "loft" into the target. The pilot would then do a wingover and get out of the target area as fast as possible. The other method was called "over the shoulder." The pilot would come completely in over the target and pull back on the stick and climb and the bomb would release and go straight up in the air. The pilot would then complete a wingover and exit the target area as soon as possible. The bombs were generally programmed to explode at 600 to 800 feet over the target.

Both of these methods were satisfactory for F2H Banshees to deliver a weapon and get away from the blast. However, for the AD-5 Skyraider, a prop plane, it was marginal whether they had enough speed to get away and survive the blast. The pilots, of course, knew this and assumed the risk. Our carrier's mission was to launch at least 30 fully loaded aircraft within the first hour of a bombing task. Sometimes, the destroyers accompanying our carrier picked up on sonar either Chinese or Russian submarines trailing our task force. Our assumption was that the carrier, being a large target, had only a limited life in the event of hostilities, and that it was important to get the strikes off the deck as soon as possible in order to complete our mission. Later when I made a second cruise as Air Group intelligence officer and also the ship's atomic weapons officer, I had access to top-secret op plans, and was able to form a better understanding of our overall attack plan as well as enemy capabilities to destroy our task force and the carrier; I determined that the carrier had a very limited survival time.

A carrier at sea is an intricate and crowded environment to live in for a number of months. You have to learn all the passageways to get from your office to your bunk, to the ready room, the mess hall, and every other place you needed to be on the ship. A carrier, of course, has a big flight deck and below that, the hangar deck where the planes are brought to perform maintenance work. Although a carrier is certainly more stable than the destroyers and cruisers that were part of our accompanying task force, in a heavy sea the carrier still pitches and rolls considerably. Occasionally, boards would be fitted to the edges of tables in the officer's dining area to keep the plates from sliding off.

As were all carriers during World War II, the Oriskany was a straight deck carrier which meant that when pilots landed, if they didn't catch one of the landing wires, the plane would strike planes on the forefront of the deck that had previously landed. To prevent this, a cable and net were strung across the deck with a mobile crane positioned behind it. In other words, if the plane missed the landing wire, it would smash into the crane parked behind the netting and cables rather than into the "pack" of aircraft parked on the foredeck. This problem was eliminated with the arrival of angled deck carriers that came online a year or two later. On my second cruise, I was aboard the Ticonderoga which was an angled deck carrier.

When not at sea, we enjoyed liberty at a number of Far Eastern ports. Yokosuka was the headquarters of the Pacific Seventh Fleet, and before that, it was the primary Japanese Naval Base during World War II. The Kamikaze pilots trained at Atsugi Airfield, which is close to the Yokosuka base, and this was the field where our pilots would fly in and out. In addition to Yokosuka, we called at Kobe, Iwakuni and Sasebo, ports in Japan, and Hong Kong, the Philippines, and Okinawa. Hong Kong was a major shopping area and each carrier was able to go there at least once on each cruise. Shopping during the 1950s was tremendously inexpensive, both in Japan and Hong Kong, as this was before the great influx of tourists. To purchase a tailor-made suit in Hong Kong was $30 or $35. Most items for sale at the PX in Yokosuka were substantially less than in the U.S. Drinks at the Officers' Club ranged from 10 to 25 cents. Liquor sold for approximately $1.00 a bottle. From each of the cruises, I bought all kinds of things, including bolts of raw silk that we used for draperies in our first home in Indian Village, our Fort Wayne neighborhood five years hence. It was common practice to buy cases of china, empty out the china, and utilize the cases to carry home liquor because it was so cheap. Of course, liquor is not permitted on any Navy ship, but there would be cases of china in everyone's office or bunk area and if you turned them over they would gurgle.

I was also amazed at the number of sailors, and officers too, who had traveled to Japan many times and had girlfriends or perhaps even a family on each side of the Pacific. These men would disembark as soon as we arrived in port and spend the entire time with their girlfriend at a place in town or nearby countryside.

On one in-port period, I was assigned as a Shore Patrol officer and performed my duties alongside a Japanese policeman, a Marine and a Navy enlisted man. While it may sound like the beginning of a bad bar joke, there was purpose to the four of us working together: if a Japanese civilian was involved in a crime, it was the duty of the Japanese policeman to handle the matter. If on the other hand, there was a Navy seaman involved, it was the duty of the enlisted seaman to take care of the offender as the involvement of a Navy officer might trigger a court-martial offense if the seaman were drunk and took a swing at the officer. As the Navy officer in this quadruple alliance, it was my job to handle any officers who got into trouble. Finally, we needed a Marine — because a drunk Marine can only be handled by another Marine! The Japanese policeman also served as our interpreter and together we inspected all the local bars, houses of prostitution, gambling, and other business of ill repute. Needless to say, I got an unbelievable tour.

Venereal Disease was very prevalent at this time and prior to arriving at each port, we were required to attend mandatory showings of gruesome VD movies, including graphic illustrations of the symptoms and side effects associated with the various types of sexually transmitted diseases. After many viewings, the men became quite familiar with these videos and would break into loud cheers when the less savory parts would come on. Because of tight health restrictions, the incidence of VD in Japan was controlled fairly well. However, in the Philippines, the rate of VD was very high. At one point, our Ticonderoga Captain mandated that VD rates would be publicized at the end of each news broadcast which we received every day over on the AP and UP wires, and which would be carried on the ship's speaker system. The announcer would go down the list of the various ship's divisions and say: "Company A, 430 men assigned, 117 on VD call," and so on through each of the divisions and then through the Air group. The smallest group was the helicopter division which only had 17 men assigned. Invariably, this group would have the highest VD rate and their name would always be read last with a great deal of derision by the announcer. Loud cheers would break out throughout the ship, "Yeah, they'd done it again!" After this happened a number of times, the Captain discontinued the announcement of the VD rate.

Going to the bathroom in Japan is a lot more informal than in the United States. It is not unusual to see men or women openly relieving themselves on the sides of country roads. This informality led to at least one embarrassing episode for me. Each squadron normally has a party while overseas and I was in charge of the party detail for ours. We rented a large room and bought numerous cases of booze for the 125 officers and men of our squadron. Some of the enlisted men were 18, 19, or 20 years old and within a very short period of time, many were very drunk. We also had entertainment — strippers from one of the local clubs. In addition, many of the men brought their Japanese girlfriends or girls they had just met. We all used the same bathroom, which included a trough along one wall for men and two commodes without doors for the women. While I am standing at the urinal, one of the enlisted men who worked with me approached me with his girlfriend saying, "Oh, Mr. Parker, I would like for you to meet my girlfriend, Miki-can." I shift hands to continue urinating and shake hands with Miki-can, who is doing a traditional Japanese bow for introductions. The situation bothered me considerably more than it did Miki-can.

Equally surprising is that I did not get court-martialed by the skipper for the ruckus behavior and unfortunate events that took place that night. The combination of booze, strippers, half as many women as men all in a too-small room filled with sailors who had been at sea for 30 days or more led to numerous fights, arrests, ungentlemanly behavior, vomiting, and torn clothing. But in the end, it was considered a typical Navy squadron party where a good time was had by all and that was the end of it.

After nine months, the Oriskany headed back to the States and our squadron was transferred from Moffett Field to Naval Air Station Alameda, across the bay from San Francisco. Pat and Pam returned to Alameda from Chicago, where they had gone to live with her folks during my tour of duty. We were given temporary housing in half of a Navy Quonset hut, which was a terrible existence for two or three weeks. When we finally got placed in a small Navy house, we thought it was palatial. In retrospect, the house was only 700 or 800 square feet, with very tiny rooms. But we were in a relatively upscale officers' housing area and quickly made friends with our neighbors in addition to the officers in our squadron.

I was transferred from the squadron to the Air Group and became the Air Group intelligence officer. Again, I felt that athletics helped me out as I had been able to play golf with Cdr. Bangs on a number of occasions, and our being partners and money winners on occasion did not hurt. Our Air Group Commander is Lou Bangs, a dynamic Naval officer who had been awarded the Navy Cross for sinking a small Japanese carrier in World War II. Cdr. Bangs subsequently became the Captain of a carrier and ultimately made Admiral.

Whenever you change duty stations — as I did from VF-194 to Air Group 9 — it was customary to call on the Commanding Officer. This was a very formal affair on a Sunday afternoon involving the officer, his wife, if married, wearing formal dress blues including sword, and placing your calling card in a silver tray in the vestibule of the CO. Pat and I made this very formal call upon Cdr. Bangs and his wife when I was transferred to his command.

In officers' housing, we became friends with an officer and his wife who lived behind us, Rick and Phyllis Conroy, who had two small children. We would often play bridge with the Conroys. Rick was a patrol plane pilot and was ultimately lost two years later when his plane went down. Rick had a big German Shepherd police dog that he kept in a fenced-in area behind their small house. Occasionally, the dog would get out and wander the neighborhood and sometimes do his business in the yard of the Alameda Base Executive Officer, a senior commander who lived down the street from Rick. On one occasion the XO picked up the dog excrement in a shovel and smeared it all over the welcome mat in front of Rick's door. Rick and the XO then got into an altercation, which ultimately went to a Captain's mast in front of the Commanding Officer of the Base. What a sorry state of affairs this was — the XO of the Base and a senior pilot in an altercation over smearing dog crap on a welcome mat. I never learned the result of the Captain's mast, but I do know that the XO was transferred very soon thereafter.

Being ashore in Alameda for six or eight months, we were able to spend time in the San Francisco area. I even enrolled in two evening courses at Boalt Hall, the Law School of the University of California in Berkeley. I would leave my office on the base at 4:30 in the afternoon and drive to Berkeley where

I had classes for two or three hours three days a week. I took these courses with the goal of ultimately taking the Bar examination and staying in California. I even looked into interviewing with several San Francisco firms, but later events compelled me to come back to Indiana. One of my friends from Law School, Bill Brown, (our anchorman on our Michigan Law School chug-a-lug team) was with one of the larger San Francisco firms. Bill was later appointed judge by then-Governor Ronald Reagan and had a long and distinguished career on the California Bench. Bill was very noteworthy because he was 6'5" and weighed almost 400 pounds. I can remember him coming over to our small house in Alameda, sitting on one of our Navy porch chairs, and having it sink clear to the ground with him.

We were also able to enjoy the San Francisco night-life scene. We went to places that later became very well-known like the Purple Onion for first wave comedians like Bob Newhart and Phyllis Diller and Miss Smith's Tearoom, a gay and lesbian hangout. These were the sort of touristy places that outsiders could go and existed before San Francisco became well-known for its diverse and beat era communities. We delighted in taking visiting friends to see all the touristy sights in downtown San Francisco, including Lombard Street (the crookedest street in the world), Coit Tower, and Fisherman's Wharf.

Before long, however, it was time to ship out for another cruise. This time our Air Group was slated to go aboard the Ticonderoga, another Essex class carrier, but with an angled deck. Two things happened just before we were ready to leave: a payment of about $250 finally came through from the Navy for reimbursement for our goods that were stolen when I was transferred to the West Coast; and I got orders to go to Navy Atomic Weapons School in San Diego. However, I was required to ship out with the rest of the Air Group, and then return from Hawaii back to San Diego.

When a carrier or any ship leaves port for an extended cruise, it is a really sad time on the dock. The wives and children come to say goodbye and everyone is crying because they will not see each other again for another nine months or so. When I shipped out with the Air Group, Pat was on the dock with Pam crying like all the other wives, but knowing full well that she was going to see me in just five days because we had planned for her to use the money we had gotten from the settlement of the Navy claim to come to Hawaii. Sure enough, when the Ticonderoga pulled into Pearl Harbor, there was Pat waving on the dock. Pam stayed behind with our friends, the Conroys. Pat and I spent three or four days at Fort DeRussy, which is on Waikiki Beach and also a Service R & R Center. The cost for a room was minimal, but Pat and I debated for a long time about whether to spend an extra one dollar to get a small cabana down on the beach (we did). We also splurged on booking a commercial flight to the Big Island where we spent five days surfing and sightseeing and stayed at an R & R Center in Hilo.

When the Ticonderoga left Hawaii for Japan, I was not aboard because I was sent back to San Diego for six weeks of special atomic weapons training at North Island Naval Air Station. Pat and Pam met me there and we got a small apartment on Coronado Island across the bay from San Diego. At this time, there was no bridge and a ferry was required to go to San Diego. The weather was beautiful and we very much enjoyed our short time stationed at North Island. I had classes every day and learned many of the intricacies and problems associated with the usage of atomic weapons.

When I completed the training and rejoined the ship, my job was to do both flight planning and to work with the Air Group ordinance officer to select weapons to be used, deciding on burst height and other aspects of each particular weapon. I was somewhat surprised to be given this training because at this point I had less than a year to go before I was slated to leave the Navy.

My plan was to rejoin the Ticonderoga in Subic Bay in the Philippines. I learned that if I missed meeting the ship in Subic Bay, the next port of call was Hong Kong, and I would not be able to catch the ship there and would have to go into Yokosuka and wait many days for the ship to arrive. Hong Kong was not a port of call to be missed.

Therefore I embarked on what I have come to call the "Trip to Hell." My flight from San Diego to Pearl Harbor aboard a Navy transport was no problem, but once I arrived in Pearl Harbor I learned that there are no Navy aircraft leaving for the Philippines for some time. I'm instructed to go to Hickam Field, the Air Force base because they have planes going to the Philippines from time to time. After arriving at Hickam, I find that all available spots on flights to the Philippines are booked. After a few hours, one Air Force personnel person tells me that he can get me on an AF cargo plane to the Philippines right away if I agree to serve as a "courier officer" delivering classified and other special mail. While I had no particular qualifications, he told me that any officer would do. They armed me with a .45 pistol and holster and turned over about ten bags of mail, which I signed for. After committing to this detail, I also learned that I would be the custodian of the body of an enlisted Navy man who had died in Washington, D.C., and was being sent home to the Philippines for burial.

A C-124 is an immense four-engine Air Force cargo plane. It is big enough to drive trucks inside through a rear cargo door. The crew sits in a cabin up a ladder and far away from the main cargo area. This was my transportation to the Philippines. I am not seated with the pilot and crew, but in the cargo area by myself with ten bags of mail, two trucks, many other types of military equipment, and a body. Two hours out of Hickam we have engine trouble and one of our port engines shuts down. We make an emergency landing at Johnston Island Air Force Base, an atoll with an airstrip located about four hours from Hawaii. We stay at Johnston Island for two days while the engine is repaired. During this time, I make arrangements with the base for two air policemen to guard the courier mail and body at all times that I am not there. We rotate shifts standing guard in the plane.

One of these guards was a tall young African-American corporal. When I came out to relieve him of guard duty, I asked him why he was standing outside the plane instead of inside the cargo area. He replies, "No, Sir, I am not going up on that plane. Not with that stiff up there. I will do my guard duty down here." I didn't argue with him.

I went for dinner that night in the small Officers' Club they had on the base. After a drink or two, I excused myself to go to the men's room. An Air Force Warrant Officer followed me in and proceeded to proposition me. This is the first and only time I have ever been propositioned by a man. I laughed nervously and quickly left the men's room. Since then I have often wondered how a gay man was able to get by in the Air Force for so long at that time as this was long before the "Don't ask/Don't tell" doctrine that came in with the Clinton Administration.

The engine is repaired, and we are off again. The plan is to refuel in Eniwetok atoll in the Marshall Islands but we are vectored away because of atomic weapon testing that is going on there. Instead, we are directed to Kwajalein Island, the southernmost and largest of the islands in the atoll. But the fog is so great we can't land. We orbit for perhaps an hour until our fuel runs low and then we are forced to make a landing. We approach the airstrip in almost zero conditions. Just before we are due to touch down, the plane pulls up very quickly. I peer out my small window and see a hangar very close off the wing. Because of the fog we had missed the runway completely and nearly landed on top of a hangar. On the second descent, the fog cleared a bit and we were able to land. The only people shakier than I were the pilots who had spotted their error at the last second!

That night the Air force officers and I decided to relax a bit by swimming in a base pool. Unaware that the pool was salt water and very dense, I dive off of a small diving board and enter the water at an unusual angle, hitting the bottom and dislocating the shoulder that I had previously injured in high school football. I was in the middle of the pool with terrible pain and nearly in shock. I am finally able to call out to the Air Force officers who jumped in and pulled me out. I'm taken to the base hospital where my shoulder is snapped back in place and taped to my chest which causes a real problem getting in and out of the plane, and later getting up and down the ladders on the ship with just one arm.

After refueling, we are off again, but then more engine trouble and this time we have to land in Guam. We spend two more days hanging around Guam while repairs are made. The U.S. military on Guam at this time is very involved in trying to capture one of the last Japanese soldiers who has not surrendered and who is still "out there" nearly *ten* years after the war is over.

Finally, about 200 miles outside of Clark Air Force Base in the Philippines, two Air Force F-86's buzz our aircraft. It seems that our pilots have failed to file the proper identification codes to enter the Philippine Air Defense Zone and Clark has scrambled fighters to usher us in. We finally land and I catch a truck ride from Clark to Subic Bay where I am finally able to meet up with my ship just two hours before sailing.

While I was having my trans-Pacific odyssey, there was much excitement aboard the ship as well. Local Communist guerrillas called the Huks had been active in the mountainous area around Subic Bay — attacking villages, burning government buildings, etc. A carrier has a detachment of Marines aboard, usually involving 30 or 40 Marines who take care of formal duties, support the Admiral, maintain the brig, and various other duties. Capt. Erickson and Lt. Richardson were the two Marine officers in charge of our detachment. Capt. Erickson was a very straight arrow-type Marine, while Lt. Richardson, a good friend of mine, was a laid back reserve. While the ship was in port, Capt. Erickson had planned a training mission ashore for the Marine detachment. They went up to a mountainous area, divided into two groups, and set up a mini-war game. One of the enlisted men was left in charge of the camp while the maneuvers took place. They tried to raise him on the walkie-talkie but were unable to do so, and they finally sent a runner back to camp. The runner finds the equipment all burned and the guard lying in the mud, presumably wounded. When they question the guard, all he can say is, "The Huks did it."

Believing that the Communist insurgents had attacked the Marine camp, the whole area goes on alert. Helicopters are launched from the carrier. Destroyers in the Bay arrange their guns to support naval gunfire in the area where they believe the Huks are. The Philippine militia is called out and an all-out hunt begins for the perpetrators.

In the meantime, my friend Lt. Harry Richardson loaded the Marine guard all covered with mud into the jeep and brought him back to the ship for medical treatment. When they get him into the sickbay and all washed off, they find that there is nothing wrong with him — he is not injured in the slightest. After some interrogation by Richardson, it is discovered that the Marine has been careless, let the fire get out of control and burned up all the equipment. The story was made up by the Marine to cover himself.

Capt. Erickson had the embarrassing job of calling off the alert with all the Naval and Philippine forces. But the officers in the wardroom do not let this opportunity pass. They secured a photo of Capt. Erickson from the Marine bulletin board, wrapped it in black crepe, put a toilet seat around it, and hung it in the wardroom over his assigned seat. Erickson took one look at this and refused to return to the wardroom for the rest of the cruise.

Lt. Richardson was the assigned trial counsel or prosecuting attorney for all disciplinary cases aboard the ship. Other than Captain's mast, the accused are entitled to defense counsel, and because Harry was a lawyer, and I was the only other lawyer aboard ship, we were pressed into service as defense counsel at a number of special court-martials. Harry and I went head to head on a number of cases, which I usually lost. After he was discharged, Harry practiced in Maine and eventually became the senior partner in a large Portland firm. He made a run for Governor of Maine but was unsuccessful. On a trip to Montreal one summer, I detoured through Maine and reunited with Harry for one day. He was a great guy and we got along very well.

I was on Commander Bangs' staff as Air Group Intelligence and Atomic Weapons Officer. As Bangs was a golfer and sometimes this meant we had to have staff meetings ashore and our golf clubs would generally come along. We would fly off the ship and head into port a day or two ahead of the ship. In this way, we played a number of the finest golf courses in Japan, the Philippines, and Okinawa and had some great golf games. One of our other golf partners was the Catholic Chaplin aboard the ship, Father Ryan. One of the special courses we played was at the Kawana Hotel in a city called Ito on the Izu Peninsula of Japan. This is a very outstanding course resembling Pebble Beach with holes along the ocean and beautiful views. It is now one of the most expensive courses to play in Japan. Our caddies were all young ladies. If you played poorly one day with the ball in the rough, the next day you might ask for the same caddy and she would refuse to go with you. "I no caddy for you, you hit in rough and I can't find ball."

In Okinawa, we played on sand greens. Once you hit the ball onto the green, the caddies would smooth down a path with a snow shovel-like rake to make it easier to putt. After putting, they would rake up the green again for the next foursome. One of the tees is on a high cliff above the ocean. A plaque near the tee indicates that from this cliff the Japanese Commander committed harakiri and jumped into the ocean just before the Japanese surrender. Hitting shots from this tee, which went either into the ocean or the deep rough, sometimes you felt like doing the same thing.

After playing a number of the courses and being at sea for many months, Father Ryan's language got pretty salty. When we returned to Pearl Harbor, Father Ryan asked the senior Pearl Harbor Catholic chaplain to play with us, a very senior Navy Captain. On one of the holes, Father Ryan hooked his ball out of bounds. He threw his club down and shouted, "Oh, Bull Shit!" The Senior Capt. Chaplain was aghast, and exclaimed, "Father Ryan, I think you have been at sea much too long."

In Kobe, Japan, we played the Rocco Mountain Course, the oldest course in Japan, and situated in a beautiful mountainous terrain. We had an all-ship tournament and at the end of nine holes, I was in the lead. However, the fog rolled in and the tournament was canceled, never to be rescheduled. Dang.

Part of my job at this time was to go to Tachikawa, a big U.S. Air Force base in Japan, and pick up intelligence photos. I would make a day-long trip from Yokosuka and a Marine guard would accompany me because these were all top-secret photos. Our Navy planes generally did photo-reconnaissance flights within 50 miles of the coast, a fast in and out flight before the Chinese could scramble the MIG-17's and our pilots were able to get back over international waters. But the Air Force had photos from much further inland. In picking up my photos, I casually asked one of the Air Force officers where they obtained these photos. He told me that I was not in the "need-to-know" category, and I could never figure it out. I thought I could identify the aircraft the Air Force had available for photo missions and I didn't believe any were capable of going inland 200-300 miles and returning without the MIGs or surface to air missiles shooting them down. About eight or ten years later, after I was long off active duty, Gary Powers, an American pilot's CIA U-2 spy plane was shot down while flying a reconnaissance mission over Russia. At once it became clear to me that the photos we had were U-2 photos taken by the Air Force.

Before the Ticonderoga returned to Alameda, I was detached from the ship and mustered out of the Navy. All of my personal possessions and the small amount of furniture that we had were repacked at the Navy Supply Depot in Oakland and shipped to Chicago. When we opened the boxes in Chicago, one of the things we found was that all the booze that I had bought so cheaply overseas had been removed and replaced with bricks. We learned later that this was a common occurrence at the Supply Depot and that the packers latched onto whatever booze they could find. Who was going to complain?

I was in the Navy Reserve for five more years after I moved to Fort Wayne. When I originally entered the Navy for a tour of duty of three and a half years, I was very concerned about how far I would be left behind in the practice of law. As it turned out, the experience that I gained in the service was very helpful and I didn't feel short-changed at all. While Pat and I made a great number of moves up and down the east and west coasts during my period in the Navy, overall it was a great experience. I strongly felt I had a significant job to do; if our squadron or Air Group was needed, we were prepared to do what was necessary. Since Korea was winding down, there was no shooting war while I was in service. But we did endure two or three minor Cold War affairs with the Chinese involving Quemoy and Matsu in which we were put on High Alert.

An interesting afterthought occurred when I returned to China with our family in 1982. While on a Chinese commercial flight into Changsha, I realized that this was one of the airfields that had been assigned to our ship as a possible target. I knew the airfield very well — where they parked the aircraft, how many barracks were located there, where the fuel storage was, and many other details. There were almost no changes since the photos I had examined in 1956. The M-17s were still parked in the same location as over 25 years earlier.

WITHIN AN EYELASH

1960

The political career of my father, Crawford Parker, had a profound effect not only on his own life but on the lives of many others, including our family. In 1956, he was elected Lt. Governor, the second-highest office in the State, and later came within an eyelash of being elected Governor.

In his various political offices — from County Clerk to Lt. Governor — he had a reputation for providing outstanding service to the public. There was never a hint of any scandal, and he was a hard-working and dedicated public servant. In fact, quite a number of projects important to the state would not have been completed without his diligence.

He ran in four statewide elections, and there are thousands of clippings about his activities. Of the hundreds of photos I sorted in going through his boxes of memorabilia, one thing is clear — he is easily the most striking person in every picture. He was very photogenic, with beautiful white hair from a young age, always a smile, and usually dressed in a dark suit that accentuated his hair. He was a vigorous campaigner and would spend whatever hours it took to meet everyone in a room and shake hands. He was almost never sick (until his later years) and really reveled in the politics of government.

Crawford Parker was born the second of ten children to Herbert and Ethel Parker in Danville, Indiana in September 1906. His father was a veterinarian but was disabled for a substantial portion of his life. While his kids were growing up, Herbert worked in the stockyards in Chicago and would take the train home on the weekend to Indianapolis and then to Danville. Notwithstanding Herbert's small salary, almost all of Crawford's brothers and sisters attended college. Most graduated from college and some went on to get advanced degrees. It is especially noteworthy that notwithstanding these humble circumstances, Crawford, his sister Lois, and his brother Will were all inductees into their high school Hall of Fame.

Crawford attended Central Normal College in Danville, but dropped out after his first year to marry Angie Lucille Bouslog, my mother, who he met at Central Normal. Lucille attended Central Normal because her father, Enoch Bouslog, had graduated from Central Normal during the 1880s. Crawford and Lucille were married in 1926 and settled down in Mooreland where Enoch Bouslog owned a small general store. My father became the butcher and both he and my mother worked full time in the store. While dad's family had always been Republicans, the Bouslogs were strong Democrats. My father and grandfather, Enoch, never discussed politics.

Dad became a Republican Precinct Committeeman in the '30s and then ran for County Clerk in 1942. He was reelected as County Clerk in 1946 and then elected President of the Indiana County Clerk's Association. He was appointed Assistant Secretary of State, and so resigned as County Clerk. While Assistant Secretary of State he was appointed to the Indiana Public Service Commission by then-Governor Henry Schricker, a Democrat. In 1952, Crawford ran for Secretary of State, was elected, and ran again in 1954 and was reelected. His terms as Secretary of State were characterized by a modernization of the Corporation and Securities Departments and upgrading of service for all of the departments. Generally, he was recognized for running a very efficient office and providing outstanding service.

While he was Secretary of State, the Republicans controlled all of the state offices. George Craig was Governor, and Harold Handley was Lt. Governor. Because of constitutional limitations at the time, the Indiana Governor could not succeed himself and could serve only one term. When Craig's term was over in 1956, Handley moved up from Lt. Governor to Governor, and Crawford was elected Lt. Governor. This sequence of events became very significant when Crawford later ran for Governor.

During Handley's term as Governor (1957-1961), two things happened that had a great effect upon the subsequent gubernatorial election. During George Craig's previous term as Governor (1953-1957), some criminal conduct had taken place in conjunction with the purchase of highway right-of-ways, subsequently called the "Craig Highway Scandals". The individuals involved were highway commissioners and associates of Craig named Doxie Moore, Doc Sherwood, and an attorney named Peak. Later during the Handley term, all three men were indicted, convicted, and served time for accepting bribes to influence their decisions to accept highway contracts.

This incident was used by Crawford's opponent, Matt

Welsh, to accuse Craig of being culpable for the crimes and by association Handley and Parker as well, because they were all part of the same Republican administration when the incident occurred. This was the case notwithstanding the fact that my father and George Craig were not friends and had almost no contact while he served as Secretary of State.

The second thing that happened involved Harold Handley's desire to go to Washington, D.C. as a Senator. The Indiana Senators at this time were Bill Jenner and Homer Capehart. Jenner controlled most of the conservative wing of the Republican party. He decided not to run for re-election in 1958, and Harold Handley ran for the vacated Senate seat while in the middle of his term as Governor. Unfortunately, Handley refused to resign as Governor after he was nominated to be Senator. Had he done so, then Crawford as Lt. Governor would have finished his term as Governor and been able to run on his own record instead of someone who served in the same administration as Craig and Handley. These two events, the Craig Highway Scandals and Handley running for Senator in the middle of his term as Governor, ended up influencing strongly the outcome of the 1960 gubernatorial race, although neither incident involved Crawford directly.

In 1958 Handley ran for Senator against Vance Hartke, the Mayor of Evansville. It was a bitter campaign. In the late '50s, manufacturing was very strong in Indiana and the Unions, particularly the UAW, were politically very powerful and had considerable sway over the Democrat party. The Republicans campaigned on the platform that Walter Reuter, then head of the UAW-CIO, would control Indiana if Hartke were elected. Crawford campaigned very hard for Handley and made almost as many, if not more, speeches than Handley did during the campaign.

Unfortunately, Handley lost the Senate seat by 244,000 votes, just two years after he had been elected Governor by a substantial margin. The newspaper clippings indicate that this was the worst defeat of a State office-holder since 1936. The voters were clearly not enamored by Handley running for Senate in the middle of his term as Governor and they proceeded to trounce him at the polls. Two years later Crawford's opponent, Matt Welsh, used Handley's unpopularity against Crawford in the 1960 gubernatorial race.

A third significant event in Crawford's campaign for the Governorship involved the Right-to-Work bill. Right-to-Work legislation effectively prohibits unions from forcing non-members to pay "agency fees" as a condition of working at unionized firms.

When a Union wins a bargaining election, one of the provisions they always desire to insert in the contract is that all employees (except management) are required to belong to the Union. This means that the Union can collect dues from all employees even if the employees have no interest in joining the Union as a condition of keeping their jobs.

The Right-to-Work law passed in Indiana in 1957, in effect outlawing the Union shop, but the Unions viewed the law as curtailing their power and did everything possible to repeal the law. With strong Union membership in Indiana in 1960, the Unions were at their greatest strength, and hence this was a primary issue in Crawford's campaign.

During the Handley administration also, there had been a long and bitter strike in 1955 at the Perfect Circle piston ring plant in New Castle. The company fired a number of strikers for picket line violations, which sent a spark throughout the union ranks in Indiana. Almost 3000 demonstrators amassed and marched in front of the plant.

Gov. Handley went to New Castle, got up on top of a police car, and tried to quiet the crowd, which was close to a riot. Later, gunshots were fired, the National Guard was called in, and people were hurt.

This episode gave New Castle a very bad reputation as a Union town and made it difficult for decades thereafter to get manufacturers to come to town. During Handley's campaign for Senator, the Right-to-Work law was a major issue and Crawford made clear that he also supported the Right-to-Work law.

As Lt. Governor, Crawford presided over the Indiana Senate. The Indiana House of Representatives, however, was overwhelmingly Democrat, as most were elected along with Hartke in the Democrat sweep of 1958. The Senate, however, was still Republican. There was a lot of maneuvering in the Senate to get Democrat members appointed to the Labor Committee. Crawford, however, was able to outmaneuver them and put a substantial majority of Republicans on the Labor Committee.

In 1959, the House overwhelmingly passed a bill to repeal Indiana's Right-to-Work law, but the Senate Labor Committee never reported the bill out for a vote and it died in the Senate. The Right-to-Work repeal effort was a huge issue in the 1959 General Assembly and Crawford was very much identified with standing up to the Unions. As Lt. Governor, he was also Chairman of the Department of Commerce, and was able to point out how Indiana attracted many manufacturing plants from other states because of the Right-to-Work Law. The Democrats, of course, tagged him as an enemy of labor.

One thing I was personally able to do to help counteract the Union opposition and support Crawford's candidacy was to get the President of the Union at Dana Corporation in Fort Wayne, Dick Darnell, a friend of mine, to oppose repeal of the Right-to-Work Law. Along with Bill Bonsib, an advertising executive hired by the Republicans, we drafted up a brochure supporting the Right-to-Work Law and Crawford's candidacy which was distributed throughout the State.

While campaigning for Handley for Senate in 1958,

Crawford was of course shoring up his own support as a nominee for Governor. There were a number of opponents early on in his own party, mostly Republicans from the Senate. However, he had worked so diligently for Handley — making many speeches and attending numerous Republican events — that he had the overwhelming support of almost all of the County Chairmen and Precinct Committeemen throughout the State. He very effectively outmaneuvered all of his opponents and was nominated by acclamation on the first ballot.

Before the State Convention, Crawford spent considerable time working to get to know all the 1,000 plus delegates, including memorizing all of their names. I remember standing in line with him as the hundreds of delegates came through a reception line, and he was able to address nearly every single one by name, knew where they lived, knew about their family, and had visited them at their home or place of business. I was amazed at his ability to recall all this information. There was no way that anyone who had not spent the time that he did was going to out campaign him for the nomination.

The only real question was who would be the Republican nominee for Lt. Governor. Al Cast was Republican State Party Chairman at the time, and he expressed an interest in running. Al was the father of Bill Cast, a doctor in Fort Wayne and a good friend of ours. Al was a possible candidate, but the Party believed that his prior connections with Gov. George Craig would create a problem and instead went with Richard Ristine.

Crawford had a very ambitious campaign platform involving the creation of new jobs, revamping the mental health department, increasing highway spending and a number of other proposals. His opponent was Matt Welsh, a lawyer and able Democrat State Senator from Vincennes. Welsh ran a very good campaign and a book he later wrote about his term in the Governor's office has a chapter on his campaign strategy.

The campaign was long and arduous. The Republicans campaigned throughout the State with a "caravan" of about 100 cars which would assemble in every county seat but also stop at many smaller towns too. Along with the caravan was a steam calliope pulled by a pickup truck. I'm not certain where the calliope came from, but it may have been from the Barnum & Bailey circus which had winter quarters in Peru, Indiana. The caravan was like a circus parade, with the cars all decorated with campaign signs and the calliope at full blast.

They usually would have a breakfast meeting and perhaps a luncheon or dinner speech scheduled in the country seat. Then throughout the day, they would walk up and down the streets of the small towns and even in rural areas shaking hands and meeting voters — a very "grassroots campaign". Considering the fact that Indiana has 92 counties, it was a very long and time-consuming process.

One morning I went with Crawford in the caravan. We got up around 3:30 or 4:00 in the morning and drove from Indianapolis to southern Indiana where we attended a breakfast meeting in one of the southern counties. We traveled around the entire morning with the caravan stopping to shake hands in every small town. Then he had a luncheon speech and after that, we caravanned again all afternoon. At dinner, there was a large rally in Jeffersonville and an evening speech. After that, we went across to Louisville, Kentucky to be interviewed on television and radio. Finally, we drove home to Indianapolis, getting in about 1:30 in the morning. The next day while I slept in, Crawford headed out on yet another caravan.

Welsh writes in his book that part of the Democrat strategy was to let the Republicans, and particularly Crawford, wear himself out with this grassroots approach. Welsh instead used TV ads, a new idea at the time, and radio to reach out to voters and didn't attempt a grassroots-type campaign.

Since the Democrats had not been in power for the last

eight years, there was no state record for the Republicans to talk about. So, much of the Republican campaign focused on how the Unions would take over the Indiana government if Democrats were elected nationally. Most of Crawford's speeches supported Richard Nixon, and opposed Jack Kennedy in the presidential race.

Welsh's strategy was to attack Republicans on the Craig Highway Scandals and link Parker closely to Handley, after he had been discredited by his overwhelming defeat in the 1958 Senatorial election. In fact, Welsh never referred to Crawford by name or even as "his opponent" but instead repeatedly called him "Handley-Parker". Welsh used it so effectively that some probably thought "Handley" was Crawford's first name.

Crawford, of course, was the most photogenic candidate. Not only was he well dressed in his bow tie and dark suit, but his wonderful flowing white hair really stood out — he looked like a politician picked by Central Casting. He easily met new people and showed genuine interest. He worked hard at remembering names and was never too busy to stop and talk to a voter. Because he knew all the County Chairman and Precinct Committeemen throughout the State, he was well-received almost wherever he went. Likewise, he knew almost all of the secretaries, custodians, lunchroom servers, elevator operators, and anyone else who worked in the State House, since he served there for many years as Assistant Secretary of State, on the Public Service Commission, Secretary of State and Lt. Governor. Many years later, when I went to the State House and the State Office Building as an attorney, people who had known Crawford years earlier, still talked about how down to earth and what a great friend he was.

Not only was the caravan an arduous way to campaign, but it ultimately took a toll on Crawford's health too. Crawford smoked and during this period, I would gather he smoked two or three packs a day. While his smoking didn't seem to bother his stamina in campaigning, I feel certain that it had some effect on the one television debate that he and Welsh did. While Crawford was very handsome, he looked tired and was not as articulate as Welsh who as a trained lawyer was well-spoken and looked fresher in the televised debate. If elected Crawford would no doubt have been the last Governor of Indiana without a full college education. He was also one of the last politicians in the state to run an entirely grass-roots campaign, refusing to run even one television or radio advertisement.

While Lt. Governor, Crawford was an extremely active politician. Not only was he running for Governor, but he enjoyed the County Fairs, the political rallies, and all the other trappings of political life. He went to every Republican National Convention. He met Senator Robert Taft, President Eisenhower, and, of course, Richard Nixon. Nixon came to Indiana for a Nixon-Parker rally that was held in Fort Wayne on the steps of the Allen County courthouse.

Crawford had his photo taken with almost every County fair queen and visiting dignitary. Herb Shriner was a fixture on national television at the time with his own variety show. He came to Fort Wayne and Crawford spent considerable time with him when together they dedicated Southgate Shopping Center on the southside of Fort Wayne. As Chairman of the Indiana Toll Road Commission, Crawford, along with Mayor Daly from Chicago, opened the Chicago Skyway. As Lt. Governor, Crawford was also the Chairman of the Agricultural Committee which was in charge of the State Fair and he was very active in the State Fair. Also, as Chairman of the Department of Commerce, he had charge of economic development and went throughout the State working to attract new jobs. He made many more appearances than Governor Handley did and was a better campaigner.

While my mother took an active interest in the campaign, she did not accompany Crawford on the caravans and only attended a few events with him in the Indianapolis area, including political rallies, fundraisers, and other social functions. She maintained her own social life, both with her old friends in the Mooreland-New Castle area and with new friends in Indianapolis.

On Election Day in November 1960, there was a large turnout. The Nixon-Kennedy contest, of course, was at the top of the ticket. There was no Senatorial race in Indiana that year so the Governor's race was the second featured race. Pat and I worked all day in Fort Wayne transporting people to the polls, and then after the polls closed, we headed to Indianapolis for what we hoped was a victory celebration. At that point, Crawford was ahead, and Nixon was running very strong in Indiana. The Lake County vote, which includes heavily Democratic Gary and Chicago suburbs, had already come in and Crawford was still ahead.

However, from the time we left Fort Wayne and arrived in Indianapolis, a second Lake County vote came in with a huge majority voting for Welsh. In fact, the majority vote was 60,000 greater than any previous Lake County vote. In the end, Crawford lost by 23,000 votes. Nixon, on the other hand, carried the State by 250,000, so there was a tremendous amount of ticket-splitting. To compound the loss, the Republican Lt. Governor, Richard Ristine, was elected. At that time, voters could split and did not have to vote for a Governor and Lt. Governor from one party. This has now changed. The rest of the Republican State ticket was elected except for Phil Wilkie as Superintendent of Public Instruction. Wilkie, the son of Wendell Wilkie, the Republican Presidential candidate in 1944 against FDR, was a maverick and the Indiana State Teachers' Association had campaigned very heavily against him. He lost by even more votes than Crawford did.

Nineteen Sixty, of course, was the year of the Chicago

vote fraud. While Nixon had carried Indiana very significantly, he lost in Chicago, and later, there was considerable evidence documenting substantial vote fraud that occurred in Chicago. Lake County, located in Indiana adjacent to Chicago, has been notorious for election fraud and there have been many investigations both before and after the 1960 election. In 1960, the Republicans controlled the Indiana Attorney General's office and they sent a number of Deputy Attorneys General and other deputized attorneys to Lake County to examine ballots and election results. A number of lawsuits were filed, but ultimately these were dismissed, and the matter was turned over to the newly convened Indiana Legislature. The House of Representatives in the Legislature was overwhelmingly Democratic, and the Senate was Republican. This resulted in a deadlock and no decision was ever made. Eventually, a significant amount of vote fraud was uncovered, but the election was not disturbed.

Like his friend and compatriot Handley in the 1958 Election, Crawford was very disappointed and embarrassed. Not only had he lost, but the Lt. Governor and the rest of the State ticket save one were elected. The Democrat strategy of utilizing television and radio advertising, hitting hard on Crawford's connection to Handley and the highway scandals, and rallying the Union troops with the Right-to-Work repeal, had been effective.

While Crawford must have been bitterly disappointed, he never talked about it and to a certain extent never showed it. He completed his term as Lt. Governor. One of the final highlights of his career was the dedication of the new State Office Building of which he had been Chairman. Because he had been such a good friend, many people in the State House took his loss much harder than he did. After his term ended, he took a position with Indiana Manufacturers Association as Administrative Vice President and continued for the next ten years until his retirement. He took no more interest in politics, never supported a candidate or got involved in any way, although he did continue with an appointment to the Great Lakes Commission, a body made up from all the states bordering the Great Lakes.

Exit polls taken of voters at the time indicated that the highway scandals, Handley running in the middle of his term, and the proposed repeal of the Right-to-Work Law, were all factors that caused the voters to split their ticket. Republicans hoped that Nixon running very strong in Indiana would help carry the day, but obviously 250,000 voters split their ticket.

Crawford's legacy in public service was that he was highly regarded for running a very efficient and productive office, with never a hint of scandal. He did a good job as Chair of the State Office Building Commission, as Chair of the Indiana Toll Road Commission that built the Toll Road across northern Indiana. As head of the Department of Commerce, he worked hard to bring industry throughout the State and also accomplished a number of specific projects like designating dual lanes for Indiana S.R. 3 between New Castle and Muncie.

Later, he received considerable publicity for an idea that he pushed through the State Highway Department — painting a white stripe down each side of highways. This had not been done previously in Indiana or elsewhere in the country, and Crawford came up with the idea while driving throughout the state and campaigning. He determined that it would be very helpful to have a white stripe down the side of the highway to better see where the edge of the road was, particularly at night.

Crawford's political career, as indicated, not only affected his life but all of our family, including myself and his many brothers and sisters who were all directly or indirectly involved in the campaign. When I decided to not return to Northern Trust after Navy service but to come back to Indiana to practice law, I interviewed in Indianapolis. However, I decided that if I stayed in Indianapolis, while Crawford was Lt. Governor and running for Governor, I would be forever known as "Crawford Parker's son." If I went to Fort Wayne, while my father was still known to a number of people, I would be able to create a career of my own. Certainly, there have been many times where people came to me as an attorney or were otherwise helpful in supporting my career because they knew my father and respected him.

When my mother died in 1965, many State dignitaries attended the funeral. Later when Crawford died in 1986, Governor Bob Orr and many other people from the State House and throughout the State came to his funeral.

In retrospect, I wonder how much difference it would have made to Crawford or the rest of the family if he had won the gubernatorial election in 1960. Certainly, he would have retained the prestige of being a former governor for the rest of his life. On the other hand, he had a good career with Indiana Manufacturers Association that started perhaps four years earlier than it would have had he been elected. Or perhaps he would have gotten a better position as an outgoing Governor, although he indicated many times that he had no desire to become a Senator or to go on to Washington. In any event, whatever job or elected post he held did not change what caused him such distress later in life and ultimately took his life — emphysema. Crawford would not have given up smoking any earlier whether he was Governor or not.

His election as governor likewise would have only affected incidentally my life and career. Our kids and grandkids would have had the satisfaction of having a grandfather and great-grandfather named as Governor, but that ultimately will not change their lives. Perhaps the most disappointing part from my perspective is knowing how hard he worked and what an outstanding job he did along the way. It was too bad he was denied the final office of Governor that he sought.

I am hopeful that my recollections might shine a light on Crawford Parker's many accomplishments in public service and inspire others to seek a similar path. Many years later, I was fortunate to receive the Individual of Integrity Award given annually by the Fort Wayne Better Business Bureau and was interviewed and asked to name two persons who I thought displayed high integrity in their careers. I named my law partner, Ed Roush, who had served as a Democratic Congressman for a number of years and did an outstanding job, and of course my father, who likewise, was very highly respected as a Republican officeholder.

RETURN TO INDIANA
1957-1967

Knowing that I would be leaving the Navy in December 1957, I started thinking a year ahead of what I would do and where we would go. One possibility, of course, was to return to Northern Trust in Chicago as that job was still available for me. On the other hand, I felt a strong pull to leave the bank and practice law. I had given considerable thought to staying in California, and pursuing a law career when I attended the University of California Law School and took graduate law courses at Boalt Hall. I also gave some thought to taking the California Bar as a number of my former classmates from the University of Michigan were practicing with San Francisco firms. However, Pat and I decided that we were looking for the Right Place, where we could raise a family and get involved with the community as well as pursue a career.

After my father had been elected Lt. Governor in 1956, I returned to Indiana for his inauguration in early 1957. I hitchhiked on Navy planes from one Naval Air Station to another and finally arrived in Indianapolis. I was able to attend the inauguration and swear in my father wearing my Navy uniform. His inauguration was a real high point for our family, taking place in the rotunda of the Capital and very well attended by Congressmen, State officials, and all of my father's political friends. The Governor was sworn in at the same time.

While home at this time, I interviewed several law firms in Indiana. One firm was Baker & Daniels in Indianapolis, where I would ultimately become a partner many years later. Another was Campbell, Livingston, Dildine & Haynie (CLD&H) in Fort Wayne. My father was friends with Von Livingston and I interviewed with Von as well as Ward Dildine, Gil Haynie, and Alex Campbell of the firm. Alex Campbell was the most colorful member of the firm. He had been a former Assistant Attorney General in Washington, D.C., and the primary prosecutor of Axis Sally and Tokyo Rose, American women radio personalities who broadcast propaganda on behalf of the European and Japanese Axis Powers during World War II. I believe they were both convicted and sentenced to death- whether this was carried out I do not know. He later became the Indiana chairman of the Democratic National Committee.

Alex was a very charismatic character. At the time of my interview, a barber came in and gave Alex a haircut. Then when the barber finished, a shoeshine boy arrived and began shining Alex's shoes. I assumed later that this show was done to impress me, but it was effective nevertheless. I decided that if these guys were so busy they couldn't leave their office for a haircut or shoeshine, there is certainly a place in this firm for a young lawyer!

Beyond the job, there were two other reasons that cemented my decision to come to Fort Wayne. My father was in

Indianapolis and would in all probability run for Governor; I very much wanted to establish a career on my own and not ride along on his coattails. Also, in the '60s, Indianapolis — sometimes called "Indy No-Place" — had job opportunities that were not as good as Fort Wayne, which had emerged from World War II with a tremendous amount of manufacturing and new industries. Later I learned that some 30,000 people immigrated to Fort Wayne during the late '50s and early '60s for jobs, including us of course. I also felt that Fort Wayne was the right-sized city where we could get involved with the community and did not present the problems of San Francisco or not having grown up on the north side of Chicago that I ran into with Northern Trust.

So, in late 1957 Pat, Pam, and I arrived in Fort Wayne. Dave Heaton, a member of the CLD&H firm, had arranged for us to rent a house owned by Robert Koerber, Sr. in Wildwood Park. The Koerbers were in Florida for the winter and this was a very nice home in a swish neighborhood and we were able to rent it for four months at a nominal price. We had no furniture. But we did have the blue and white Plymouth that I bought when I graduated from Law School, a small savings account, and some stock primarily invested in Reynolds Tobacco that I had bought while at Northern Trust. Eventually, all of our personal goods in storage at the Naval Depot in Oakland, California, were shipped to us.

The firm's ability to get the Koerber house for us on a short-term rental turned out to be a very good first step for our entrance into the Fort Wayne community. Living in Wildwood Park we were able to meet many new friends and neighbors which would not have happened if we had moved into an apartment house elsewhere in the city. We also met a number of our friends through the Newcomer's Club. The President of the Newcomer's Club was Joanne Haag, who was the wife of Vernon Haag, the new President of the ITT plant, who had just been transferred to Fort Wayne and they moved in near us in

Wildwood Park. The Vice President of the Newcomers Club was Paula Parrott, the wife of Bob Parrott, who was Executive Vice President of Central Soya, another major company. Later, Pat also became an officer of the Club. In sum, moving into Wildwood Park and joining the Newcomer's club allowed us to meet many business executives, young professionals, and make life-long friends.

Campbell, Livingston, Dildine & Haynie occupied the 15th floor of the Lincoln Bank Tower. The total office space was probably 10,000 square feet and in that, we had ten attorneys, several support staff, a reception area, a small library, and an even smaller conference room. To say that we were crowded was an understatement. My office was about six by eight feet, just enough room for a desk, a swivel chair, and one additional small chair. Dave Keller and Bill Fagan were located next to me and their offices were equally as small. The large corner offices were assigned to senior partners Von Livingston, Ward Dildine, and Alex Campbell. Gil Haynie, Tom Yoder, and Dave Heaton had other smaller offices. There was not a square foot wasted on the entire floor.

As indicated, Alex Campbell was the most well-known of the partners. Alex tried condemnation cases for Indiana-Michigan Electric Company (I&M) and he always dressed for the part. When he went out with the jury to view an area being condemned, he wore old boots and drove a station wagon with rusted out rocker panels so that they would view him as just another small-town lawyer. On the other hand, when Alex went to Washington, D.C. for legal work, he wore a homburg, an overcoat with a velvet collar, and a white silk scarf. He took Washington dressed like the most sophisticated lawyer from Wall Street. Alex became involved in a bitter divorce with his first wife, Eleanor, and then remarried. Alex was also passionate about horses and sadly died from a heart attack pulling his horse trailer on the way home from the Rose Bowl Parade in California where he had participated.

Von Livingston was the lead attorney for Indiana-Michigan Electric Co. and probably earned more than any other lawyer in the city. Von had practiced with a large firm in Chicago and was a very precise and excellent lawyer. In my early years with the firm, I worked under Von's tutelage. He would heavily mark up my memos, letters, and every document I wrote until I learned that nothing left the office unless it was properly done. While I learned a great deal in law school, there is nothing like having a tough mentor when you start to practice law and many of the good habits I developed were really forced upon me by Von Livingston.

Von had a number of clients, but the largest was I&M, a division of American Electric Power (AEP) based in New York. Any time anyone called from AEP, we all jumped into action as the I&M account was such a large part of our revenue. On one occasion, Donald Cook the President of AEP, called for Von and the young receptionist answering the call said, "I'm sorry, Mr. Livingston can't come to the phone at this time because he is in the bathroom." Later when Von returned the call, Don Cook kidded him about being in the bathroom. Von was so embarrassed about this incident that he promptly fired the receptionist.

When Alex Campbell became the County Chairman, there were always a number of political hangers-on who would come and sit in our small lobby to wait for Alex with hopes of getting some type of a party job. One fellow in old beat-up clothes would sit there for days on end hoping to get a glimpse of Alex and make his pitch for a job. Gil Haynie came in one day and saw this fellow and went back to Von Livingston and said, "Von, Don Cook from AEP has just dropped in unannounced and needs to talk with you now." Von, of course, jumps up, puts on his coat, straightens his tie, and bustles out to speak with Don Cook only to find Alex's hanger-on in the lobby. In later years, Von developed Alzheimer's and would commonly forget names and even where he was. It was really a shame to see one of the most brilliant legal minds in Fort Wayne deteriorate to that extent.

Ward Dildine was an attorney for Home Telephone Company and did primarily corporate law. He was also the office manager and controlled billing, administration, and other office matters. Ward had a very nice lake cottage at Clear Lake, and he would invite the three young associates, Dave Keller, Bill Fagan and myself up to visit, usually at the start or end of the summer when we could help him put in or take out the dock at his cottage. I keenly recall two or three years where I stood in my swimsuit in the cold water on a cold spring or fall day putting in or taking out Ward's dock.

The firm was organized shortly after World War II. Alex Campbell brought to the firm clients he had while serving as U.S. Attorney and Attorney General. Von Livingston brought Indiana-Michigan Electric Company as a client. Ward Dildine brought the telephone company, and the fourth partner, Dick Teeple, was married to Helene Foellinger's sister, who owned the News-Sentinel, one of two major newspapers in Ft. Wayne. Both Teeple and his wife were killed in an aircraft accident before I arrived.

Joining the firm shortly after Teeple died was Gilmore Haynie. Gil had been in the Navy during World War II, and served as a "beach master" at the Normandy invasion on D-Day. Gil had many interesting stories to tell, not only about the war but about the many trials in which he had been involved and about Alex Campbell too, as he was an Assistant U.S. Attorney when Alex was U.S. Attorney in Fort Wayne immediately after the war. Gil was one of my very good friends in the firm and also a very respected trial lawyer. He got a number of outstanding verdicts trying negligence cases in northern Indiana. Gil and his wife, Mary Ann, were also well known socially in town. Gil was President of Fort Wayne Country

Club, an avid golfer, and a good bridge player. Gil was also a pipe smoker and during this period I was a pipe smoker as well. We spent a lot of time buying different types of tobacco and blending and comparing our pipes and tobacco.

Gil Haynie was a great storyteller and it was always a treat to have a new person come into the office because we would get to hear Gil tell all of his stories again. Gil and I went duck hunting together for two or three years. One time we went hunting at the Kankakee Game Preserve along with Dr. Carl Keck, a very proper and well-known physician. We were sitting in a blind along the river very early one cold, dark morning when Dr. Keck fell into the water. We fished Carl out and drove him sopping wet to a little town nearby where he sat at a laundromat in his underwear while his hunting clothes dried. I can only imagine what ladies who came into the laundromat early in the morning thought about finding this well-known doctor sitting in his underwear.

Another time I went with Gil to the 18th floor of the Lincoln Tower to settle a case for a client with Arthur Parry, an older attorney, who represented the insurance company involved. Arthur was notorious for being very tight with the insurance company's money and guarded it almost as much as he did his own. Our client had lost a leg and Gil had settled the case with the adjuster. Arthur's only job in the settlement was to prepare the release. It was summer, very hot and all the windows were open in Arthur's office on the 18th floor because there was no air-conditioning in the Tower. Arthur, seeking to reduce the payout, proceeded to berate our client, arguing that it was an unjust settlement, he was robbing the insurance company, and so on. Our client, with one leg and on crutches, listens to this diatribe for about ten minutes then suddenly jumps up and grabs Arthur by the collar and says in a low voice, "Listen here, you old son-of-a-bitch, I'm going to throw you out the window." Gil and I grabbed our client and Arthur in time to prevent this from happening. Arthur signed the release and we got our client out of there as fast as possible.

Another time Gil and his friends pulled a trick on Jim Jackson, a fellow attorney. One of the men in the group had picked up a porno magazine while in France, probably nothing more than Playboy, but still fairly risqué for the time. They were passing it around among the group and Jimmy Jackson put the magazine in a law firm envelope, printed with Jackson & Parrish as the return address, and sent it to the home of another fellow in the group. Gil, who was Assistant U.S. Attorney at the time, worked out a scam with Bob Biteman, the local Postal Inspector, to put postage on the envelope and postmark it. Gil then instructed Bob to call Jimmy Jackson and indicate that he was responsible for sending pornographic material through the mail — a federal offense — and that Bob was required to refer the matter to the U.S. Attorney's office for prosecution. Biteman and Gil continued to carry out this charade for several days, suggesting that the matter was going to be sent to a Federal Grand Jury. All of the group, except Jim were in on the joke and Jim was beside himself with concern that he was going to be indicted by a Federal Grand Jury for distributing pornography. Finally, some time after putting Jim through an ordeal of conferences with the Postal Inspector and the U.S. Attorney's office, the group sprang the joke on Jim that it was all in good fun! After a month or two, Jim finally got over it, but Jim's wife did not speak to any involved for many months.

My starting salary was $6,000 a year, which was about the same or maybe even less than I had been making as an officer in the Navy. However, I was able to negotiate an arrangement where I got a 15 percent commission of any business that I brought in. The firm did not expect me to bring in much business, and therefore, never expected to make any payments to me with this arrangement, but this turned out not to be the case. The hourly rate for attorneys at this time was $15.00 per hour, and there was also a Bar Association fee schedule: preparing a deed was $8.00; handling a divorce was $100.00; etc. Later, these Bar Association fee schedules were declared to be in violation of restraint of trade by a case in Arizona.

When you begin the practice of law, it is amazing to discover the things that you don't know and which were not taught in Law School — how to draft a pleading, how to work with secretaries, how to keep time, how to deal with clients, etc. When I came to CLD&H, Von Livingston implied that if I worked with him, I would eventually be able to take over the Indiana & Michigan account, which was one of the largest accounts in Fort Wayne at the time. A lot of my early work was doing research for Von, much of it connected with Indiana & Michigan rate cases pending before the Public Service Commission. I also did some trial work with Gil Haynie, interviewing witnesses, doing background investigation, and attending the trial in what is known as "second seat" capacity, where I would take notes and provide information to Gil as the lead attorney.

I assisted Gil with a case in Federal Court. Again, our client had lost a leg in an auto accident. Bill McNagny, another very good Fort Wayne trial attorney, was on the other side of the case. After Gil made his closing argument to the jury for the plaintiff, Bill closed for the defendant insurance company. Bill was not only very bright but also quite witty and some of his statements had the judge, jury, and everyone else in the courtroom laughing. When Gil got up to make his rebuttal, he was also laughing and said, "You know, Mr. McNagny is one of the funniest people I know. His wit is outstanding." Gil continued to praise Bill's sense of humor at length and then at the end said this: "The only person that wasn't laughing, if you noticed, Ladies and Gentlemen of the Jury, was my client who lost his leg. This case is his only opportunity to be compensated for losing that leg and to him, there is nothing funny about this entire matter." Gil's rebuttal completely undercut McNagny's brilliant and funny closing argument and the jury returned with a very sizable verdict.

I went to Justice of the Peace Court on various types of cases. Because the maximum limit in J.P. Court at that time was $500, all of these were small. But this is how I learned and gained experience, by going into Small Claims Court or the Justice of the Peace Court on minor matters.

Joe Christoff, another life-long friend, was City Court Judge at this time and Joe had the ability to designate judges pro-tem when he was on vacation. Joe designated a number of his friends to sit in as judge pro-tem including Howard Chapman, Otto Bonahoom, and myself. We got $15.00 for a morning's work and got to witness a procession of drunks, minor traffic accidents, domestic arguments, minor assault cases, vagrancy, and every other type of case imaginable, usually 40 or 50 of them each morning. Most would plead guilty and there were standard fines that we would levy. Occasionally, a case would be set for trial to be heard at a later time, or sometimes we would set off an hour or two at the end of the session that day to actually hold a trial. If the case was a traffic offense, usually the police officer would testify and perhaps the defendant would take the stand. Sometimes the defendant would have a lawyer, but generally, this was not the case. By going to J.P. Court, Small Claims Court, and City Court I picked up a great deal of experience about how to deal with other members of the Bar, the police, and city officials.

In my second or third year of practice, I began to pick up a few clients of my own. Mostly, these were representing small corporations, partnerships, or friends who owned businesses or referred their friends in business. The latter arrangement is how I met Doug and Joan Lawrence. I drafted a partnership agreement for what was then called Schenkel & Lawrence (later Schenkel & Schultz), one of the major architectural firms in the region. Schenkel & Lawrence started in a small loft room over a lumber yard on Wayne Trace in Ft. Wayne. Through Doug Lawrence, I also met Leonard Murphy from Van Wert, Ohio, who would become a very good client and lifelong friend. Through Doug, Leonard, and DeNeal Hartman, an accountant, I began picking up some practice on my own.

During this period, I was truly a "general practitioner" doing everything: writing wills, handling real estate transactions, divorces, going to Small Claims Court, helping senior attorneys with major cases, drafting agreements, and almost anything else that came in the door. While I was developing my own practice, to a certain extent it took me away from the Indiana & Michigan work that Von Livingston had indicated I would handle. However, I came to believe that there was only a partial commitment by Von that I would follow him with Indiana & Michigan. I don't think that he had any real intention of giving up this client for a long time. Moreover, I'm not sure that I would have been nearly as effective as Von in representing I&M.

One day Gil came to my office and told me that Jimmy Jackson of Jackson & Parrish, (the same attorney implicated in the earlier porno magazine story), was named the Special Judge for an interesting case in Superior Court that involved an Amish divorce, a very rare event then and now. When we got there, the courtroom was completely filled. On one side, representing the wife, was David Peters. On the other side, representing the husband, was Louis Dunten. Both of these attorneys had no love for each other and were from the old school where they did a lot of colorful things that the judges would not tolerate now.

Peters drafted a divorce complaint for the wife in which he alleged that the husband had made "unusual demands" during their 18-year marriage, including a demand to have sexual relations a minimum of 12 times daily. The complaint goes on to describe in detail that in a typical day, the couple would have relations two or three times after getting up in the morning, then in the middle of the morning, before and after lunch, and so on throughout the entire day. Surprisingly, the couple only had two children, two young girls who sat in the adjoining law library while the case was being tried.

When all of these colorful allegations made their way around the bar, the attorneys, their secretaries, and many people in the Courthouse all decided they had urgent business that required their presence in Superior Court. A great number of the Amish community attended as well, including a surprising number of young girls.

In addition to the sexual allegations, the wife's complaint stated that the husband did not do much work around the farm and that she had to do it all. The wife then testified to these allegations and withstood a withering cross-examination from Louis Dunten. During one particular trial session dealing with splitting up the property, there was testimony about the farm animals that they had, including horses, cows, pigs, sheep, etc. At this time, I was standing at the back of the courtroom with Gil and he took out his yellow pad and wrote something on it. He then called the bailiff over and sent the note up by the bailiff to the Judge. The Judge unfolded the note, got a big grin on his face, and began to snicker. He brought down the gavel and called, "Recess." Everybody adjourned for a temporary recess. I went over and picked up the yellow sheet that Gil had written. It said: "Dear Judge, I represent the Society for the Prevention of Cruelty to Animals. Please do not give those sheep to that man."

Another job I did during my early years of practicing was to examine abstracts. All of the title work for real estate transactions required the preparation of an abstract which would be sent to an attorney to review. The attorney, after reading the abstract, would write a formal opinion indicating that the title was good or that it had this or that problem. It was not unusual to take home two or three abstracts every night, and the review of abstracts and handling real estate transactions was a big part of many attorneys' work, particularly young attorneys. All of this work is now handled by title insurance companies.

In Fort Wayne, we moved a number of times during these early years. We first lived in Wildwood Park during the winter of 1958. Then we moved to Terrace Road, north of downtown Fort Wayne, into a furnished house owned by Bob Shambaugh, who was the brother of a friend Max Shambaugh, and was then working as a professor of music at Louisiana State. We had only one car and I usually rode the bus to and from downtown, although sometimes I would walk the 10 or 15 blocks.

While we were on Terrace Road, Carole was born. While Pat was in the hospital, she met Joan White, who was in the hospital for the birth of their daughter, Leslie. Ed and Joan White would become good friends and also were founders of the Bowmar Instrument Company, which became the inventor of the handheld calculators in the mid-'70s selling under the brand name — the Bowmar Brain — before becoming a casualty of the calculator price wars with Texas Instruments.

After living on Terrace Road for about two years, we moved to South Anthony and lived in a small apartment that was part of a city housing project for a period of time. Then we moved to Smith Street, just at the south end of the intercity, and lived in a house we rented from Peoples Trust Bank. At this point, we had acquired a few pieces of furniture and I got a U-Haul trailer for moving. It was common at this time to hire day workers from the Fort Wayne Developmental Center on the northside of Fort Wayne. The center had a number of patients who were developmentally disabled but interested in working at odd jobs in the community with a great deal of supervision. On the day of our move to Smith Street, I picked up John from the center who had been recommended by a friend. He was big and strong, but with the mental capacity of a young child. He and I unloaded our small couch off the truck and attempted to carry it into the living room of this little house. But the couch wouldn't fit through the door. I looked at it and tried various maneuvers to force it to fit through the door but finally gave up. John then says to me, "Max, Max, if you will just take the door off the hinges, I think we can get it through." And, sure enough, we took the door off the hinges, and the couch went right through. John was certainly smarter than me.

After we had been in Fort Wayne for about three or four years, we bought a lot in Indian Village, a new suburban neighborhood southwest of the city. The lot cost $6,000. We then asked our friend and architect Doug Lawrence to design a house for us. The house cost $25,000 to build and we borrowed $15,000 on a mortgage from Lincoln Bank, paying five percent interest or $124.00 per month. The remaining $10,000 we got to pay for the house and purchase new furniture came from money that we had saved while in law school and during the Navy.

When we moved into the Indian Village house in 1962, we sent out a Christmas card showing all of our addresses for the ten years since we had been married. There were 22 different addresses, including all of our moves in the Navy, Pat's move back to Chicago while I was out on cruise, and all of our recent moves in Fort Wayne. We listed each address and then crossed out all but the last, 2500 Wendigo Lane. At the bottom of the letter, we commented that it is "Hell to stay ahead of creditors."

While we were in Indian Village, we became good friends with the Mort and Freddy Frank family, who lived on an adjacent street, but our lots touched in back. We remained close friends even after we both moved from Indian Village. The Franks had two boys, Bob and Bill, and a daughter, Sally. Carole and Sally were the same age and were inseparable growing up. They would climb up the various crab apple trees in the neighborhood, and tease younger sister Kristi unmercifully.

At this time, we also had a great dog — Kokie, a standard poodle that we got as a pup. Kokie got 128 out of a possible 130 points in training at obedience school. One of the tests was what was called "the long sit." The handler (me) leaves the dog, commanding it to "sit and stay," then walks away. All of the dogs are sitting obediently while the handlers walk clear across the room. However, two of the dogs get into a fight and all hell breaks loose — all of the dogs begin fighting, running around and barking. In the midst of all of this chaos, Kokie is sitting there very patiently waiting for me to give the command "free." Later on, Kokie was injured in a car accident and had a leg amputated. Even with three legs, Kokie was still the best dog around.

While we lived in Indian Village, Pam entered Elmhurst High School and at some point began dating. Pat and I were very concerned, not about Pam being out on a date, but about possible car accidents. Sometimes when Pam's date arrived, Pat would meet the date while Pam finished getting ready to go out. In the meantime, I would sneak out the back door and check out the date's car, to see if he had safe tires, etc.

One year we had a Halloween party in Indian Village, making a "Tunnel of Horrors" with cardboard boxes all through our garage. We hired Madison and Lou, two bartenders at the Chamber of Commerce who were used for many parties. When Madison arrived an hour before our Halloween party to set up the bar, he was driving a shiny new T-bird. He asked me whether he should park it in the back of the house. I said, "No, Madison, park it in front where we can show it off because it will be much nicer than the cars of any of our friends coming to the party." And it was.

During this period, we had several young girl students who would live at our house while attending Fort Wayne's International Business College. In exchange for room and board, they would help Pat with getting dinner on the table and babysitting the kids for a few hours on the weekends. We had a very good experience with the first student, Charlotte Wine, who came from a farm near Portland, Indiana, and we kept up a correspondence with Charlotte over the years. She subsequently married and has a family of her own, still living in the Portland area where her husband was general manager of a manufacturing plant. Our experience with the other two girls was not as successful, but overall the program provided us with an extra pair of hands while the kids were young and also helped the students attend college.

Our real savior during this time, however, was Cora and Henry Blanton. Henry Blanton had been a fireman on the Pennsylvania Railroad before he retired. Cora was an excellent cook, quilter and would buy and sell antiques. The Blantons never had children of their own but started as babysitters to our kids and later became almost like foster grandparents, particularly to our youngest, Kristi. A friendship developed that continued even after all the daughters left for college and really until the death of both Henry and Cora Mae in the mid-1980s.

When the Blantons were in their 80s, their home in south Fort Wayne was broken into by two young punks, one with a gun. Henry was not deterred and chased them out of the house with an ancient double-barrel shotgun, which he fired in the air as they ran down the street. The story made the front page of the Journal-Gazette with a photo of Henry holding the gun.

During these early years in Fort Wayne, we met many couples who would be our friends for years, including Irv and

Jane Deister, Leonard and Peg Murphy, Ed and Joan White, Doug and Joan Lawrence, Ray and Rosemarie (Banks) Lavender, Mort and Freddy Frank, Joe and Ginnie Christoff, Howard and Betsy Chapman, John and Joan Pichon, Dick and Sunny Helstrom, Bob and Margaret Klingenberger, Marge and Stu Cavell, and many more.

Both Pat and I got involved with a number of community organizations at this time as well. Pat was particularly active with the Junior League where she served as President and there was an extensive article about her in the Journal-Gazette including a great picture of our entire family. In 1967, I received a Presidential appointment to the Northern Indiana Selective Service Appeal Board. This was during the Vietnam war and thankfully no publicity was ever released as to the composition of the Board.

The latter was very interesting in that our board heard all the appeals for deferments for the northern half of Indiana during the war. We met monthly to review written petitions. There were no hearings but we abided by a number of strict rules to make deferment decisions. Certain occupations such as teachers were entitled to automatic deferment. Others who had been deferred for college but had now graduated were subject to being drafted. I was on this Board for at least five years including a period of time in which I served as Chairman. There were five of us on the Board and we had to be very careful about who was told about our service. Needless to say, our meetings were closed and there was no publicity. When my term was finished, I received a very nice Presidential citation for my service, but I was very careful in ever mentioning that I was involved. It was a difficult job that somebody had to do.

During the summers, we rented a place "at the lake," usually Lake Gage where we vacationed for a number of years. We rented a cottage on the north side of the lake for a few years, and then later an A-frame on the south side directly across the bay from Doug and Joan Lawrence's cottage. We spent many pleasant summers at Lake Gage and this is where we taught the girls to water ski.

Also, during this period of time, our friends George and Judy Edwards, had a good-sized cruiser and we traveled on their boat on Lake Wawasee and later on Lake Michigan and Lake Erie. On one particularly memorable trip to Lake Erie, we stopped at Middle Bass Island to spend the night after boating all day. When we checked into the little hotel, the receptionist looked at George and said, "Mr. Edwards, do you want the same room that you and your wife had last week?" Whereupon Judy exclaimed, "Last week! You said you were in New York on business." The divorce was filed about two weeks after that.

We also were able to get the "Governor's Cottage" at Indiana Dunes State Park for a week for three summers through my father when he served as Lt. Governor. There were 105 steps from the beach up to the cottage and my father went there once and vowed never to return. The cottage was large — room for eight or ten couples — and we took a whole group of our friends and had a great time.

During the winter we started taking the kids to northern Michigan to ski at Boyne Mountain and Boyne Highlands. This was always a crazy experience, requiring us to leave Fort Wayne on a Friday afternoon, drive six hours to northern Michigan, ski Saturday and Sunday until 4:00 and then drive home. The traffic coming down I-75 in Michigan — usually in a snowstorm — would be terrible.

Shortly after we moved to Indian Village, Kristi was born. Pat recalls sitting through the D-Day war picture *The Longest Day* right before going to the hospital. At this time, Leonard Murphy was dating Peggy Frank Huber who lived down the block. Leonard would stay with us occasionally rather than driving back to Van Wert, Ohio. Sometimes on Sunday morning, the kids would get up and go in and bounce on "Uncle Leonard" on the couch. We would lock our bedroom door so they couldn't get in and Leonard would be forced to read the funny papers to them, usually after a hard night out on the town and going to bed late.

Our kids often played in the park just a block away from our house and attended Indian Village Elementary School and later Kekionga Middle School. The Pocahontas swimming pool was just on the other side of the elementary school and park and we all spent considerable time at the pool. The kids joined the swim team and were coached by Bob Armstrong who led an undefeated team for seven years and would later become mayor of Ft. Wayne.

After I had been with the firm eight years, it became apparent that this job was going to be a dead-end street and it was time to move on. A number of attorneys had already made a decision to leave the firm for similar reasons, including Dick Doermer, Barrie Truemper, and others. There was an unwillingness of Von, Ward and even Gil Haynie to share with the associates any of the monetary benefits of the firm, and the matter was further complicated by the fact that Bill Fagan, Dave Keller and I were all hired at approximately the same time and the senior partners felt obligated to keep our compensation the same.

Through the development of my own clients, I was steadily spending much more time doing my own work and creating considerable business for the firm. I spent a lot of time talking with Gil Haynie and Von Livingston about my concerns and proposed a variety of ways to figure out a way for me to stay with the firm, but to no avail. The matter caused me a lot of personal distress and I eventually developed ulcers. Although it now appears that ulcers are caused more by a virus than stress alone, I am certain that my high level of stress at this time fueled my gastronomic complications.

Originally, I made a plan to leave with Phil Burt to start a new firm. We tried to get Gil Haynie to join us and practice together but Gil was unwilling to do that. Phil also backed out and stayed with the firm a while longer after I left, before ultimately taking a job with a separate firm.

At this point, I had been with the firm for almost ten years and I had made the decision to leave. Finally, I asked Bob Hoover if he would join me. Bob, who had joined Campbell Livingston just a year earlier, was working closely with me and together we spent almost all of our time on business that I had generated. So, Bob and I left together in March of 1967 and formed our own firm, Parker & Hoover. We rented a space from Leonard Murphy in what was then called the Strauss Building and is now called the Murphy Building. We both went out of our way to maintain a very good relationship with our old firm and were careful to give them credit on billing time performed at the old firm on matters that went with us. Likewise, they were careful to give us credit for any matters that continued and stayed with them. As a result, we remained good friends with all of the people in the old firm after we left. Ward Didine commented to Von Livingston later that Bob had been successful one year in winning the Bar Association golf tournament and I had won the next year and he joked, "Well, Von it's a good thing those guys left, because all they did was play golf anyway."

During the period I was with Campbell Livingston, my mother had a stroke in Indianapolis and died. At just over 60 years old, this was very unexpected and a tragic loss. From my mother, I had inherited my incentive to read and to learn many new things. She was very much ahead of her time in her ideas about nutrition, filmmaking, and many other areas. She was always very careful about keeping a proper diet.

Shortly after my mother died, four young contemporaries on a fishing trip to Canada went down in a plane in Lake Huron off Alpena, Michigan in June, 1966. Because the waters were 55 degrees, they did not survive very long. Among these were two of our very close friends, Doug Lawrence and Gordon Banks. In addition, were Stan Knapp and Don Irving. The four left 13 children among them. I was notified very shortly after this happened and drove to northern Michigan along with Irv Deister to identify the body of Gordon Banks, who the Coast Guard had found earlier that day. Some of the other bodies did not come up for two or three weeks because of the cold water but eventually, they were all recovered. I made a number of attempts, including renting a plane and flying over the lake area, to try to locate the plane. We even talked about renting a submarine to try to find the plane and hopefully determine what had caused the accident. But the wives of the four were not in favor of this and we were never able to find the plane or discover the cause of the accident. My final theory was that they had run out of gas on one wing tank, had lost power, and the plane had gone down in the water before they could shift to the other wing tank.

One of the best things that a young attorney can have is a mouthy client. Some clients never say a word, even if you do an outstanding job. If someone asks them about you, they might say, "Oh yes, he is okay," or some other unremarkable statement. Leonard Murphy on the other hand was one of those people that if you were "his attorney" you were absolutely the best attorney ever and he would tell everyone about how good you were. DeNeal Hartman, who was Leonard's accountant, and I got a number of clients because of Leonard touting about what a terrific job we had done for him. To detail all of the deals that Leonard Murphy was involved in and what a colorful character he was would unduly prolong this tale. Leonard was the type of person that could tell an off-color story in mixed company and get away with it because he had such an infectious sense of humor and a great laugh. I was one of the pallbearers at Leonard's funeral. We were standing outside of the church after the funeral and one of the other pallbearers looked down the street and saw a big moving truck nearby. He remarked, "My God, look at that, Leonard has found a way to take it with him!" Another pallbearer chimed in, "Yes, I'll bet it's filled with Scotch, too." Whereupon the last pallbearer replied, "Yes, but it won't last Leonard until we get there." Leonard Murphy was one of a kind.

Another interesting client I had during this period was the Tamarack Mountain Ski Resort in Angola, Indiana. This was the development of a new ski area that within a very short two or three years went into hard financial times. I worked with one of the principals, Chuck Priest, to try and raise funds to keep the business afloat. We flew to two or three places in Chuck's aircraft to try and raise money but without success. Finally, we drove to Elkhart to meet two contacts suggested by an acquaintance of Chuck's in the back of a nursing home. These individuals supposedly represented the Teamsters Fund out of Chicago. Chuck was told to bring cash to Elkhart to pay the contacts a finder's fee. I was bothered that we had to pay the finder's fee upfront and that it had to be cash. I was not for doing the transaction at all, but Tamarack was in such sad financial straits that we felt compelled to explore all possibilities. Chuck and I met with the Teamsters representatives, who appeared to be con men of the worst sort, including obvious gun bulges under their coats. At some point, I became very leery of the whole transaction and kicked Chuck under the table before excusing myself to go to the bathroom. In a few minutes, Chuck came to the bathroom. We grabbed our coats and left quickly out the back door.

Another interesting client involved hog buyers out of Nashville, Tennessee. Kennett Murray was the largest hog buyer in the Midwest with multiple stockyards in Indiana, Ohio, Illinois, Kentucky, Tennessee, and Georgia. These yards were all arranged as partnerships with local entities, with one master partnership operated out of Nashville. Each year Carl Lipp, who was the accountant for Kennett Murray, and I would travel to Nashville to handle the big partnership meeting. Guys who run stockyards can be pretty rough characters, and these meetings were always characterized by a lot of disagreement, considerable arguments, and large amounts of drinking. In earlier years, some of the partners had gone to jail for fixing the scales at the Indianapolis stockyards, and this hung over the head of the partnership. I represented this client for a great number of years before they eventually split up.

There is real value in practicing law with and being tutored by good attorneys. You learn to do things in the proper way and to never let anything go out of the office unless it is 100 percent correct. Von Livingston received his training in a large Chicago firm where this was the standard and I was fortunate to receive this training under Von, and was able to pass this on down to Joe Kimmel, Larry Shine, and others. As a matter of fact, they had a name for me — "Red Pencil Mac" — for the markups that I did to their documents before they went out. I also learned the value of timekeeping. The practice of law is subject to so many daily interruptions, that unless you are diligent with the timekeeping, you do not have adequate information when it comes to billing. This would become very important in the next phase of my practice, when I have to depend mostly upon myself to get out the bills and collect sufficient funds to keep the doors open.

Left. Mac's mother Lucille at 3 years old with grandmother Molly Bouslog, circa 1906. Below Right. Mac's grandfather Enoch (Neve) Bouslog, circa 1890 Mac still has the beaver top hat. Below Left. Mac's great grandmother, Amanda Peckinpaugh, a stern and no-nonsense lady. She had 8 children by Abraham Wesley Bouslog, and after he died, another 3 children by Henry Veach.

Above. Crawford Parker, 3rd from left, with his eight siblings, circa 1938. Left. Mac at 12 years old with his hunting dog Vicki. Below. Lucille Bouslog Parker, circa 1921.

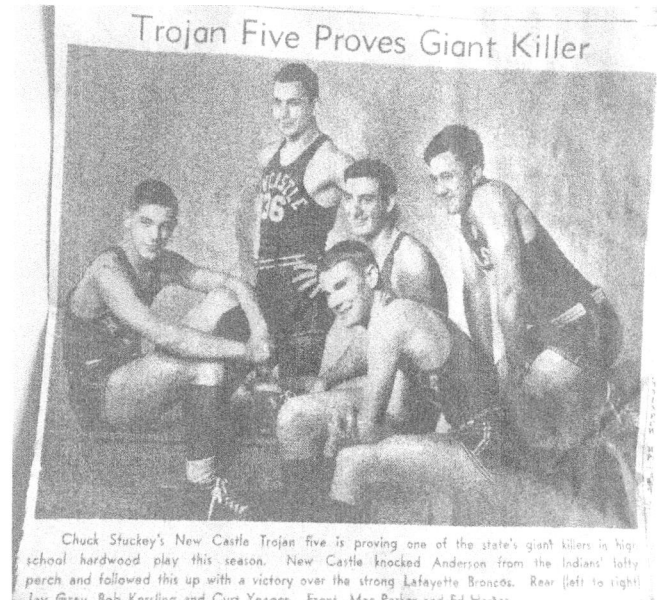

Above. New Castle Trojans, 1946. Below. Mac long jumping in high school.

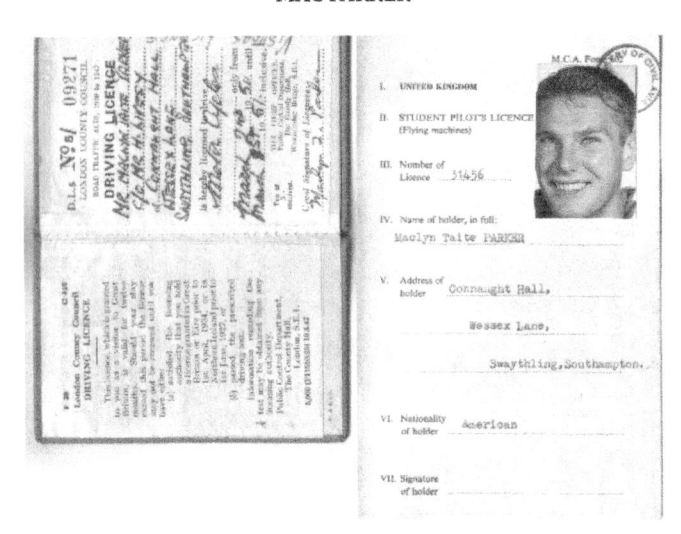

Above. London motorcycle driver's license and student pilot's license. Left. Mac on rugby team during year in England. A

DePauw Basketball, 1951.

MAC PARKER

THEY'VE SEEN A BOOK BEFORE

One of the worries that Coach Jay McCreary doesn't have about his DePauw basketball team is scholastic eligibility. Eight of his Tigers are holders of Rector scholarships for good grades. Four of the eight are starters on the 14-man squad that has won 9 of 11 games. Here Lee Hamilton, of Evansville, the team's leading scorer, paces the eight in a session with the books. Others are, standing, left to right, Mac Parker, New Castle; Kent Guild, Fairland; Truman Brandt, Nashville, Ill., and Clyde James, Marion; and, kneeling, Russ Freeland, Lawrenceburg; Gene Gephart, Ashtabula, O., and Harry Stewart, Indianapolis.

Above. DePauw basketball team, 1951. Holding book is DePauw center and former congressman Lee Hamilton. Below. Mac pole vaulting at DePauw.

LANDING IN THE RIGHT PLACE

Pat and Mac, DePauw, 1951.

Above Left. Aboard the aircraft carrier Oriskany, 1955. Above Right. Navy officer, 1955. Below. Officer's housing at Naval Air Station Alameda, 1957.

Pat and Mac's wedding, 1952.

Above. Mac swearing in Crawford as Lt. Govenor, 1956. Right. Lucille Bouslog Parker, during Crawford's gubernatorial campaign, 1960.

Above Left. Crawford's 1960 campaign postcard. Above Right. Nixon campaigning for Crawford, 1960. Below. Crawford and Mayor Daley opening the Chicago Skyway, 1958.

Christmas letter sent in 1960 showing 17 moves since 1952.

ON OUR OWN
1967-1981

The period from age 35 to 50 is supposedly one of the most productive periods of a person's life. Generally, by the time you reach 35 you have achieved some stability with your career and are in a position to make a contribution to your family and give back to the community in which you live. This was certainly no exception with our life in Fort Wayne. The 14 years from 1967 through 1981 were very productive years for Pat and me, a period when we were primarily in our 40s.

So many things happened during this period to our family and me personally that it will require a page or two just to list them, let alone elaborate on the details. In 1971 we moved from our home in Indian Village to Covington Lake, a new addition in a relatively rural suburb southwest of Fort Wayne.

As a result of this move, our kids changed schools from Indian Village Elementary and Elmhurst High School to Aboite Elementary and Homestead High School, both part of Southwest Allen County schools. During this 14-year period, all three kids finished high school and either completed or were in college. The net effect was that Pat and I went from having a very active household of five and being deeply involved with the daily schedules of our children at the beginning of this period to reordering our priorities and conversing with our kids by phone at the end in 1981.

During this period, I left Campbell, Livingston, Dildine & Haynie and started a law practice with Bob Hoover. I became involved with Flint & Walling, a company in which we invested considerable time, and later on, considerable money, at least for us. I also became involved as an attorney for a number of suburban utilities going through bankruptcy, which proved to be a 10-year project for me and our small law firm. I served as Chamber President, Rotary President and Quest Club President. Pat became Junior League President and involved with McMillen Center for Health Education, and the Fort Wayne Sister City Committee.

We made investments in various real estate ventures, first with Doug Lawrence and later with DeNeal Hartman and Jim Schenkel. Bob Hoover and I also invested in Dot Group with Paul Fischer.

We started to play tennis at Wildwood in the 1970s and this has remained a sport that both Pat and I, and later our kids, have played.

Our family also took a number of trips overseas during this period, including a trip to Japan in 1977, which included Hong Kong and Thailand. We bought our first condominium in Aspen, Colorado, and also a retirement house for Pat's folks in Arizona. There were many other events during these 14 years, but these are the major ones.

Leaving Campbell, Livingston, Dildine & Haynie and striking out on my own with five mouths to feed at home was not an easy decision. As indicated previously, I made many attempts to try to work out a long-range situation with CLD&H, but without success. I finally made up my mind to leave and Bob Hoover, after a great deal of soul searching on his own, decided it was worth the risk to join me. Bob says that he will never forget Tom Yoder telling him after we made our announcement to leave that "this was the biggest mistake of his life." As Bob looked back on it, it was one of the smarter decisions of both of our lives.

We arranged space for our firm with our good friend and client Leonard Murphy in a building he owned, then called the Strauss Building, and now called the Murphy Building. Leonard had an office area that was furnished and we rented the office and bought the furniture.

To add to our problems as a startup firm, the telephone company errored and left us out of the new telephone book. They tried to rectify the error by including us in an addendum to the phone book which they put out later. As it turned out, it didn't do any lasting damage, but we were very concerned at the time as this was the primary source of contact and advertising in an age before the internet.

When we first opened, we had no secretary. Pat came in and worked part-time until we were able to hire someone. One day, our friend Joanie Lawrence agreed to come and answer the phone while Pat went to lunch. Like a smart aleck, I told one of our clients, Bob Borger, that he should meet our secretary (meaning Pat) because I was sleeping with her. After our conference, Bob jokingly says to Joanie (unfortunately a new young widow at the time) "I understand you are the secretary Mac sleeps with all the time." Joanie almost fell off her chair and there were red faces all around.

A week or two later we hired our first secretary, Jeri Behr, who worked for both Bob and me for about a year. She also did the bookkeeping, along with some help from Pat. At some point, we hired Marilyn Rentschler as a bookkeeper, and she remained with us for about 15 years.

During the first year, our fees were small but we made enough to pay all of our bills and to have an income too. The firm grew gradually over the 14-year period. Leonard Murphy, DeNeal Hartman and many others were not only friends and business associates, but they also helped us get the firm started. Some years we worked very hard, putting in 1,900 to 2,000 hours each. And because both Bob and I were young, diligent, upbeat, and involved in the community, we were able to attract a number of clients. From a small two-man office, we began to build a reputation and establish a small corporate practice. As we got busier, we decided to hire an additional attorney. Devon Weaver was our first associate. Devon stayed with us for two or three years and then left for Lincoln Life.

I then recruited Joe Kimmell out of the University of Michigan Law School. We felt very fortunate to get Joe because his family had a third-generation law practice in Vincennes, Indiana which Joe could have joined. Later we got another outstanding associate when Larry Shine joined us, and shortly after that, we also brought in as a partner Ed Roush who had been a three-term Congressman from our Fourth District, but was defeated in a redistricting. Ed was a wonderful fellow but had been out of law practice for a number of years and it took a lot of time to get Ed back to where he could be of value to the firm. Ed later ran for Congress, was re-elected and left the firm but we maintained a nice relationship with Ed until his death years later. Dave Keller had been with CLD&H. He left the firm after I did, went into another partnership for a few years, but that broke up and Dave became available so we brought him into our firm to handle litigation. We brought Ken Waterman in for the same purpose.

During this period many of our administrative staff joined us as well. Brenda Richardson joined us in 1976 and has been my secretary and assistant for over 42 years. The firm's name over the period began as "Maclyn T. Parker (Bob elected not to be a partner the first year) then "Parker & Hoover", then "Parker, Hoover & Roush", and finally "Parker, Hoover, Keller & Waterman" (PHK&W), which it remained for most of the last years of the firm.

Of the clientele that I had built at CLD&H, we were fortunate that most went with us when we started the new firm. We were very careful to not take any old clients of the firm and as a result, we got along very well with our former partners, associates and staff. We arranged to clearly divide matters based on the date we started the new firm; if we completed the matter, we paid the old firm for the prior time and if they completed the matter, they paid us. This arrangement worked quite well and both the new firm and the old firm were happy, and we continued to remain good friends for many years.

Our billing rates during the early years of the firm were $35.00 to $45.00 an hour for partner time and $15.00 to $20.00 for associates. By 1981, this increased to $75.00 an hour for partners and $40.00 to $50.00 for associates.

We took on almost any type of case that walked in the door, from writing pension plans and handling labor negotiations to divorces, wills, real estate transactions, litigation, and bankruptcy cases. I would talk up Bob as an expert on labor, pensions, and many other areas of the law. We had various contacts in Indianapolis and elsewhere that we could call on a consulting basis when we needed to get up to speed on a new matter. Bob says that we would often meet with a new client who would explain his problem and during the meeting, Bob would excuse himself to call up one of our consultants and then report back on the action we should advise the client to take. Leonard Murphy also talked us up as two of the world's greatest attorneys and this helped expand our reputation in the community.

During this period, I also served as attorney for Richard Cole and Flint & Walling Company in Kendallville, and became attorney for John Pichon, the Trustee in a major Chapter 10 Reorganization involving ten utilities. This work is detailed in later chapters.

The Flint & Walling bankruptcy required a substantial portion of my time and I turned over a number of my clients to Bob Hoover, Joe Kimmell, Larry Shine, and others in the firm. After the utility's reorganization ceased and because of the good job that both John Pichon and our firm had done, John was appointed as trustee for the reorganization of a small airline, Hub Airlines, that served Chicago and also a number of cities around Fort Wayne. Again, I was appointed as attorney for the Trustee. While not nearly as large as the utility case, the airline was hazardous because it flew many planes and passengers every day. We worried about the maintenance of the aircraft and the safety of the passengers and crew, and we were glad when the matter concluded.

As a result of the utility work, the firm got larger and we were able to attract a number of corporate clients. Sometimes our clients came by happenstance and there are a number of examples of this. One of these was Glenbrook Shopping Center. Stu Cavell came from Zionsville to open a Ford agency in Fort Wayne. He had a small place over on East Washington and was looking for a larger location. We went to Chicago and met with the developer of Glenbrook, Landau & Hyman. Paul Clay, from Landau & Hyman, was originally from Indianapolis and had served briefly in the legislature with my father, and was responsible for the new Fort Wayne shopping center. Landau & Hyman had previously used another attorney in Fort Wayne to get the land rezoned for Glenbrook, but wanted to have a permanent attorney in Fort Wayne so Paul called our firm. Bob took over the representation of Glenbrook and did an outstanding job for a number of years. His representation of Glenbrook was a prime reason that he decided to specialize in real estate law.

Another client that came through a unique set of circumstances was an insurance company called Franklin National Life. When I was with CLD&H, Louie Palumbo came and asked Alex Campbell to form an insurance company. Alex didn't know the first thing about how to do this and turned it over to me. While I did not know much more, I dove in, formed the company, and got it qualified under Indiana insurance laws. Later, when Alex left CLD&H, he took the client with him. However, after Alex's death, they sought me out and for the next ten years I served as the general counsel for Franklin National Life. The company originally did quite well, but later made a very unprofitable investment by buying Club Olympia, a Fort Wayne athletic club and its adjoining office building. This ultimately led to the demise of the company and sadly the suicide of Louie Palumbo, the president.

Gerson International Corporation, Hy-Matic Manufacturing, Materials Handling Equipment Corporation, Dot Corporation, and Paul Fischer were all substantial clients during the early years as well. In addition, I handled a few personal injury cases that were settled for some significant amounts, and did real estate rezoning while representing Mutual Security Life and North American Van Lines.

Other noteworthy clients we served include Thunderbird Boats in Decatur, still a large luxury boat manufacturer, Fort Wayne Lincoln-Mercury, Jerry Watson Ford, Souder's Furniture, Old Fort Supply, and Superior Ball Joint. Also, Wick's Pies from Winchester, Indiana, which still makes cream pies exported all over the Midwest, Dana Corporation, Weatherhead Division, LML Corporation, makers of float boats, Bowmar Corporation, maker of the Bowmar Brain, all the Dot

Group subsidiaries located in Illinois and South Carolina, Bob Thomas and his various Ford and Lincoln subsidiaries located in Birmingham, Alabama, and Charlotte, Virginia, and Ted Brehm and the development of Arlington Park.

Sherman Armstrong was a client from Winchester whom I got involved with through Jay Conrad. Sherm was a real character. Through his company, Armstrong Mould, he owned race cars and was a two-time USAC National Sprint Car owner champion. One of his drivers was Janet Guthrie, the first woman race car driver. Sherm said she knew more bad language than any man he ever met in his life. Sherm had two cars in the Indy 500 for a number of years.

Running a law firm is just like running any other small business — it takes considerable time and no small amount of planning. Payrolls have to be met every week, rent and other bills have to be paid, and invoices need to be sent out. Clients put off paying legal bills perhaps more than many other types of businesses and the aging of receivables is always a problem. Another problem is in trying to get the attorneys in the firm to stop handling the client's work long enough to send out bills, or to follow-up with clients to make payment on a timely basis. We would have weekly billing sessions in which we would go over accounts receivable and all of the unbilled time. We had a line of credit at the bank to carry us, but in general, we had sufficient balances to meet our obligations and we used our line of credit very sparingly. After all expenses were covered, we would determine how much was left over for our partnership draw. I made sure that all of the young partners and Bob received a draw before taking one for myself. We were also very careful about our expenditures. When the IBM mag card typewriter came on the market, we agonized a long time before laying out $400 to purchase one.

In addition to PHK&W developing a number of corporate clients, I learned from Von Livingston the importance of setting up monthly and quarterly retainers with clients. This was helpful in that it gave us a steady source of revenue. It also benefited retainer clients who were given preferential treatment and outstanding service, including knowing their businesses so well that we could sometimes assist them with legal problems before they would arise.

During this period, we also did a lot of work for Flint & Walling which was making a number of acquisitions. I would meet with John Pichon and Bill Macomber for a number of hours each week concerning both Flint & Walling business operations and their legal problems. Through Flint & Walling, I met Richard Manoogian and we ended up doing work for Masco Corporation, a large New York Stock Exchange company.

Paul Fischer worked at Lincoln Life and later left to start a business brokerage firm. Paul was instrumental in selling Howard's Photo Lab to Guardian Industries in Detroit, the world's largest manufacturer of architectural and automotive glass (until it was bought out by Koch Industries in 2017). This was a sizable sale at the time and Guardian sent their attorney, Oscar Feldman, to Fort Wayne to negotiate the sales contract with me. Later we went to Detroit to close the deal. It was a cold winter day with lots of snow on the ground, and Rod and Phil Howard, the owners of Howard's Photo Lab, chartered a plane to take us to Novi, Michigan, where Guardian Industries' office was located. The CEO and primary owner of Guardian Industries was William Davidson, who had been an Admiral in the Navy in World War II. He looked every bit the part — tall, distinguished, gray hair, and very urbane looking. There had been a public issue of Guardian shares a number of years earlier, but Davidson decided he didn't want public shareholders so he purchased back the outstanding shares with $400 million of his own money. Davidson built Auburn Hills Stadium outside of Detroit and was the owner of the Detroit Pistons for a number of years until he died in 2009.

Upon arriving at the Detroit airport Davidson sent his personal limousine with chauffeur and beautiful interior and lap robes to keep us warm. During the final paperwork, Davidson came in and we all stood to greet him, befitting the respect to which he was due. Davidson then informs us that one of the matters that Oscar Feldman and I had negotiated, to-wit a guarantee by the parent corporation on the lease for the premises that the Howards were retaining, would not be possible because he would have to footnote this on his financial statements. I said, "Mr. Davidson, do you mean that you will not permit the guarantee on the lease after Mr. Feldman and I negotiated this?" Davidson said, "That's correct." Whereupon, I began to pack up my file and asked Rod and Phil Howard and Paul Fischer to get their coats because this was a deal-breaker and the sale was off. Davidson left the meeting but Oscar Feldman stayed behind. As Paul, the Howards and I walk down the hall to leave the building, Oscar Feldman chases after us and says that Mr. Davidson has changed his mind and that we would go ahead with the deal after all and they would permit the guarantee. My little bluff had worked even though Rod and Phil Howard and Paul were having heart attacks thinking that their sale was going down the drain. But Davidson got his small revenge in the end sending us back to the airport in a Volkswagen bus, a far cry from the limo we arrived in. The bus had no heater and we nearly froze before we got to the airport.

Another memorable matter was when Leonard and Leo Murphy sold a motel on the Indiana/Ohio state line to a group from Cincinnati. The motel had a very shady past and was used as a haven for prostitutes. The only way Leonard was able to keep it open was that his attorney in Van Wert, Ohio was also the County Prosecutor. Leo and I met up with two men from Cincinnati at Leonard's office in Van Wert and they brought all cash in a brown paper bag to purchase the motel. Leo and I counted it and closed the deal. About a month later, the Prosecutor closed down the motel. We very carefully watched for men in raincoats from Cincinnati for a long time afterward.

We had a young and very vigorous firm — I was the oldest member of the firm, in my 40s, Bob was in his 30s, and Joe, Larry and all the rest were in their 20s. Although we worked hard, we had a lot of fun. When Bob retired from Baker & Daniels, we had a small party bringing together many of the attorneys who had been with the firm before we merged in 1981 and we wrote up stories and tall tales about the old days, which got better over the years with each new telling.

Because we were young, energetic and the firm was growing, we were able to attract very high caliber people to join us. After our merger with Shoaff and then Baker & Daniels, both Bob Hoover and Joe Kimmell served terms as Chairman of the Management Committee of Baker & Daniels, the firm's highest management position. Larry Shine and Steve Hazelrigg are very well regarded and outstanding attorneys, and Paul Mathias was elected to the Appellate Court. Our staff members all proved to be outstanding as well, including Brenda, Sarah, and Georgia who all stayed for many years.

One of the office highlights each year was the annual Christmas party in which we invited all of our clients. A great number of our clients would attend this party and it would last from early in the afternoon to very late in the evenings. (Parties like this undoubtedly don't happen today because of strict enforcement of DUI laws.) We also had a Christmas party each year just for the staff. One of these was very memorable — it was at the Sands Nightclub in Northcrest, on the north side of Fort Wayne. The party lasted until 2:00 or 3:00 in the morning. During this period Ed Roush was running for Congress and we decided about 1:00 that we needed to get Ed out of there because we were afraid that as rowdy as the party had become, someone would call the police and Ed's name would appear in the paper while he was a candidate. Fortunately, nothing did happen, but we left without paying the bill which was $2,000 or $3,000. Marilyn Rentschler had to call the Sands the next day and apologize that the place had closed before we paid our bill.

As I look back on PHK&W over 20 years after the merger with Shoaff, Keegan, Baird & Simon, it was really an idyllic period. We were all young, everyone got along fairly well together, we had a lot of work to do and everyone was busy. The firm was growing and revenues were increasing, and we were able to give raises every year. Above and beyond that, there was a good deal of camaraderie in our small firm — something that is much harder to achieve as a firm grows larger. We had acquired a good reputation in the community and several other firms approached us about merging before we made the decision to go with the Shoaff firm. Personally, I was quite proud of the firm and the people that comprised it. Having started with only Bob and myself, in 14 years we grew to eight attorneys, plus another eight support staff. While we didn't have the long history of a Barrett, Barrett & McNagny or Shoaff, Keegan, or even of our old firm, CLD&H, we had enough expertise to compete with them for good clients. For this reason, I was very hesitant about merging with anyone. However, Bob finally convinced me that we could grow even faster with a larger base. particularly with an old-line firm with good clients like Shoaff, Keegan.

During these 14 years, I also became involved with the purchase of real estate. First of all, with Doug Lawrence — we were jointly involved in building an office building on Coliseum Boulevard at the time of his death in the aircraft accident in Lake Huron I mentioned earlier. Jim Schenkel, who was Doug's partner in Schenkel & Lawrence, Joanie Lawrence, his widow and I would later become partners in the building and would ultimately sell the building to Schenkel & Lawrence. We bought other real estate, principally farms in St. Joe Township and eventually a farm near Southtown Mall.

Building our house in Covington Lake took a lot of time and effort. Pam was in a class called Miss Gates Dance School, and while waiting in a line at her dance class, I talked to Dave Ray, who had a lot in Covington Lake he wanted to sell. We previously had bought a lot on the other side of the lake but decided to buy Dave Ray's heavily wooded lot instead and sold the other lot. We had Roy McNett design our house and then had both Roy and Amos Lengacher bid on building the house. Amos Lengacher came in substantially lower than Roy McNett, and so we hired him to build the house. There were many decisions to be made during the building and Pat carried the load on most of these.

The American Bar Association had a trip to England and Europe over the summer of 1971 and Pat and I had planned to go. But because we anticipated that a number of decisions needed to be made on building the new house during this time, Pat decided to stay home and Pam traveled with me to London, Paris and Rome. As it turned out, many of the house decisions got postponed during the two weeks we were gone and poor Pat missed the trip to no avail.

Fort Wayne became involved with a Sister City — Takaoka, Japan — and in 1976 we had a teen-aged girl, Keiko Ikadai, from this city who stayed with us for almost a month. We maintained a relationship with her family and with the Sister City Committee ever since, and in 1977 we made a trip to Japan and on to Hong Kong and Thailand with our whole family. We took another family trip to Egypt which included treks to Cairo, Luxor, Abu Simbel, and later stopped in Rome, for the Rotary International Convention. During this period, Pam traveled to South America and lived for the summer with a family in Bogotá, Colombia. These were all very memorable trips and I will tell a few stories in a later chapter.

Also, in 1976, after having been on the Board of the Fort Wayne Chamber of Commerce for a number of years, I was elected as President. This was the first of two stints, as I was nominated to be Chairman for another term in 1991. Just before this, we had a downturn in our economy in 1974, and I was instrumental in starting an economic development group called the Horizons Council in 1976. This became a major economic development organization for the City of Fort Wayne for a number of years. I also was instrumental in forming the Chamber Foundation during this period, including meeting with the IRS in Washington DC to get final approval for the organization. I was subsequently elected President of the Foundation and continued in that capacity for over 40 years.

FLINT & WALLING
1960-1980

One of the things I have always maintained about the practice of law is that it's never boring. When I first got involved with Flint & Walling in the 1960s, little did I know that it would be a story that I would be intimately involved with for the next 20 years, and then would continue to be involved with for another 40 years and the foreseeable future, through a foundation created by Dick Cole, the majority stakeholder of Flint & Walling.

Flint & Walling started in 1854 before the Civil War and will celebrate 166 years in 2020. At one point, it was one of the largest manufacturers of windmills in the United States. A number of Flint & Walling windmills are still operating throughout the country. A windmill museum was started in Kendallville by Flint & Walling employees, some who began their employment in the windmill days.

When I became involved in the early '60s there were two divisions, a water pump division and a gray iron foundry. Richard (Dick) R. Cole became President in 1950 after he purchased a substantial block of stock. During the Depression, Cole had purchased Kendallville Foundry stock at a time when the hard-pressed foundry paid its employees in stock instead of cash. Many of the employees didn't want the stock and they would sell the shares to Dick Cole at 25 cents a share or whatever small amount he would pay.

Cole was a good businessman, but also a life-long bachelor with a mischievous personality. He was arrested frequently for drunken driving and once for drunken flying of his airplane. He would become involved in brawls in bars and he wrecked a number of cars. He went to rehab institutions on a number of occasions but then would fall off the wagon again. None of this played very well in the small town of Kendallville.

There are so many colorful stories about Dick Cole that it would be difficult to relate more than a few. Only very recently did the Cole Foundation approve a request by a local group to do a public service announcement acknowledging the connection between Dick Cole and Flint & Walling. We decided that sufficient time had elapsed and not many in Kendallville would remember Dick Cole or raise their eyebrows about saying any good words about him.

Certainly, Cole was community-minded when he created the foundation. However, most of the value of the foundation was actually created by the acquisitions that we made later in Flint & Walling which caused the value of the Flint & Walling stock to increase substantially.

Dick's chauffeur was W. T. Jackson, an African American

from Fort Wayne. W.T. was more than a chauffeur, he was Dick's man Friday, keeping Dick out of trouble and fixing problems in his wake. W.T. made sure that Dick got home after hitting the bars. One time when Dick was away at rehab, W. T. took it upon himself to go through the factory in Dick's golf cart and give orders to the foreman for Dick. This incident did not set well with the Union members who filed a grievance and called a strike. As attorney for the company, I was called, and the Union representative told me the walk out was due to W.T. giving direct orders to the foreman, bypassing management and Union representatives. I called W. T. and asked him to meet me in a drug store in Avilla. I convinced him that Dick would be very unhappy if he learned about the strike and that we should do everything possible to get them back to work. The Union representative indicated the only way they would return would be if W. T. apologized to the foremen and Union representatives. I persuaded W. T. to do this and the strike was settled.

After Dick's death in 1965 (not in an accident surprisingly but unexpectedly of pneumonia and heart disease), I went to Ludington, Michigan to meet with the manager of a company in which Dick held an interest. The manager relayed a story about his last meeting with Dick, about six months before his death. He said that while flying his plane from Kendallville to Ludington, Dick radioed someone at the field to call the manager to ask him to drive out to the small grass field that passes as an airport for a meeting. Dick landed the plane midway down the field and when the plane finally stopped, the propeller was turning over against a small fence at the end of the field. He turned the plane around to face the other direction and they had their meeting right there by the plane. Throughout the meeting Dick drank liberally from a pitcher of martinis that he sat on the plane seat. By the end of the meeting, it was dark. The manager tried to persuade Dick to stay at a hotel in Ludington, but to no avail. Dick flew back to Kendallville that night, still drinking from the pitcher of martinis.

While he was President of Flint & Walling, Dick ran the Company in a very erratic fashion. He would call a Board of Directors meeting and then sit in his office busying himself with various other work for an hour or two while the board members — who were mostly employees or small shareholders — sat waiting in the boardroom. Sol Rothberg, a Fort Wayne attorney, was Dick's confidant and advisor for about three years. At some point, Dick and Sol had a falling out and Dick came to Von Livingston of Campbell, Livingston, Dildine & Haynie to extricate himself from Sol as his attorney. At the time, Dick was in one of his alcoholic depression moods. After a good deal of persuasion, Von and Ward Dildine were able to convince Dick to effectively buy out Sol by paying him a substantial retainer fee.

It was at this point that Campbell, Livingston, Dildine & Haynie became counsel for Dick Cole and Flint & Walling. Over time, I was brought in to do minor matters. Dick and I got along quite well and soon he began calling the office to ask for me specifically to handle matters for him. I made trips to Kendallville often and ultimately became not only the attorney in our office who handled all Flint & Walling matters, but Dick's personal attorney as well.

Dick created a foundation called the "Olive B. Cole Foundation, Inc.", named after his mother, through Dick Shook, an attorney in Washington, D.C. There were few assets in the foundation and I eventually re-incorporated it and Dick funded it with additional gifts. In his will, Dick left Flint & Walling stock in trust for his mother—to ultimately go to the Foundation after her death. In addition, his mother possessed Flint & Walling stock in her name, and this ultimately passed to the Foundation as well through her Will. After both Dick and his mother passed, their controlling interest in Flint &

Walling, which was approximately 55 percent, passed to the foundation.

Dick died in 1965, naming Lincoln National Bank in Fort Wayne as Executor of his estate and Trustee of the trust created for his mother. The house where they lived in Kendallville was ultimately sold and his mother moved to the Towne House in Fort Wayne, where she lived until 1968, dying at the age of 93. The Lincoln Bank, as Executor of the estate and Trustee of the trust, held the controlling interest in Flint & Walling. The balance of the Flint & Walling stock was held by the Macomber family, the Park family, and a number of small shareholders.

After Dick's death, William B. Macomber, who was then Vice President of Flint & Walling, became President. William B. was in his late 60s or early 70s at the time and also had medical problems. While he had been with the Company for a great number of years, he was not a leader. The company remained profitable during his tenure, but started to drift. Through friends Irwin and Jane Deister, I met William A. Macomber, or Bill, Jr., his son, who at the time was an engineer working for Aro Corporation in Bryan, Ohio. Bill, Jr. was married to Irv Deister's sister, Elise. John Pichon, Jr. was the trust officer at Lincoln Bank assigned to the Cole estate and trust. I discussed with John the possibility of bringing Bill Macomber, Jr. into the Company. While Bill did not have any management experience at that time, we thought that we might be able to give him enough assistance to stabilize the Company.

After a great number of discussions, Bill Macomber and I also persuaded John Pichon to leave Lincoln Bank and come to Flint & Walling as Executive Vice President. For the next 11 years, from 1967 through 1978, when final control of Flint & Walling was sold to a subsidiary of Masco Corporation, Bill Macomber as President, John Pichon as Executive Vice President, and myself, as Secretary, constituted the Executive

Committee, and with the assistance of the Board, directed the Company.

Flint & Walling sales at the time were $9.8 million and the net income was $640,000; the only two divisions were the Pump Division and the Kendallville Foundry. As the Executive Committee, we met about every two weeks over the next 10 or 11 years to review finances, plan acquisitions and make most of the major decisions involved with running the company.

In 1968, we had an opportunity to purchase Paramount Tube, a manufacturer of square and rectangular paper tubes, located in Interstate Industrial Park in Fort Wayne. Bob Weimer was the operating executive and ended up staying with the Company. While Paramount was small, it was a very profitable company during the years that Flint & Walling owned it.

Masco Corporation was organized by Alex Manoogian in 1929 and was a small screw machine company in Detroit. The company stayed relatively small until Alex Manoogian purchased the rights to the single-handle faucet, which ultimately became Delta Faucet, now a leading company in the plumbing business. Alex's son, Richard Manoogian, joined Masco in the '60s. By the time Flint & Walling became involved with Masco in 1971, their sales were in the 100 million range. Richard, a Yale graduate and perhaps in his early 30s at the time, was very interested in growing Masco.

With the Cole Foundation having all of its assets in Flint & Walling stock, we felt it prudent to diversify. Also, under the Internal Revenue Code, 501(c)(3) private foundations were not allowed to have a controlling interest in a company. So to diversify and meet the IRS code we determined to sell almost one-half of the Flint & Walling stock held by the Foundation to Masco. So in 1971 Masco acquired 30 percent interest in Flint & Walling, and Richard Manoogian came on the Board of

Directors.

In 1972, we made the decision to acquire Utah-American Corporation which was owned by the Frank Pyle family in Huntington, Indiana. This was a manufacturer of loud speakers, primarily for the automotive market. In addition to a plant in Huntington, they also had a plant in Guttenberg, Iowa (on an island in the middle of the Mississippi River). Subsequently, we made the determination to start a speaker operation in Nogales, Mexico, and Nogales, Arizona, with the manufacturing plant located in Mexico and the warehouse across the border in the United States. I made a number of trips to Nogales, Arizona, in conjunction with starting this plant. Through 1973 and 1974, the speaker business was expanding and very profitable. However, beginning in late 1974, OPEC restricted oil imports to the United States, which caused a recession. The auto business declined, which in turn substantially affected our speaker business. At about the same time, many of our customers started manufacturing their own parts or purchasing speakers offshore. From 1974 on, the speaker business went south. In 1973, we also made the acquisition of Parker Industries, owned by the Hank Parker family (no relation to me), located in Silver Lake, Indiana. This was a manufacturer of small grain wagons and large metal trash containers.

As a result of the acquisitions of Paramount in 1968, Utah-American in 1972, and Parker Industries in 1973, Flint & Walling sales shot up from $9.8 million in 1967 to $41 million in 1974, net income increased from $640,000 to $2.3 million, and shareholders' equity increased from $4.7 million to $13.4 million.

At this point, Masco Corporation was very interested in buying the balance of Flint & Walling stock and offered us Masco shares in exchange at a very acceptable price. This deal turned out to be far much more advantageous than the one we eventually took with Masco. If we had taken Masco's first offer, the Cole Foundation and three of us as managers — John Pichon, Bill Macomber and myself — would have owned shares in Masco Corporation rather than the cash deal we got. The shares would have been worth considerably more and we would have also avoided a capital gains problem. While John Pichon and I were in favor of accepting Masco's first offer, Bill Macomber was not and Masco would not proceed unless we were all in agreement.

Masco Corporation in the early '70s was one of the fastest growing companies on the New York Stock Exchange with a 20 percent annual growth rate of sales and income. They made a significant number of acquisitions each year and by the early 1980s, their sales had gone from 100 million to over a billion dollars. Masco, however, made a management decision in the early '80s to get into the furniture business, buying a number of the large furniture manufacturers in the country as well as many other types of home furnishings, fabrics, etc. Coupled with the recession of '82-'84, this 10-year foray into the furniture business turned out disastrous and almost sank the company. However, Masco eventually worked its way through these financial problems and by 2003 was strong and profitable again with sales over $10 billion.

Through Masco, we met not only Richard Manoogian, but a number of other good people, including, Sam Cracchiolo, the director of development, Sam Valiente, who handled investments, Jerry Bright, the corporate attorney, and later John Leakley who succeeded him. Dick Mosteller was chief financial manager, and Don Rabahy was involved with finance. We were invited to attend Masco management meetings for a number of years. These were normally held in Detroit and involved bringing in Masco management from all their divisions, both in this country and abroad. Some years the meetings were held at Boca Raton or other Florida destinations, and families were invited to stay for three or four days at high-end resorts with much entertainment in addition to the corporate meetings.

During the period that Bill Macomber, John Pichon, and I made up the executive committee of Flint & Walling, we also offered to purchase any Flint & Walling shares that became available on the market. I purchased a significant number of shares from another director, Ferris Shafer, and gave him a note for the purchase price.

As indicated, after 1974 we started incurring losses with the Utah speaker division. In 1975, these losses were $35,000; in '76, they had risen to $700,000; in '77, a million dollars; and in '78, $513,000 before we ultimately closed down Utah Speakers after unsuccessful attempts to make a sale.

By 1977, the net profits had decreased from $2.3 million in 1974 to $1.2 million because of the Utah Division losses. The remaining divisions remained profitable but because of Utah we were no longer a growing company. Masco at that point offered us $14.00 per share, which was a lesser price than the stock offer they made earlier. Bill Macomber decided to put together his own group to purchase the company, consisting of Don Perrey, a local realtor and investor in a number of businesses. He offered $15.00 per share. However, there was a real question about whether Macomber and his group could come up with the actual financing to make the purchase. But that point turned out to be moot because Masco offered $18.00 per share and the Cole Foundation, which at that point owned 162,000 shares worth approximately $2.9 million indicated that they would sell to Masco. At this point, Masco owned 42 percent of Flint & Walling through earlier purchases, and the Cole purchase would give Masco a 54 percent control of the company. Masco then decided to purchase all of the shares that any shareholder wanted to sell. They made a June 23, 1979 offer to Flint & Walling shareholders to purchase shares for $18.00 each. Because the purchase was for cash, all of the shareholders had capital gains taxes to pay.

Bill Macomber was very unhappy that John Pichon and I did not go along with his purchase offer for a lesser price and our social relationship with the Macomber family was terminated by the Macombers. This also involved Bill's brother-in-law, Irv Deister and Jane Deister — very good friends — and left many of our other friends in the middle. Leonard Murphy commented at the time that this matter will not be cleared up for 20 years, and that prediction turned out to be correct. After about ten years, we had a speaking relationship with the Macombers and the Deisters but almost no social contact. Bill Macomber eventually bought G & L Company, a Fort Wayne company involved in construction and rigging and proceeded to operate it until his death in 2001. Our friendship with Elise and the Deisters has been on good terms for the last number of years. But the experience was very traumatic for both Pat and I because the Perrey's, Macomber's and Diester's had all been very close friends of ours and this episode forced an abrupt change in our relationships for a great number of years.

After the sale to Masco Corporation, Don Rabahy from Detroit was named as President to run Flint & Walling. I continued as attorney for Flint & Walling for another six or eight years during which time Flint & Walling acquired Holman Boilers in Dallas, Texas, and Richards Tool in Rhode Island. John Pichon and I continued to attend the Masco Management meetings until approximately 1985 when the disastrous furniture business era and recession made it necessary for Masco to cut back the number of people attending the meeting.

As a result of being Dick Cole's attorney and involved with Flint & Walling, I have continued on the board of the Cole Foundation since Dick Cole's death in 1965. The foundation at the time of Richard Cole's death had a value of approximately three million dollars; the current value of the Foundation is over $30 million and grants over the years have exceeded $50 million. Some of our large grants have been to the hospital in Kendallville, to East Noble School for the Cole Auditorium, for the Cole YMCA in Kendallville, and each year we give in excess of $250,000 for scholarships to students in Noble and other counties. At one time almost all of the grants went to Noble County, but with the start of the Dekko Foundation in Noble County we have branched out to include Noble, DeKalb, Steuben and LaGrange counties as primary regions of interest.

THE INBALCO CASE
1969-1979

My friend, John Pichon and I were involved in one of the highest profile, longest running, and most involved legal cases in Fort Wayne for many years. This was the bankruptcy and reorganization of a number of sewer and water utilities serving not only suburban Fort Wayne, but also Carmel and West Lafayette, three of the fastest growing areas of Indiana. These utilities were the sewer and water service for thousands of customers and there were many millions of dollars of assets and hundreds of creditors involved.

The matter started in the 1960s, when extensive development in the suburbs surrounding Fort Wayne was beginning. Development in these regions was restricted, however, by the lack of sewer and water service. For various reasons, the City of Fort Wayne elected not to extend sewer and water lines into these outlying areas. Developers were faced with the choice of homeowners putting in their own septic tanks and digging wells, or building and operating a small sewer and water utility serving only one subdivision. A small utility was a complicated endeavor and few developers had either the expertise or inclination to do.

Entering into this scene were Dick and Bray Barnes, two Canadian brothers who somehow ended up in Fort Wayne in the early '60s. The Barnes brothers developed the concept of creating regional sewer and water utilities to link together a number of subdivisions. The areas developing the fastest around Fort Wayne at the time were St. Joseph and Aboite

Townships.

The Barnes went to the Indiana Public Service Commission and obtained a Certificate of Territorial Authority (CTA) to be the exclusive service provider for sewer and water in the geographical areas covered by the CTA. They were able to get CTA's for a substantial part of both St. Joseph and Aboite Township and also large areas around Carmel and West Lafayette, regions all growing very rapidly at the time.

When developers put in a subdivision, they would install sewer and water lines and turn these over free of charge to the utility companies formed by the Barnes to operate. The Barnes would then obtain financing to drill deep wells to provide the water, and construct a sewage treatment plant to process the sewage. In some instances, they were able to arrange a connection with the sewer and water utilities of the City of Fort Wayne to provide the water or to process the sewage.

The building and operation of the well fields and sewage plants as well as interconnecting the lines installed by developers was not only a costly venture but often took months or even years to complete. The Barnes were able to obtain financing from a number of insurance companies, from Lincoln National Bank locally and Continental Illinois National Bank in Chicago. The main water utility was called Puritan Utilities; the main sewage utility was Diversified Utilities. In addition, they built and operated Clearwater Utilities, Pine Valley Utilities, American Suburban Utilities and at least one or two other companies together with their contracting company, the Utility Development Corporation. The plants operated for a number of years and the Barnes employed a good number of people, owned considerable construction and servicing equipment, and were serving about 8,000 customers.

The Barnes relied on the sewer and water fees paid by customers to repay the substantial up-front capital they borrowed to build the operations. However, the amount they could charge customers was regulated by the Public Service Commission and rate increases always lagged behind capital requirements. This led to the Barnes becoming overextended in the late 1960s and Lincoln Bank, Continental Bank and a number of other creditors filing a petition for bankruptcy. Because this was an operating utility, it was necessary to keep the plants open and operating. The petition was ultimately changed to a Chapter 10 Reorganization under the Federal Bankruptcy Act.

Prior to the bankruptcy, there were numerous lawsuits by creditors repossessing almost all of the trucks and other equipment used to service customers. Once the bankruptcy was filed, there were no funds in the checking account and almost all the employees had quit because of non-payment of salaries.

Lincoln National Bank, as the primary local creditor, and Continental Illinois National Bank as a large creditor, along with two large insurance companies controlled the appointment of the Trustee. Mike Beatty, the President of Lincoln Bank, had previously worked in the trust department with John Pichon and asked him to take on the position of Trustee of these utilities in bankruptcy. John, who at the time was Executive Vice President of Flint & Walling, agreed to have his name submitted and requested I be appointed as his attorney. Both of our names were submitted to Judge Jesse Eschbach, Federal Judge for the Northern District, and after a hearing we were appointed.

As John and I faced the first days of the reorganization, it was a daunting task. There was no money, no equipment, no employees, and 8,000 customers depending upon these utilities for sewer and water service. Our first job was to petition the court for authority to borrow funds to pay salaries to rehire some of the former employees. These employees in turn would try to operate the company, service customers and collect outstanding accounts. Our next task was to petition the court to get back some of the trucks and other equipment which had been repossessed by creditors. All of these petitions were filed in Federal Court before Judge Eschbach, a very excellent and no-nonsense judge. As this was my first experience in bankruptcy court, I spent many hours of book work trying to understand this whole area of law which was absolutely new to me. Almost every attorney in town represented a bank or creditor of one or more of the companies in reorganization. At the first meeting of creditors before Judge Eschbach, over 100 attorneys showed up.

With the Trustee authorized to borrow funds to pay salaries, we were able to hire back some employees, the most notable being Vern Gore, who had been the financial officer for the Barnes. Vern stayed with the utility not only through the entire reorganization but for many years afterward and eventually ended up as the chief operating officer.

There was a tremendous amount of unraveling involved before we could start preparing a Plan of Reorganization because of the complexity of the number of companies involved, each with different or some of the same creditors, and some creditors were secured while others were not.

The utilities reorganization became almost a full-time job for me. We did not have enough people in our small law firm to handle the legal problems involved and hence we had to hire new people. I turned over a number of my clients to other members of the firm. I was surprised when Jim Dumas, an older attorney in Ft Wayne, told me on the street one day that the utilities reorganization would be the largest piece of legal business in Fort Wayne for years to come and that it would take ten years to work through all the issues with the various corporations and creditors. He was more than right on both counts. We didn't finish up until almost 1980.

Each corporation was different, serving different areas, some sewer, some water, and some both. Each corporation also had different creditors. And, of course, there was a whole host of operating problems. Many sewer and water lines had been put in without adequate inspection and there were many maintenance problems. Further, the sewage treatment plants were constructed on the cheap and breakdowns were constant. The improper processing of sewage resulted in a number of complaints to the various public health authorities and the Indiana Public Service Commission.

In addition, the sewage and water rates were inadequate to sustain the operation. This necessitated numerous petitions to the Public Service Commission to increase the rates. Each petition resulted in objections from customers, community associations, businesses and many others, both on the basis of cost and inadequate service.

While we held CTA's on very developable land around Fort Wayne, West Lafayette and Carmel, we had no funds to build the required plants. Therefore, developers and others who wanted to get into the water and sewage business were constantly fighting to take away our CTA's. We resisted these efforts on grounds that the CTA's were important assets of the corporation, and that we would sell them if we could not build the plants and develop the area ourselves.

All of this necessitated many hours both in Court and before the Public Service Commission. Ultimately Judge Eschbach turned the matter over to Judge Robert Rodibaugh, the Bankruptcy Judge for the area, who traveled to Fort Wayne from South Bend three or four times a month. Each time he came, the utility matters would occupy a substantial portion of his docket. Like the heavy blue drapes in the courtroom, John Pichon and I became fixtures in the Federal Court House because it was important to keep the utilities operating. The Judge would sometimes bend the rules in our favor even when the law was not exactly on our side. John still talks about one particularly spirited controversy we had with an attorney from South Bend. He had excellent arguments and the law was in his favor, but the Judge ruled against him. He scoffed afterwards that, "the Judge's robe is hanging out of Parker's pant leg."

Because of the legal work involved, we added a number of people to our law firm. Devon Weaver came as an associate and then we hired Ed Roush as a partner. Ed was a wonderful fellow. He had served in Congress for a number of years and was defeated after his region was redistricted. He worked with us for three or four years and we got him involved with the utility work. Ed ended up returning to Congress for two terms and then came back to work for the utility as their attorney. He stayed with the utility for a number of years after the reorganization was completed doing their Public Service Commission work. Because of the heavy workload on the Trustee, John Pichon brought on Bill Latz, a former state representative and former vice president of Wolf & Dessauer, as a co-Trustee. This worked quite well as Bill was a very affable and well-spoken businessman. However, I had a number of experiences at the Public Service Commission with Bill as my witness. But he was unfamiliar with testifying and would get stage fright and was almost unable to answer questions on cross examination.

Putting together a Plan of Reorganization involved years of work because of the great number of corporations, creditors, inadequate capital, and many other problems. The group that ultimately worked to put the plan together was attorneys Roscoe Nash and Walter Knudsen from Chapman & Cutler in Chicago, who represented several insurance company creditors, along with Howard Chapman, who represented Lincoln Bank, Jim Barrett III, who represented Lee National Corporation, John Pichon and myself. We met constantly in the boardroom on the second floor of Lincoln Bank.

Roscoe Nash and Walter Knudsen from Chicago were both characters. Roscoe was the older attorney and had a lot of bankruptcy experience. Walter's main claim to fame was that he would have at least double martinis at lunch, and still be able to function in the afternoon. Roscoe explained to me once that the reason these matters take so long is not only the complexity of the issues, but because the reorganization plan has to be voted upon by each class of creditors, and involves many compromises. He pointed out that it takes a long time for the creditors to move from wanting 100 cents on the dollar to accepting five cents to get the deal over and done.

We were involved with almost every developer in the region. Two thorns in our side were Elmer Mackey and Joe Zehr. They opposed us on many issues and their attorneys were constantly present in the courtroom to make objections. John as Trustee for the case and me as the attorney got paid for our work by submitting detailed fee petitions to the court, copies of which went out to all the attorneys. We submitted a fee petition about every three months for both the Trustee's fees and attorney fees. Each petition not only required a great deal of preparation but involved both John and myself testifying with respect to the hours we worked, our hourly rate, the associates who worked on the matter, and details about exactly what everyone did. These petitions were scrutinized by all the other attorneys and while we eventually prevailed and received most of the fees requested, it was not without considerable effort.

During all the years on this case, John and I made numerous trips to Indianapolis where we worked on rate cases and other matters before the Public Service Commission. It was interesting that some of the people I met at the Public Service Commission had been there during the time my father had been a member of the Commission in the '50s and also when he had been Secretary of State and Lt. Governor. I received a great deal of help in preparing cases and settling and resolving matters that I would not have received but for the goodwill that I inherited from him.

Gradually over a period of time, one by one, the cases started to be resolved. Some of the corporations were sold off and the creditors were paid with the proceeds. Some of the territories were sold to the City of Fort Wayne, but this caused even greater problems. Bob Armstrong was Mayor and Bill Salin was his City Attorney. Our utilities served some of the areas that the City wanted to annex or had already been annexed to the City. The City received a number of complaints about our service and improperly functioning plants. The City attempted to buy a portion of the utility in St. Joseph Township, but at a price the major creditors considered inadequate. We made arrangements to sell it to another purchaser and Bill Salin put up a substantial objection. In the meantime, we finalized the Plan of Reorganization and planned to sell off the balance of the operating corporations that had not previously been sold.

The case became known as the "Inbalco Case", as that was the name of the company that ended up owning the major portion of the utilities at the end of the reorganization. The name was derived from the five major creditors: "In" from the insurance companies, "ba" from the banks and "l" from Lee National, also one of the major creditors.

As trustee, John was charged with trying to find a buyer for the assets in reorganization. I tried to assist by getting in touch with Jay Conrad, another client of mine from Berne, Indiana, who had been involved with a number of investments. Jay and I then talked with DeNeal Hartman, my friend and accountant. They wanted John and I to be involved since at this point, we had many years of experience in operating the utilities. John, however, had had enough of late-night phone calls when a plant broke down and said," no thanks" I indicated an interest, petitioned the Court for approval, and offered to resign as attorney for the Trustee if I became involved. The judge approved this decision, but was not particularly happy that I would become an investor given that I had been involved as an attorney for the Trustee since the beginning. Noting the judge's displeasure, I got the message and withdrew from the investment group.

Still, my consideration of being a part of the investment group and petitioning the Court was enough to give the City a pretext to urge a separate creditor to include me in a lawsuit against the major creditors and the Trustee. They claimed that I was prejudiced against the City's attempt to purchase a portion of the utilities. The fact of the matter was that the City was offering a rock bottom price that the major creditors refused to accept.

In any event, I had to obtain Tom Logan as my attorney, depositions were taken, and because the utilities were high profile, the newspapers covered the lawsuit almost every day. The case against me was ultimately dropped on summary judgment and never went to trial. However, I learned my lesson. While there was no direct conflict, there was an appearance of a conflict of interest which the City exploited to try to obtain the purchase at a low price. Incidentally, years later, the City paid substantially more than the price they had offered to the trustee and other investors to purchase just a portion of the utilities surrounding Fort Wayne.

DeNeal Hartman and Jay Conrad and two gentlemen from Ohio, Jim Noneman and Doyle Hartzog, eventually bought and ran the utility for a number of years, although with a great deal of controversy and headaches. Because of the original faulty installation of the lines and plants, there were constant breakdowns and customer complaints. However, Jay Conrad lived in Berne and Noneman and Hartzog lived in Ohio, and none read the Fort Wayne newspapers or cared about the controversy. DeNeal Hartman eventually gave up his accounting practice and retired to Florida, so then none of the four were local. Vern Gore was the main operating officer and ran the utilities from 1979 for about 11 years and then it was sold to AquaSource. It has since been sold again to a large New York Stock Exchange company. There are currently over 25,000 customers in Allen County alone, and AquaSource has poured considerable money into upgrading the facilities, although it is still not without controversy. At some point, the water service alone was purchased by the City of Fort Wayne, as I indicated previously, at a considerably greater price.

Utilities that serve thousands of customers are very high profile. John as Trustee and myself as his attorney worked very hard on this case for nearly ten years to maintain water and sewage service. Notwithstanding all of the conflicts encountered, we were proud of the job we did. I learned a good lesson about "even the appearance of conflict of interest" and with the problems that Hartman, Conrad and other investors had after the sale, I was certainly glad I decided not to participate, but was sorry I had even considered the possibility.

BRANCHING OUT

1982-1996

From 1967 through 1981, much of my time and efforts were devoted to starting and building a law practice with Parker, Hoover, Keller & Waterman and the work with the reorganization of the utility companies. But after the firm merged in 1981 with Shoaff, Keegan, Baird & Simon, management of the firm was shared with others and I had time to devote to other matters. This led to me becoming involved in a number of areas beyond the practice of law.

This 12-year period from 1982 to 1994 also brought a great number of changes in our family. By 1982, all of our daughters had graduated from high school and either graduated or were in college. Pam started at DePauw and later finished at Indiana and Portland State University, where she earned a degree in accounting. Carole finished high school at Culver in 1978 and then went to Vanderbilt, graduating in 1982. Kristi finished high school at Homestead and then went to Colorado College, and then on to Kennedy School at Harvard.

The daughters leaving our school system meant that I was no longer able to spend time hassling the Superintendent about dismissing Homestead for "snow days" every time there was a light snow. I would regularly attend school board meetings and point out to the Superintendent and the entire board examples of kids attending schools in states where "snow days" were unheard of, such as North Dakota, Colorado and other places with significantly more snow than Fort Wayne. I wanted to believe my harassment had some impact because the district is now very reluctant to dismiss school for snow days — although many attribute this change to the Indiana legislature passing a law requiring "snow days" to be made up later in the spring, and not my harassment.

When the kids began to think about which colleges they might attend, I put a string on a pencil and drew a 300-mile circle around Fort Wayne, indicating that I would like them to go somewhere inside this circle. This encompasses quite a large area including all of Indiana, most of Ohio, Illinois and even into Wisconsin, and also includes schools in large cities like Chicago, Detroit and Cleveland. I figured 300 miles was far enough to be away from home but close enough to get there and back in a day if needed. Pam went to DePauw for three years and later attended Indiana University in 1980 — both well within this circle. Carole strayed 104 miles outside of this circle and attended Vanderbilt in Nashville. But Kristi blew my idea completely when she decided to go to Colorado College, graduating in 1985, and then to Harvard Kennedy

School in 1989.

This 12-year period also saw a number of other major changes in our family beginning with the loss of Pat's father, Earle Opie in 1982, at age 81, and my father, Crawford Parker in February of 1986, at age 79. Both Earle and Crawford were strong, energetic men their entire lives and it was hard to see them suffer from illnesses in their waning years. Earle had Alzheimer's for nearly a decade in his last years, and Crawford was on oxygen from emphysema, contracted I'm sure from his many years of smoking.

We lost my grandmother, Mollie Bouslog, in 1972 at age 96. I had established a trust many years before her death to pay her expenses for a nursing home. After this, the only survivor of our parent's generation was Pat's mother, Millie, who lived a relatively healthy life until age 92, passing in 1995.

This period also saw two marriages in the family: Pam and Rodney were married in 1984 in a wonderful ceremony at First Presbyterian church in Fort Wayne. Carole and Dan were married in Ashcroft, Colorado in 1989 in a mountainous meadow near Aspen. Both weddings and the receptions were outstanding, due of course to Pat's diligent planning.

With the merger of Parker, Hoover, Keller & Waterman and Shoaff, Keegan, Baird & Simon in 1981, the name changed to Shoaff, Parker & Keegan. The management of the law firm also changed; instead of an informal arrangement where Bob Hoover and I made most of the decisions, there was now a four-person management team composed of Tom Shoaff and Reed Silliman from the Shoaff firm and Bob Hoover and myself. Later when we merged with Baker & Daniels in 1989, an Indianapolis management team took over and I was no longer involved. While I was somewhat disappointed with this new arrangement, I was also relieved to no longer carry the major responsibility for both procuring a great portion of our law business since 1967 and also making most of the decisions to manage the firm.

My practice with clients continued about the same. I was involved with a number of corporate clients — doing merger and acquisition work for Flint & Walling, Masco Corporation and others. Through our trips with the Sister City Committee in Takaoka, Japan I was able to develop some Japanese clients and these proved quite interesting.

Thunderbird Products, the manufacturer of Formula boats, Burlington Air Freight and local Ford and Lincoln-Mercury distributorships also continued to be good clients during this period. However, not devoting time to law firm management and delegating some of my law work to younger partners, allowed me to free up time for other investments and community organizations. Life settled into a more predictable pattern.

After we sold Flint & Walling to Masco in 1978, John Pichon and I stayed involved with Masco as members of the Management Committee. Our duties were not onerous but we were able to attend the annual Management Committee meetings which were normally held at Masco headquarters in Taylor, Michigan. On at least two occasions, the meetings were held in Florida, one at the Boca Raton Hotel and the other at Turnberry Resort. At the meetings in Florida, the whole family was invited and we enjoyed four to five days of meetings and entertainment on a grand scale. Noteworthy speakers, for example Alan Greenspan, were always brought in by Masco to cap off the meeting. My relationship with Masco exposed me to a high-powered manufacturing organization listed on the New York Stock Exchange with outstanding people who not only operated in the major financial centers of Detroit and New York, but overseas as well.

During the late '70s and early '80s, I also became involved with various partnerships to purchase real estate. This began with Les Gerig, DeNeal Hartman and Jim Schenkel. We purchased four farms in St. Joseph Township. These would later be sold for housing developments. Much of this land went to Arlington Park, a very sizable development with over 1,000 homes. I also purchased with Bill Moser, Hartman and Schenkel, a large farm on the southside of Fort Wayne which was sold off to develop Southtown Mall and also a large apartment development. While these real estate partnerships were generally profitable, they required a lot of time and tied up investment funds. Our purchases were not always in the right locations and we ended up holding onto properties for many years before a viable sale came along. Buying and holding real estate for future development takes a lot more work and patience than it appears at first glance. Also, since these matters normally require a great deal of legal work, I ended up contributing many hours of legal services for free to the partnership.

During this period our family also became more involved in skiing. We began this sport many years earlier, beginning with trips to Michigan in the late '50s and early '60s, and by 1962, we made our first trip to Colorado. On this trip, in company with Jack and Kathleen Summers, we traveled by train and bus and skied a number of different places, including Aspen Highlands and Arapahoe Basin. Because of a snowstorm, our bus had difficulty getting over Loveland Pass (long before the Eisenhower Tunnel was built) on the way back to Denver. We tried two or three additional passes before we were finally able to make it through. But we missed our train to Chicago and had to catch a later train where we didn't have seat reservations. We parked temporarily in a club car with a group of young skiers from Chicago who were drinking heavily. One of them threw a full can of beer the length of the car almost hitting Pat and Kathleen Summers. I jumped up and threatened to tear into this group of five or six much younger and bigger guys. Luckily, Jack Summers' better judgment prevailed, talked me down and encouraged us all to leave the club car instead. We eventually found separate seats scattered throughout the train. After skiing, riding the bus and missing our train, we were dead tired. At 3:00 in the morning, as the train stopped in Lincoln, Nebraska, a nice elderly gentleman got on the train, nudged me and said that I was in his reserved seat. I replied that I was too tired to move and that he would need to find another seat. He must have done so, because I never heard from him again — a story I still remember and regret.

After this first trip, we went to Colorado almost every year, spending at least 25 Christmases in a row in Aspen. We would go for two weeks, the required time to guarantee accommodations. Sometimes we traveled by plane, usually through Chicago, and we spent at least three Christmas days or eves in either O'Hare Airport or Stapleton in Denver when the plane was delayed or snowed in. For a number of years, we also drove. During the early years, we drove a station wagon with all of our gear packed on top. We would normally stop somewhere in Kansas and stay overnight, but this was a problem as we had to unload our gear from the top of the car. Later, when the girls got their driver's licenses, we would drive all night, getting into Aspen late in the afternoon in time to unpack, eat dinner, and go to bed early in order to be ready to ski the next day. We had many wonderful Christmases in Aspen. One of my favorites was at the Blue Spruce, a modest motel by Aspen standards. We arrived Christmas eve and there were no Christmas trees to be found in town. So Pat erected a Christmas tree made from all of our ski poles and strung lights and ornaments and tinsel on it!

We met many great friends skiing — the Bledsoes from Terre Haute, Indiana, the Lovetts from Owensboro, Kentucky, and of course our good friends from Fort Wayne, Ed and Joan White. Ed and Joan owned a condominium in the Fifth Avenue, and we went to fabulous New Year's Eve parties there for a number of years.

One of my favorite stories about skiing with the Whites was that Ed and I were booked to ski with a deep powder group on the backside of Aspen Mountain, a relatively rare tour at the time. Joan was to drive us to our pickup point that morning. Unfortunately, Joan did not have time to dress, so she just put on her house slippers and robe over her nightgown to drive us. By the time we arrived at the pick-up spot, the jeep that would deliver us to the snow cat had already left. Ed drove his Cadillac up the narrow road to where the snow cat was, but unfortunately there was no turnaround. Hence, it was necessary for Ed to back the Cadillac almost a half a mile down this very narrow and twisting lane while the jeep followed with Joan and I and the jeep driver. This was early in the morning, the temperature was well below zero, the jeep had a canvas top and no heater, and Joan in slippers, bathrobe and nightgown was freezing. The Whites had a lot of words when we came home from skiing that night.

Later, after Ed and Joan divorced and Ed remarried Nancy, we met John and Sandra Day O'Connor through Nancy. Nancy had been secretary of the Arizona Bar Association and had met Sandra, who was a local court judge and later an Appellate Court Judge in Phoenix. The O'Connor's came skiing with the Whites on a number of occasions and we developed a friendship before she was appointed to the Supreme Court. John O'Connor was always a more adventurous skier than Sandra who was generally very cautious. One day when the Whites, the O'Connors and the Parkers were skiing together, I suggested that we go ski "Back of Bell No. 2." Everyone protested saying, "That run is too difficult for us." I said "just trust me". I made this decision because I had noticed from the lifts that the snowcat had cut all the moguls off that morning. While the slope is steep and a double black diamond, I knew it would be manageable without moguls. We skied Bell No. 2 two or three times and felt pretty proud of ourselves.

At an after-ski party, someone asked Justice O'Connor about her skiing that day and she proudly relayed how we had skied Bell No. 2 that day. Several friends noted the difficulty of this run and praised her bravery. Whereupon, daughter Carole pipes up: "Oh, yeah, they catted all the moguls off Bell No. 2 last night — it was so easy!" The moral of this story is that even a Supreme Court Justice is not above bragging rights about her skiing and there are times when young people should learn to keep their mouths shut.

John O'Connor and I had a conversation one evening about our kids coming to visit us at Christmas. John stated that if you made the reservations, bought the airline tickets, mailed the tickets, and promised to house and feed them, your kids would actually visit you over Christmas. I lamented that this would likely be the case until we go on Social Security. And John retorted, "No, not our Social Security, until our kids go on Social Security!"

After renting hotel rooms in Aspen for a number of years, in 1978 we decided to buy a condominium at the Chateau Dumont, located near the bottom of Little Nell. The manager of the Dumont was a very colorful character named Buddy Wallen, who always cut a few corners managing the condominium. One owner in the condominium association was a woman from Canada and also an accountant. She claimed that Buddy was charging the association double for towels and other linens being replaced. She sought out the suppliers and got copies of actual invoices to reveal that Buddy had been trumping up extra invoices which he had not paid.

While the Dumont was fine, after six years we did an exchange into the Durant, which was a much nicer condominium on the other side of Little Nell with a view over the city and up Aspen Mountain. The condominium was previously owned by a woman from California and had been decorated to the hilt. She had used mirrors at strategic places to make all the rooms appear larger and expand the views of the mountain.

After owning the Durant from 1984 for 20 years, we finally put it up for sale. After about four months on the market, the condo sold. The good news is that we got almost 100 percent of our asking price. The bad news is that we probably didn't ask enough.

Another sport in which our family became very involved during this period was tennis. Pat and I played in mixed doubles tournaments at Fort Wayne Country Club, and I participated in a pro-am that was played each summer at the Club. This was a tournament where Club members partnered with pros. I was fortunate to win this on three occasions, once with a pro who would wolf down vodka and tonics between matches. He was so good, however, that drunk or sober he carried us through. Pat and I also both played in various tennis leagues, usually under the name of Volvo or USTA. Our respective teams would generally win the local competition and then would qualify for the Northern Indiana region played in either South Bend or Fort Wayne. If we were successful in regionals, we would go to Indianapolis for the Indiana Championship. If we were successful in Indianapolis, we would attend a six-state tournament held either in Indianapolis or Kalamazoo, Michigan. While our team finished second on two occasions, we were never able to win the six-state regional. Had we won, we would have qualified to play in the Nationals, usually held in Phoenix or L.A. We were never able to accomplish this, but I am still proud of our many achievements in these tournaments.

In addition to the Fort Wayne Country Club and USTA, we also played in various tournaments at Wildwood Racquet Club and in the City of Fort Wayne tournaments. Some years I was lucky in winning City Senior Doubles in the over 45 and over 55 brackets, and one year, I was able to win both brackets. After 1999, however, I stopped playing in the USTA league that I had played in for 20 years, and played only with a doubles group on Tuesday nights. During this period, particularly during the '80s, tennis was a big factor in our lives and we played two or three times weekly in the winter at Wildwood and outdoors during the Summer. We met a lot of great friends through tennis, and Pat played and had lunch with her group weekly.

One good friend I met through the Fort Wayne Fury was Earl Goode. The Fury was a professional basketball team in a minor league that I was involved with from 1988 to 1999. It consumed a large part of our lives during these years and is detailed in another chapter. Earl was the Regional Vice President of GTE (now Frontier) in Indianapolis. GTE at the time was very involved in all types of sports advertising, including sponsoring the Seniors Tour golf tournament held at the Broadmoor Club in Indianapolis, Tampa, and elsewhere. Earl invited me to participate in the pro-am portion of the Seniors Tournament in Indianapolis, in Tampa and best of all, at Kapalua in Hawaii. The Hawaii trip was a great week for both husbands and wives. We stayed in the Kapalua Hotel and had an excellent time both playing golf and touring Maui. On at least two occasions, our Senior pro was Dave Stockton, one of the best putters and shot-makers on the Senior Tour.

Another highlight was going to Florida and playing at the Bay Hill Club with Arnold Palmer, which he owned. On another trip to Latrobe, Pennsylvania, we not only played golf with Arnold but spent the day at his home. His wife, Winnie (unfortunately now deceased as of course is Arnold) was a very gracious host with a good sense of humor. On a tour of their home, she shook her head when spying a pair of Arnold's shorts flopped in the corner of the bedroom. "I can't get that damn kid to pick up." Near the swimming pool was a neat little sign which I am sure Winnie installed for Arnold's benefit: "Please do not walk on the water."

When we played at Latrobe with Arnold, Jim Kelley from Fort Wayne was also in the foursome. As we walked the course, Arnold knew every maintenance worker and stopped to talk. It is easy to see why Arnold was so popular — he was truly a man of the people and made time for everyone.

On the Latrobe course with Arnold, I was very fortunate on the front side. I chipped in on one hole, hit a long putt on another hole, and as we got ready to tee off for the ninth hole, Jim Kelley quietly leans over as says, "Do you know that you are two under par and leading Palmer by two strokes?" Surprised by this news, I said "I am?" Immediately after this exchange, I hooked the ball out of bounds for a two-stroke penalty. Palmer and I tied on the front side, and he played with another group on the back side. My one great chance to beat Palmer and I blew it!

Once when we played with Palmer at Bay Hill, Dr. Steve Beering, the then-President of Purdue, was in our foursome. While he was an outstanding President, his golfing skills were minimal and I was surprised he had the nerve to accept an invitation to play with a pro like Palmer. Ten on a hole was a good score for him. But Arnold Palmer was most patient. He would help Dr. Beering line up his shots and give him tips on putting. This was really above and beyond the call of duty and in stark contrast to Ray Floyd, and some of the other pros in the pro-ams, who would rarely even speak to their amateur partners.

At the Senior Pro-Am in Tampa, a photo was taken of Arnold and me, with Pat between the two of us. We sent the photo out as part of our Christmas card that year with the caption: "Outstanding golfer Pat Parker and two of her pupils." It brought a great response from friends!

In addition to skiing, tennis and golf, I was generally able to get in at least one hunting trip each year. We have a group that went to the Meier Pheasant Farm, south of Elkhart where they raise and release pheasants. Usually five or six of us would make up a party and the Pheasant Farm would provide the dogs and the trainer. As you hunt through the cornfields, you will see pheasants running ahead of you. At the end of the field, they have cut the last 20 corn rows and the pheasants are reluctant to run across the bare ground so they bunch up at the end of the field. When all the hunters arrive, the dogs are turned into the field and pretty soon a number of pheasants will go up. Usually it is pretty good shooting, although a lot of the pheasants do get away.

After the hunt, we would sit in a small shack, drink beer and tell tall stories while the farm crew cleaned the birds for us. It is a great day of hunting without having to travel to North Dakota or Nebraska for a week. When the girls were young, I would also take them duck hunting and bring ducks home to clean. With lots of persuasion, they would help me clean the ducks too. We would dip them in paraffin and hot water before taking the feathers off.

In the early '80s, Al Zacher, Bob Hoover, Joe Gerson and I formed a little real estate partnership called the Reindeer Group and we purchased about 20 acres of property near the Ft Wayne airport. In 1985 I decided to build office warehouse buildings on this property and engaged Dan Lawrence and his company, Construction Inc. They erected two office warehouses, one in 1985 and one in 1986. While these buildings were good income producers over a period of time the venture was not without maintenance and other problems. Although I did have a good general contractor, there are many decisions that must be made when you get involved in building and leasing property. In the end we made a little money and I can say that I spent time as a real estate developer and property landlord.

Another ad hoc hat I have worn in my career is that of investment advisor. Starting back in law school when Pat worked full time and I worked part-time, we had a few extra dollars and decided to invest it in a mutual fund called The Canadian Fund. It never did very well and we ultimately sold it. After that, I invested primarily in the stock market when I worked at Northern Trust, and the few extra dollars we earned were put into stocks — principally Reynolds Tobacco. The stock grew and we used the proceeds to make a down payment on our first home in Indian Village. After that, I had some investment success off and on throughout the years. For many years, I had a knack for putting money into stocks during the good times when prices were high and then unfortunately selling at the wrong time when the downturns would come. In the '80s, I turned to investing in mutual funds and tried to pursue a more long-term strategy, principally investing with the Vanguard Group which had a new approach that focused on broad index funds and low fees.

After our law firm merger with Baker & Daniels in 1984, I was appointed to the Baker & Daniels Pension Committee, which at the time was almost wholly invested in treasury bonds. I became Chair of this committee in the early '90s and continued in this capacity for the next 13 years. During this time, the Baker & Daniels Pension investments went from a few million dollars to over 100 million. I was able to get the Baker & Daniels 401(k) plan transferred to Vanguard in 1991, and set up investment managers for the HR-10 in 1992. Throughout the years, I worked with our consultants to select investment managers and funds and monitored the performance of the B&D investments each quarter. At this time, I also began reading a number of investment publications and books and attending seminars on investment management and was able to educate myself to make better investment decisions, particularly involving mutual funds.

At a 75th birthday party held for me by the law firm, Joe Kimmell relayed a story about an end-of-the-year meeting of the firm in which the managing partner Brian Burke asked,

"Which partner do you think produced the most money for the firm this past year?" Several partners guessed the names of several of our partners with major corporate clients, particularly those from Indianapolis. Then Brian replied, "Nope, it was Mac Parker, who made us almost $8 million dollars last year from increases in our HR-10 and 401(k) investments." While Brian was being very generous, as it was the manager's and stock market that produced the $8 million and not me, I certainly appreciated the compliment. The firm has been very pleased that I put in place the new management and investment of our pension plans back in the early '90s, and this served us very well when the stock market went up during this period.

In addition to Baker & Daniels, I have spent about 40 years on our church investment committee, which also began quite small and has grown considerably. In the late '90s, I also took over the investment of the Olive B. Cole Foundation funds. This gave me a basis to work with investments with three different entities, and also the opportunity to compare the performance of different managers and investment styles. The total assets of these three entities exceeded $150 million, a sizable portfolio.

While I certainly would have made a number of different investment decisions over the years, I believe that having an asset allocation plan and sticking to a rebalancing policy pays off over the long term and enables you to sleep better at night when there are substantial downturns in the market.

My restless nature and interest in sports also got me involved with pro basketball during this period of my life. I will leave for a separate chapter my involvement with the Fort Wayne Fury, which occupied a substantial portion of my time from 1989 through 1995.

During these years, we were also able to travel quite a bit. We took some trips with our entire family, some with a portion of the family, and some with just Pat, myself and other friends. Most of these trips are detailed in separate notebooks with photos and a diary of the trip. Some of these trips were to our Sister City in Takaoka, and one very interesting trip was to Takaoka and then on to Jinzhou in Manchuria, the northern part of China. Also, we traveled to Egypt in 1984, to the Soviet Union with Howard and Betsy Chapman, to Germany just after the Berlin Wall fell in 1991, and with the entire family down the Colorado River through the Grand Canyon.

John and Joan Pichon had a home in St. Croix in the U.S. Virgin Islands for a number of years and we visited them there on a number of occasions. One time we sailed with the Pichons throughout the British Virgins. Pat still chides me but I lament we did not buy real estate there as the Road Town area of the British Virgins is so beautiful.

For a number of years, I was a member of the Defense Orientation Conference Association (DOCA). This is a group of mostly retired military men and women and has a mission of continuing education of its members pertaining to national security. We traveled to military bases in the continental U.S. and Alaska as well as Brazil. We would also attend annual meetings in D.C. and receive briefings from high Pentagon officials on world affairs and national defense matters.

In 1991, while deeply involved with the Fort Wayne Fury, the incoming President of the Chamber of Commerce was unable to serve, and I was asked to take over the Chairmanship of the Chamber again. One noteworthy event was the Chamber's Annual Meeting at which Pat and I persuaded Justice Sandra Day O'Connor to be the guest speaker. It was the Chamber's largest annual meeting ever with over 1,000 people attending. Sandra and her husband, John, stayed at our home for two or three days and Pat and I very much enjoyed having them as guests, including playing tennis and sightseeing around Fort Wayne.

Another investment endeavor started with my friendship with Jack Hoffer. We secured 15 or 20 investors and formed a new trust company — Northern Indiana Trust Company — with two or three employees and an office on the west side of Fort Wayne. Unfortunately, Jack viewed the job more as a retirement position rather than one in which he would go out and spend time soliciting new accounts. The net result was that it bounced along for four or five years and we ended up selling it to a local bank. As investors, we came out with all of our money, but it was by and large not a very profitable enterprise.

In May, 1994, I turned 65 and in November Pat joined me and we both became eligible for Medicare. This turned out to be very fortunate because in December of 1994, I was diagnosed with prostate cancer and this opened a new, if not welcomed, phase of our lives.

Pat threw a 65th birthday party for me at our home with about 30 of our friends invited. She contracted for a trained pig act for the event. The pig — actually a 300 lb. sow — was ushered into our family room, where she did little tricks like blowing a horn, dropping balls in a basket, etc. The pig was supposedly house-broken, but evidently "not feeling well" this night as her trainer later explained. The pig began to urinate, and went on and on. Pat rushed to the kitchen, got a pan, which the pig filled to overflowing. Meanwhile the assembled guests were rolling on the floor with laughter. Someone kept a movie camera rolling, and the footage was worthy of being sent to the "World's Funniest Home Videos".

COCKROACH BASKETBALL
1988-1999

While I always had a consummate interest in sports, during the next decade this led me in a direction which I had never anticipated. As Fort Wayne emerged from the early recession in the 1980s, I became increasingly concerned about the need to pay special attention to attracting young people back to Fort Wayne. I recognized that this is a complex problem involving good jobs, educational facilities, quality of life, and interesting opportunities in sports and entertainment.

This problem became one of the principal reasons why I got involved with the Fort Wayne Fury and the Continental Basketball Association (CBA). For the next 12 to 13 years, I became engrossed in the world of minor league sports. All the publicity, thrill of winning, agony of losing, financial problems, and every other aspect of owning a basketball team became a major part of our lives. For at least five years, I was directly involved in signing every check for the Fort Wayne Fury, the City's CBA team, on a daily basis.

The impetus for bringing the CBA team to Fort Wayne began with an unanticipated connection relating back to my father. In 1987, I attended a ceremony in Indianapolis for the opening of a time capsule at the State Office Building. My father had been the Chairman of the State Office Building Commission some 25 years earlier when the time capsule was originally dedicated. At the ceremony, I met a gentleman from Indianapolis, Phil Conklin, who had known my father when he was Lt. Governor. Phil told me that he was interested in the CBA and in possibly bringing a CBA team to Indiana. At the time, he was dealing with a man from Rockford, Illinois named Jay Pohlan. Phil had an option to buy a CBA franchise which Pohlan owned. Phil and I talked and agreed that Fort Wayne might be a good market for a CBA team.

Phil, a friend of his named Tommy Thompson, and I attended a CBA board meeting in Denver in the spring of 1988. In the meantime, Phil's financial deal with Jay Pohlan had fallen through, so Phil, Tommy and I talked to the CBA about obtaining a new franchise directly from the League. The cost was $500,000, which could be paid over four years. In addition, a Letter of Credit of $100,000 would be required.

Shortly after our initial discussion with the CBA, a firm from Chicago, Kemper Lesnick, associated with the Kemper Insurance Group, purchased an option from the CBA to locate a team in one of five different cities. The cities were ultimately narrowed down to just two: Fort Wayne and Sioux Falls, South Dakota. Representatives from Kemper came to Fort Wayne and met with the Fort Wayne Sports Task Force, the predecessor of the Sports Corporation. After two days of investigating Fort Wayne, Kemper ultimately decided to exercise their option and locate the franchise in Sioux Falls. Fort Wayne was very taken aback by this decision as Sioux Falls is a much smaller city and didn't have the rich sports history of Fort Wayne.

Over the next year, on various trips to Colorado to ski, I would stop by the CBA office in Denver and meet with Jay Ramsdale, the CBA Commissioner at the time. Ultimately these visits resulted in me obtaining an option to bring a CBA franchise to Northern Indiana and in the Spring of 1989, I put up $25,000 for this purpose. Later in November, I put up an additional $25,000 for the option. After several meetings and cocktail parties where Pat met a number of people who own CBA teams — all of them losing money — she asked me why I would do something like this. I confess I never had a good answer for her.

Phil Conklin, Tommy Thompson and I then started to look at places to locate the team. Since we could go anywhere in Northern Indiana north of Interstate 70, we looked at Muncie and Anderson, in addition to Fort Wayne. We looked at the Wigwam in Anderson, which has only a high school floor, and at the Ball State gym in Muncie. One reason we decided to take the option on all Northern Indiana was so we would have a little negotiating room with Fort Wayne. As soon as we received favorable terms from the Fort Wayne Coliseum, we did not proceed further with other locations.

At this point, the planning began in earnest. We had to figure out what it was going to take to buy the franchise, put up a Letter of Credit, raise the money to employ a staff, and get a team off the ground. I talked with John Weissert, who was then the president of the Fort Wayne Sports Corp., and he put me in touch with Jay Frye, who had previously tried to bring a minor league baseball team to Fort Wayne. Jay then contacted Denny Sutton who had also been involved in the attempted purchase of a minor league baseball team and the three of us formed the initial investor group for the Fort Wayne Fury. We were also three old basketball "jocks" — trying vicariously to get back into the game!

At this point, Phil Conklin and Tommy Thompson decided to drop out since they lived in Indianapolis and the new team would be located in Fort Wayne. Phil did come to the opening game in November 1991 and I kept in contact with him for a few years.

Although we had decided on Fort Wayne, the CBA still had to approve the city and set the terms for operating the franchise. In late 1989, I wrote to Irv Katz, then Commissioner of the CBA, who had succeeded Jay Ramsdale, and invited him to come to Fort Wayne for a visit. (Jay Ramsdale was unfortunately killed in a very high-profile aircraft accident in Sioux City, Iowa, where a United Airlines plane crashed, killing almost everyone onboard.) Irv Katz came to Fort Wayne, reviewed the Coliseum and other facilities and gave his approval.

Jay Frye, Denny Sutton and I then attended a CBA Board of Directors meeting in Denver in May 1990 where we agreed to the terms to purchase the franchise. The terms were that the purchase was contingent upon our signing a Coliseum lease, selling at least 1500 season tickets, and putting up a $100,000 Letter of Credit. When we arrived back in Fort Wayne, we were met at the airport by crews from all three of the local TV stations, and all the newspapers. The next day, the headlines all read: "CBA Basketball Coming to Fort Wayne."

Fort Wayne was overjoyed because at the time there was no professional sports teams in the city. The two minor league teams here previously — the Fort Wayne Komets of the International Hockey League, and the Fort Wayne Kicks of the America Soccer Association — had either failed or relocated out of the City. Soon afterwards, however, the Franke brothers, local FT Wayne residents, bought another IHL franchise from Flint, Michigan, and brought professional hockey back to Fort Wayne.

The CBA or Continental Basketball Association, is sometimes called either the "Crazy Basketball Association" or the "Cockroach Basketball Association." The latter name arose because some said, like a cockroach, you could never kill it or get rid of it. The CBA league actually began as the Eastern Basketball League in the late '30s and is older than the NBA. It has a history of being in and out of many, many cities, perhaps 75 to 100 in all, over the years. It has been in Alaska, a number of cities on the West Coast, many cities in the Midwest and South, and even some on the East Coast. The cities range from Portland, Maine to Pensacola, Florida to San Jose and Bakersfield in California, and Fairbanks, Alaska.

In many cities, the franchise would be brought in by a single owner with money or perhaps a small group. The team would play for two or three years, achieve a lot of local publicity and notoriety, then the novelty would wear off, fans would look elsewhere for the next new thing, attendance would fall off, and the owner would either sell the franchise or go into bankruptcy.

This has been the history of the CBA since the '50s. But in the late '80s, they negotiated a contract with the NBA to become the "Official Developmental League." This meant that any NBA team had a right to call up any player in the CBA on 48-hour notice. That player would stay with the NBA on a ten-day contract. This new contract enabled the NBA to get an immediate replacement from the CBA if they had an injury or problem with one of their regular NBA players. The players' contract could then be renewed for an additional ten days if needed. If it extended beyond 20 days, then the NBA team had to keep the CBA player for the rest of the season. For this right, the CBA was paid various amounts, usually a million and a half to two million dollars a year. Most of these funds went to the league office and enabled management to live lavishly and travel extensively. Unfortunately, each of the CBA teams in the league struggled financially under this contract and faced the perennial problem of having their best players pulled at any time during the season.

CBA rules were the same as NBA rules with two differences: the CBA league allowed one additional personal foul for a total of six, and was on a "quarter point" system. This system awarded one point for each quarter and three additional points for winning the game or a total of seven points for the entire game. The number of points was critical for determining league playoffs, regardless of won and lost records. The purpose of the quarter point system was to keep fans involved throughout the entire game. Otherwise, if a team fell way behind in the early periods, fans might leave. But if a team won the last quarter or two, they would still get points out of the game and that might help them achieve a better playoff status. There was even a quarter point clock that scored the points for each quarter. There was always a big flurry of activity toward the end of each quarter, similar to the end of the game.

I have always thought the quarter point system was a very good idea. It achieved a lot of extra interest in the CBA and kept most of the fans there until the game was over. Also, at each CBA game there would always be two or three NBA scouts. The players were aware of this and played especially hard when they knew there would be a lot of scouts there or scouts from a particular team in which they were interested. Overall, CBA players played much harder than those in the NBA. The players were basically young guys hoping to get a chance at the "Big Dance" — the NBA. Occasionally the CBA league would also include former NBA players who for one reason or another had been passed over and were hoping to get called back to an NBA team. The NBA connection was overall a mixed blessing. It gave the CBA league more class and ensured a lot better play from team members. Still, the call-up provision constantly forced CBA coaches to rebuild their teams with new players and it discouraged fan loyalty as favorites they hoped to see at a game would suddenly get called up to the NBA and be gone.

Irv Katz stayed as CBA Commissioner only a short time and was succeeded by Terdema Ussery, who had been the staff attorney for the CBA. Terdema was the Commissioner most of the time I was active with the CBA. He ultimately went on to a very good job with Nike and handled sports promotion for many of Nike's outstanding athletes, including Michael Jordan.

In addition to being a training ground for NBA players, the CBA was also a training ground for referees and coaches. Three CBA coaches who went on to the NBA and achieved outstanding records were Phil Jackson, who won NBA Championships with both the Chicago Bulls and the Los Angeles Lakers; George Karl, who was with Seattle and more recently Minnesota; and Flip Saunders, who I knew very well, and who went to Milwaukee. Many books could be written about the CBA and all of the various crazy things that went on in the league. However, there is only one book of which I am aware of called *On the Rim*, about the "Albany Patroons", when George Karl coached the team in the late '80s.

After Denny Sutton, Jay Frye and I returned from Denver and the publicity died down, we had to go about the business of developing a plan to field the team in Fort Wayne. Through the CBA Board, I met Tom Rubens, the General Manager and one of the owners of the Grand Rapids Hoops, which had started about three years earlier. From Tom, we got a lot of good advice, particularly in the financial arena, of what it would take to get a team off the ground. We determined that we would need to raise at least $750,000. Of this, $300,000, or $100,000 each, would come from Jay, Denny and myself, and then we would get 12 investors to put up $37,500 each. We decided to form a corporation with "A" and "B" shares and qualify it as an S-Corp so that gains and losses could be passed directly through to the shareholders. Because we understood that a minor sports team cannot be run as a committee operation, we decided that the "B" shares would have full voting rights and the "A" shares would have limited voting rights. Under this scenario, if the "B" shares (owned by Jay, Denny and I) all voted together, they would have control of the corporation. But if one member holding B shares voted with the A shares, then the A shares and the one B share would have control. In other words, if Jay, Denny and I all continued to work together, then the operations would be left up to us. But if we were not able to get along, then the A shares and one B shareholder could effect a change of management.

I wrote up a private offering memorandum to sell $450,000 of the A shares. This memorandum included a complete description of the CBA, the history of many of the teams, cities they had been located in, the financial difficulties of running a minor league franchise, the fickleness of the fans, our personal resumes, how we proposed to raise and use funds, and all the other risks involved. I gave this memorandum to Jim Aschleman, a securities attorney from our Indianapolis office to review and he indicated that we had enough "caveats" to meet the criteria for accredited investors. An "accredited investor" is an SEC term defined as someone who has a very substantial income or assets over a prescribed amount.

I then talked with three friends who I believed might be interested in becoming investors. I advised them that we were hopeful that this investment would not be a complete bust, but that they should view it as more of a community contribution rather than a money-making proposition. I told them that we hoped to bring some excitement, fun, and goodwill to the community, and that we intended to at least break even or perhaps a little better.

I talked with Dick Doermer, Jim Vann and Tom Eckrich, each of which agreed to become an investor. Tom Eckrich and I went to see Dick Freeland, who also agreed to be an investor, and I also met with Tom Kelly. Tom Eckrich later ran into financial difficulty and was unable to continue, but I always appreciated his initial help. After this, Maury O'Daniel, Dick Waterfield and Gary Probst came in as investors. Later, Tom West, Dr. Al Stovall, Tom Jehl, Stan Lipp, and Ted Nowak joined us. This was our original group. Because of their reputations in the community, after Dick Doermer, Dick Freeland and Jim Vann joined the group, it was no problem to attract other investors. People called, asking to join.

Later investors included Tim Borne, Doug McKibben, Mike Thomas, and others, but the above names, plus Denny, Jay and myself were the original 15 investors in the Fort Wayne Fury. In fact, we hardly had any turndowns.

The final investor group was a "Who's Who" list of the City of Fort Wayne. I doubt seriously whether it would have been possible to put together a better group from the standpoint of community visibility. We asked that they not only become investors, but season ticket holders and that their business should consider buying a box, becoming a sponsor and attending games. Almost all agreed to do these things and hence we ended up with a broad base of support from top level community leaders. This was the real secret to getting the team off the ground in the early years.

In launching the team, there is little more we could have done to be successful. We established a Finance Committee that I met with on a monthly basis which initially included Gary Probst and Dick Waterfield and later Maury O'Daniel, all well-known and successful Fort Wayne businessmen. Denny, Jay and I divided up management of the Fury. Jay and Denny ran promotion and overall team management and I took care of the finances. We hired a general manager, Rich Coffey, who at the time was a basketball coach at Hamilton High School, north of Fort Wayne. Our Assistant General Manager was Art Saltzberg, a well-known local sportscaster, and Scott Sproat was in charge of Sales and Promotions. Danielle Taylor (later Talarico) was one of our first employees to handle all administrative matters. My long-time administrative assistant, Brenda Richardson, became the team statistician. Gerald Oliver was our first coach. Waterfield Mortgage had previously purchased the old First Federal Building on Court Street which we utilized as the Fury office until it was later demolished and we moved to the Standard Federal Building.

Later, Rich Coffey would leave and go to Hartford as their general manager, and Art Saltzberg took over as general manager. Art and I worked very well together and met frequently to review finances and other aspects of the operation. We spent time from May 1990, when we received the franchise until November, 1991, getting organized. During this time, we sold season tickets, over 2700 in all — substantially more than the 1500 required by the league — and a great number of sponsorships.

We formed a Fury dance team and conducted tryouts at the Performing Arts Center. We had over 100 attractive young ladies show up — from high school girls to mothers with children — many with very strong dancing ability, and for the first two or three years, the Fury dance team was pretty good. Jokingly, we told Tom Jehl, one of our investors and well-known as a shopping center developer, that he was in charge of selecting the dance team, but luckily he deferred to a professional dance coach! Later on, I brought home one of the Fury dance costumes for Pat to try on. She looked pretty good in the tight leotard and skirt and somewhere there is a great photo of Pat as a Fury dancer.

We also had to finalize our lease agreement with the Coliseum. Our rental rate declined as attendance increased: at

2500 or less fans, we paid $1200 per night, at 3,000 it declined to $800 and at 4,000 fans, our rental rate was zero. The reason for this declining scale is that the Coliseum received parking and concessions revenues and the greater the attendance, the greater their receipts from parking and concessions.

We conducted a very extensive "Name the Team" contest that ran in the newspapers with over 22,000 entries from 13,000 participants. We finally decided on a winner and had a big press conference to announce it, which included Donnie Walsh, General Manager of the Indiana Pacers, who came to Ft Wayne for the announcement. The name "Fury" was selected among a number of other top entries — such as "Generals," "Rivermen," and "Xpress" — and in retrospect I think it was probably the best choice. The name "Fury" was submitted by 49 different people and we later drew those 49 names out of a hat to decide who won the contest.

Opening night on November 8, 1991, was a sell-out crowd of over 8,200 people. The Mayor issued a Proclamation naming this "Fort Wayne Fury Day." The Lt. Governor, later Governor, Frank O'Bannon attended, along with Senator Dan Coats, Congresswoman Jill Long, and many other politicians and notable community members. Many of the Directors, including Jay, Denny and I, dressed in tuxedos and we stood at all the doors greeting our new Fury fans as they arrived — shaking hands with each one.

Our opening game was against Columbus, Ohio and because it was a sell-out, it was televised locally over WKJG. The halftime entertainment was a bungee jumper who leaped from the rafters of the Coliseum. Although the jump was fine, he got hung up and someone had to send up a knife to cut the rope and lower him to the floor — an anticlimactic ending. Unfortunately, we also lost our first game to Columbus, but it was a great night, and no one cared because pro basketball was back in Ft Wayne! There had been two other attempts since the Zollner Pistons to have a team but they were short-lived. This was a solid operation, with good funding from many well-known people and with an NBA contract. The newspaper and television coverage was phenomenal and tickets were in high demand.

In retrospect our team was really terrible that first year, with a record of 21-35. Still, everyone had a tremendous time and that first season we broke all the attendance records for the CBA, with an average attendance of over 5,800. And during the entire decade that the Fury was in Fort Wayne, we either led CBA attendance or were second.

Even though our team never achieved outstanding success on the court, we always had great halftime entertainment. Often, we would book acts from the West Coast and split expenses with the Indiana Pacers, the Chicago Bulls or one of the other NBA teams. The acts would play various arenas over a five-day gig for one set price. One of the notable acts was the Chainsaw Juggler, a crazy but entertaining guy who juggled three running chainsaws. The Coliseum insisted that we put down special plywood to protect the floor in case he dropped one. Another unique act involved the Dynamite Lady, a woman who was placed inside a coffin-like box, and then the box was blown all apart. Still other acts included the Dallas Cowgirls, the Bud Light Daredevils, the Jesse White Tumblers from Chicago, and the San Diego Chicken. One of the crowd favorites that returned every year was Christopher, a man from LA who did a dance act where he stood in the middle of what looked like five people but which were really two dummies in front and two dummies behind him, all connected to his hands, arms, and legs with rails so that they all moved simultaneously. We also had a number of cute dog acts. And, of course, the Fury dancers danced at halftime and sometimes during quarter breaks.

There was also all kinds of promotional entertainment

paid for by sponsors: a fan seated in a chair at the free throw line trying to shoot a basket, little kids shooting from various places on the court and getting paid for each basket made, little race cars, sack races, fans dressed in heavy suits like sumo wrestlers, etc. Sometimes a blimp would fly above the audience and drop tickets for free pizzas. The Fury mascot named "Jam" would roam through the audience and engage fans. Choreographing all the entertainment and hoopla was a huge part of the total evening's production. Some fans admitted that they came just for the halftime entertainment and didn't stay to watch the rest of the game.

The players were a great cast of characters too. Many of them were young players straight from college who had not been drafted into the NBA, but were one step away. They played in the CBA with dreams of getting a call up and joining an NBA team. Their play was very hard and energetic, if not as polished as the NBA players, and they would race down the boards and dive on the floor for loose balls. During the first season, there was a salary cap of $125,000 for all ten players for the season (November through April). The players had individual contracts so while the best players were paid more, some of the players received less than $10,000 for the entire season, although the team also paid for a good portion of their meals and room. Still, as indicated, the salary was not the reason they played, but rather their hope to get a call-up to the Big Dance.

Later on, the salary cap was revoked in a case in which the NBA and CBA were deemed in violation of antitrust laws. This caused an escalation of salaries and increased the annual cost from $125,000 to $300,000 and $400,000 in later years. This increase in salaries ultimately caused real financial problems in the CBA.

We tried to select players who had played at Indiana University, Purdue or one of the other Indiana universities. Jay

Edwards, who played at Indiana, was a long-time member of the Fury, and a very good scorer. Jay was also a perennial problem because he had a host of young ladies interested in him. At one point, we employed Jay Frye's brother as a roommate to Jay to keep the young ladies at bay. Jay's brother indicated that Jay would sometimes have one young lady in his room and another waiting for him down the hall. Jay Edwards also refused to play in one city and we found out later that there was a paternity suit pending against him there and two or three garnishments on his salary for child support.

Damon Bailey, an outstanding player at Indiana, was a real crowd favorite when he joined the Fury. Probably one of the best players we ever had was Lloyd Daniels, nicknamed "Sweet Pea". Lloyd had a knack of taking over the game in the last quarter and scoring at will. He was eventually called up by the LA Lakers and played the rest of the season with them. Travis Williams and Moochie Norris were other players who were with us and went on to very creditable NBA careers. Our best team was in January 1995, with Sweet Pea, Jerome Harmon and Mark Strickland. Unfortunately, all were called up, and we had to rebuild from the ground up.

One continuing problem with the players was drug tests. The CBA had a policy of doing random tests on the players. The normal procedure was to take two urine samples, sending one in for analysis and holding the other in case it was needed later for confirmation of the first. Shortly, after we acquired a player named Treg Lee from Grand Rapids, he was hit with a random drug test and the sample came back positive for marijuana. We met with Lee and he swore on a stack of Bibles that the test was erroneous and that he was "clean". Under the CBA policy, in order to send in the second sample, the player must agree to not contest the first sample and put up $100 of his own money to pay for the cost of processing the second sample. Although Lee seriously swore that he was clean, he was unwilling to put up $100 of his own money to prove his case. The net effect was that he was suspended for a number of games.

There were 28 home games and 28 away games during the regular CBA schedule plus also an All-Star and playoff games, if the team made the playoffs. So, there were usually games every week and sometimes twice a week. Going to the games was always exciting. When Pat and I arrived at the Coliseum, we would always check the parking lot first to see how many cars were there, hoping that we would have a good crowd. After seeing a full parking lot, sometimes we were disappointed to find that there was a dog show, home show, or other event at the Expo Center — in another part of the Coliseum.

The opening of each game was always a highlight. The lights would be turned off and a series of colored spotlights would shoot around the Coliseum, along with smoke on the floor, music playing and a grand introduction of the players. On special occasions, live fireworks were added.

Because of the good players on every team in the league, games were usually exciting and close. In order to save money, the CBA used only two referees and not three like the NBA. This meant that the CBA referees made a greater number of bad calls than their NBA counterparts. Sometimes the referees would decide that a play was too rough and they would call the game very close so that fans only got to watch players walking from one end of the court to the other to shoot free throws. Occasionally, the Fury would be up five or six points with only a minute to play and somehow, we would manage to lose the game. In one game, when Rick Barry was coach, we were up three points with less than five seconds to play and the ball out of bounds. Scooter Barry, Rick's son and one of our players, threw the ball in, the pass was stolen, the opponent's player threw up a long three point shot which was successful and tied the game, and then we lost in overtime. Heartbreaking!!!

To get the crowd excited about the game, Jam, the Fury mascot, would chase after the referees. This got so bad that at one point the referees ejected Jam and had deputy sheriffs take him away. This gave rise to a great publicity stunt in which we took photos of Jam in jail and asked fans to help us spring him. We also gave away free tickets to church groups and inner-city kids interested in seeing the games, giving them special rooting sections.

In 1994, we hosted the CBA All-Star Game and this created a lot of extra publicity. A number of alum NBA players came and spoke to various groups of school kids that we brought to the Coliseum. At one point, we had 30 or 40 busloads of kids from not only Fort Wayne, but the surrounding regions to hear the NBA players give inspirational talks on staying away from drugs, working hard, staying in school, etc.

By 1992, the Fury was very high profile, with big newspaper and TV coverage every day, but we raised it up a notch by hiring Rick Barry, an NBA Hall-of-Famer as our coach. Our publicity went from local to national articles in magazines and newspapers including USA Today, Sports Illustrated, The Washington Post and a number of others throughout the country. While Rick Barry was high visibility, he was unable to produce a winner, and he didn't get along with the players. This problem was compounded by the fact that he brought in his son, Scooter, as a player. While Scooter had great ability, it caused some discord on the team. Finally, after a losing record, we had to ask Rick to resign. He refused to do so, and we had to terminate him. This made headlines around the country as it is not easy to terminate an NBA Hall-of-Famer.

Because of the intense competition among teams, the CBA Board meetings were always fraught with politics. There was always considerable jockeying with either the Commissioner or the Commissioner's office for favorable rulings on player suspensions, trades, and more from the league. This was coupled with the fact that we had a high turnover of Commissioners and the league office moved from Denver to St. Louis and finally to Phoenix over a number of years.

The gentleman who was probably the best coach during the entire run of the Fury was Mo McHone who received a great deal of press coverage. Mo coached the CBA team in Birmingham, Alabama, before he came to Fort Wayne. While in Birmingham, Mo had gone through a divorce and later became involved with a beautiful young woman who he brought to Fort Wayne. Mo spent more time with his girlfriend than the team and we ultimately had to terminate him for not producing a winner. Within a day or two of our termination meeting, there was an unfortunate accident. Jam, the mascot, hit a toy nerf ball as part of his halftime entertainment and the head of the golf club flew off and hit Mo in the testicles. Poor Mo was ushered out of the arena and spent the third quarter in First Aid. He finally returned before the end of the game, but it was a most ignominious end to his coaching career with the Fury. Mo went on to another CBA team and proceeded to win at least one and possibly two championships, something that eluded him during his time with the Fury.

During 1993, when things were still going very well with the Fury, a part of our ownership made a play for the San Antonio Spurs. This may sound a bit like the mouse crawling up the elephant's leg, but it had some substance. Jay Frye had contacts with the managers of the very sizable arena in St. Petersburg, Florida and they were looking for an NBA team to play there. The San Antonio Spurs had fallen on hard times in San Antonio and were up for sale. We put together a group of Fort Wayne heavyweights, Gary Probst and Dick Waterfield as well as Jay Frye, Denny Sutton and myself, and made the trip to St. Petersburg where we met with arena officials and a number of bank officers.

We determined that we could borrow almost the entire purchase price for the franchise and put together an offer of $68 million. Unfortunately, a group that wanted the Spurs to stay in San Antonio put together an even larger offer and were successful in keeping the franchise. Later, when the Spurs won the NBA Championship, we lamented the fact that we had been beaten out in the acquisition.

As stated earlier, CBA has been in and out of a great number of cities over its more than 50-year tenure. After the first two or three years in Fort Wayne, the novelty wore off and the franchise was ready to move on. We came in during the late '80s and early '90s when the CBA was at its strongest — with the NBA contract, salary cap, high visibility and solid financing. However, after the NBA lawsuit declared the salary cap illegal, the CBA began a downward trend with all teams forced to pay higher salaries and barely hanging on. In addition, the NBA teams began looking to Europe to resupply players, creating further competition for the CBA leagues.

Because of community ownership, the Fury held up fairly well — although we were never able to produce a winner. By 1994, attendance was down, expenses were up and we were now talking about losing money and making capital calls from directors instead of distributions to them. The early aura had worn off and this was further complicated by the turnover of coaches.

At this point we began to look for ways to reduce costs, payroll, and fixed expenses. I approached the Coliseum with various proposals to revise our rental arrangement but to no avail. Some of the directors were not inclined to put in additional capital. We became like many other past CBA teams — looking for a way out.

We met a number of times with one group who wanted to purchase the franchise and relocate it to a suburb of St. Louis. These meetings became known to the media and elicited considerable publicity about whether the Fury would remain in Fort Wayne or move elsewhere. At this point, Jay Frye and Jay Leonard indicated they would like to buy the shares which Denny and I owned and become controlling partners of the Fury. After some negotiation, Denny and I sold our controlling shares but kept other shares so that we continued on as shareholders and directors but were no longer responsible for management of the Fury.

This occurrence was a complete change but not entirely unwelcome. For a period of five years, I had signed every check and taken the lead in every financial transaction for the Fury. Not only did I go to all the games, but I sweated over all the losses and was constantly concerned about revenues and expenses. As the wins dwindled and losses mounted, there was much disagreement between Jay Frye on one hand and Denny and I on the other. Much of this was typical of any business situation: when the profits roll in, everyone gets along. But when the losses mount, the trouble begins. Some coaches maintained that we weren't able to produce a winning team because Jay became overly involved with the coaching strategy and player trades. Whether this was true or sour grapes, we may never know. During the time the Fury was in Fort Wayne, we had transitioned from Gerald Oliver to Mo McHone to Rick Barry to Clifford Ray to Bruce Stewart to Gerald Oliver again and finally to Keith Smart. There is no doubt that coaching turnover hurt the team, but we were never able to settle on a good coach. Fans complained about this as well as problems with the NBA calling up key players and forcing us to constantly rework the team.

Finally, with many teams in disarray and losing substantial amounts of money, yet another change in the Commissioner, and moving the Commissioner's office from St. Louis to Phoenix, the NBA contract was put in considerable jeopardy. Some franchises, located in the same city for many years, gave up and were moving elsewhere or going inactive.

At this point, in 1999, Isaiah Thomas came along. Isaiah had been an outstanding player in college at Indiana and then enjoyed a long career with the Detroit Pistons. Isaiah had also coached the Toronto Raptors, an NBA team, but either resigned or was fired. He was looking for something new to do and he had some cash. Isaiah proposed to handle the escalating salary problem by imposing a cap on what was paid to players through the "one owner" system. This was a method to get around the anti-trust ruling, because there would be no conspiracy if the entire league was owned by one entity. He bought the entire CBA league for about $10 million dollars.

Everyone assumed that Isaiah had an arrangement worked out with David Stern, the Commissioner of the NBA, to increase the NBA contract or modify its terms favorable to the CBA. But this did not happen. Shortly thereafter, Isaiah was offered the head coaching job for the Indiana Pacers and he lost interest in the CBA. Without strong leadership, a bad situation turned worse. The corporation that Isaiah formed to take over the CBA went into bankruptcy, leaving people who had put up money for season tickets and many creditors holding the bag.

Under Isaiah's original deal with the CBA, he paid the franchise owners differing amounts depending upon season ticket sales, revenues, etc. He purchased the Fort Wayne franchise for $1,120, 000. The owners received some of this in cash and the balance by note. After the league went into bankruptcy, Isaiah tried to renege on the notes. Fortunately, there was a personal guarantee by Isaiah on the notes to buy the Fury, thanks to Denny Sutton and myself. After Denny threatened to file a lawsuit, Isaiah eventually paid off the notes. The net effect was that of the initial investments made in the Fury, almost everyone got their money back through cash distributions and a final payment by Isaiah, and the season ticket holders got their money back.

Some thought that this was the end of the Continental Basketball Association, but it was not called the "Cockroach Basketball Association" for nothing — it was tough to kill it. Some owners bought the naming rights out of bankruptcy and started the league up again. The "new CBA" played for a number of years in many of the same cities where it existed before, but with reduced attendance, fewer expenses, no NBA contract, and considerably less media exposure. Jay Frye bought the name "Fort Wayne Fury" and talked about reviving the team in Fort Wayne, but it never got off the ground. In the end, the NBA started their own "NBA Development League" and this was finally the end of the Cockroach League.

Of the many projects with which I have been involved over the years, the Fury was the highest profile and carried more media attention than anything else. People still talk about the Fury with great hope and nostalgia about returning to the great old days of the early '90s in which there were exciting games, great halftime acts, and large crowds. It was a very exciting period in my life and I will always fondly remember the many good aspects and forget all the financial troubles and other problems. I met many wonderful people and made a number of lifelong friendships.

BIG BUMPS IN THE ROAD
1995-2005

Beginning in late 1994, I was confronted with a situation that, while not hindering me from carrying out my daily activities with family or practicing law, was nevertheless a big bump in the road. A rising PSA discovered in 1994 was constantly in the back of my mind for the next five years and actually continues to the 2020s. I went through a number of biopsies before doctors determined that this was indeed prostate cancer.

A prostate cancer biopsy is not a fun endeavor. A tube is inserted in your rectum and through the tube a long hollow needle is inserted into the prostate through the wall of the bowel. The needle has a spring-loaded small knife which is used to take a tiny specimen within the prostate. This is usually done in the doctor's office or at the hospital, and without anesthesia.

The PSA test taken in the doctor's office indicated a rising PSA, but the first three attempts at a biopsy did not reveal anything definitive. Finally, in early December 1994, I went to Indiana Medical Center in Indianapolis, and on the day before Christmas, I received a call from my doctors stating definitively that the rise of my PSA was indeed caused by prostate cancer — a wonderful Christmas gift!

Once the discovery was made, I faced a more definitive question: what to do about it? My diagnosis coincided with the rise of Google; Pat and all three of my daughters were very helpful in going on the internet and coming up with various recommendations, histories of other patients, etc. I also went to the library and did considerable research. One of the articles I turned up was called, "The Cutters, the Burners and the Freezers." It indicated that surgeons (the "cutters") almost without exception recommended prostatectomy; the radiologists (the "burners") supported radiation; and another group of doctors (the "freezers") advocated utilizing cold temperatures to freeze the cancer in the prostate. Almost everyone I talked with or sought advice from had different suggestions and articles were very self-serving depending upon the author. Both surgeons and radiation oncologists indicate that there are almost no side effects and no incontinence resulting from their particular procedure. What you find is that there is a lot of misinformation and that the side effects are considerably greater than they want you to believe.

After much consultation with my local urologist, Dr. Chris Stiedle, I decided to undergo surgery — a prostatectomy — in March 2005 in Columbus, Ohio, with Dr. John Burgers, who had trained at John Hopkins in Baltimore, the leader in prostate surgery. Preparing for the surgery is almost as difficult as the surgery itself. I went to the Red Cross and stored a pint of blood in case I needed blood during surgery. Also, the day and the evening before surgery necessitates drinking a considerable volume of liquid and utilizing Fleet enemas until you feel your insides have almost turned out — worse than preparing for a colonoscopy!

The surgery was early in the morning and I awakened from the anesthetic around 11 AM. The surgery involves almost a 12-inch incision below the navel and takes considerable time to heal. In the hospital, however, they have you up and walking around almost immediately and they also place inflatable stockings around your legs. This is to prevent blood clots from forming in the legs while you are inactive and in bed. The stay in the hospital was four days. On the fifth day, Pat put pillows in the back of our car and drove me home from Columbus.

At the time of the surgery they do a biopsy of the removed prostate to determine the advancement and aggressiveness of the cancer. They determined that the cancer had spread from the prostate to at least one of the lymph nodes and seminal vesicles. They also determined that the cancer was one of the most aggressive types — or a '10' on a Gleason scale of 1 to 10. My surgeon, Dr. John Burgers, shared this information with Pat immediately after the operation, but they elected not to tell me for a number of months.

After surgery, the procedure is to get a PSA every 30 or 60 days; once the prostate is removed, there should be no PSA whatsoever. If PSA is anything other than 0, it means there are still cancer cells in the body which are emitting the particular type of protein that the PSA test picks up. For 18 months, my PSA tests were all 0. Then, however, my PSA went up slightly. Because my cancer had been determined to be a very aggressive type, Dr. Steidle was quite concerned. He started me temporarily on a treatment called "hormonal therapy" in which I received a monthly shot of Zolodex and took a daily pill of Casodex. The purpose of hormonal therapy is to reduce the production of testosterone by the body. Prostate cancer feeds upon testosterone and the reduction of testosterone is one of the primary methods used for treatment.

I was faced with the problem of how to deal with a recurrence. Should I stay on hormonal therapy, try radiation, chemotherapy, or another method of treatment? During this period, I became acquainted with Dr. Dan Paflas, a partner of Dr. Bill Cast, a good friend. Dr. Paflas also had a very aggressive form of prostate cancer which had spread considerably before he was diagnosed (unfortunately, he later died from the cancer). Dr. Paflas was being treated by Dr. Howard Scher at Sloan-Kettering Cancer Center in New York. Dr. Scher was very well known, had been interviewed on a number of national television programs, and was rated one of the top doctors in the area of prostate cancer. Unfortunately, he was not accepting new patients. Daughter Kristi worked at the time with Bob Craig, director of the Keystone Center, who had contacts with Sloan-Kettering. Through Bob I was able to get in to see Dr. Scher.

Dr. Scher recommended that I do radiation and stay in New York for the duration of the radiation which would require 35 treatments spread over seven weeks. I inquired whether there were other options closer to Fort Wayne and learned from Dr. Scher that the University of Michigan had been very successful in developing a new three-dimensional method of providing radiation. The traditional method involves a patient lying on his or her back on a table with radiation targeted from overhead at one area of the body. However, because this method also presents a danger to the bowel, urethra, bladder and other organs in the vicinity, the radiation dosage must be reduced. With the 3D radiation, they are able to increase the dosage by radiating from not only overhead, but from all sides of the body, and hence more specifically target the prostate region without harming other organs.

Based on this knowledge as well as the more convenient location, I made the decision to have my treatments at the University of Michigan hospital in Ann Arbor. For seven weeks during the summer of 1997, I drove to Ann Arbor almost every weekday — over a two-hour trip each way. Pat accompanied me on most days, although friends joined me a few times as well. After the first week, I fell into a pattern. I would go to my office in the morning and then meet Pat at 2:00 in the afternoon at the Marriott parking lot on the northside of Fort Wayne. She would leave her car parked there and we would drive to Ann Arbor arriving around 4:45. I would get the last treatment offered each day just before 5:00. We would then go out for dinner at one of Ann Arbor's many excellent restaurants and stay at a motel overnight. Sometimes we would even play tennis or go swimming in the evening. Then the following morning, I would get one of the first treatments at 7:30 or 8:00, drive back to Fort Wayne and go back to my office to work that afternoon. Pat and I joked that anyone who observed our frequent meetings at the Marriott and leaving one car parked there must have assumed we were having an illicit love affair!

Radiation side effects bother most people. Fortunately, I got along very well, and was even able to play tennis, swim and go to the office. Sometimes, the treatments would leave me feeling tired late in the afternoon, but by and large, I felt pretty good.

I learned early that a key aspect of these daily treatments was about being lined up precisely on the table to ensure that the radiation beams would not damage the surrounding organs. This process is done initially by computer which determines the exact location for the radiation and the dosage and then creates a personal Fiberglas form or "cradle". When you arrive for treatment, the radiation therapist would get out the cradle with your name on it and position it at the exact same place on the radiation platform. It takes the therapist about five minutes to prepare you for treatment after you undress and put on a hospital gown. It takes them a few more minutes to position you precisely on the table. The radiation itself takes less than five minutes.

Because of the large number of people undergoing radiation at the hospital each day, this is a bit of a production line. I learned that it is very important to cooperate fully with the therapists to make sure that they were very careful in lining me up properly. I took them apples and various other gifts, learned all of their names, about their kids, and where they had gone to school, so that I became more than just another number that they had to deal with. I thought this was particularly important when I came very late in the afternoon and the therapists had spent a full day treating many, many patients. Whether this was actually helpful or not, I will never know, but I had no side effects from the radiation. As I learned from my dad many years before, a personal touch and kind words can never hurt.

After the radiation was completed in September of 1997, I went off hormonal therapy. Unfortunately, about five or six months later I had another recurrence as the PSA indicated that there were still cancerous cells at some place in the body. The problem with the PSA test is that it is good at detecting whether cancerous cells exist but not where; they could be in either the prostate area or any place else throughout the body. Dr. Steidle put me back on hormonal therapy with a monthly shot of Zolodex and daily Casodex pills. After going back on hormonal therapy in 1998, I traveled to Sloan-Kettering annually to see Dr. Scher. During this period, I got a PSA every 60 days, and later every 90 days. All PSA's from 1998 until 2003 were zero and I continued on hormonal therapy.

The lowering of testosterone levels makes many people very tired and a decrease in activity is usually accompanied by a weight gain. However, Sloan-Kettering advised me to go on a low-fat diet and to take vitamin E, selenium and soy extracts — all expected to further decrease testosterone levels. For over five years, I was very religious about the diet, eating almost no fat and being very careful about my diet in general. Pat, who was trained as a dietician, was excellent at keeping me committed to this diet. Even now, while I do eat some items that contain fat, I am still on a very reduced fat diet and Pat is very helpful in planning and cooking.

After three years of the hormonal therapy and restricted diet, I read in several publications and on the internet that I should consider "intermittent hormonal therapy" where you go off the shots and pills for a period of time to see if the PSA returns. In July 2003, with Dr. Scher's and Dr. Steidle's advice, I went off hormonal therapy and for the next two years my PSA was zero. Unfortunately, cancer cells have a way of mutating and lying dormant for years and then coming back. During this period, I had posted a note on my mirror that said, "Pray to God but don't stop rowing."

For a period of five years, the cancer situation was at the top of Pat's and my mind, and actually the whole family, because of the aggressive cancer and the fact that treatment was a lot more primitive. This was accompanied by some changes in lifestyle and starting to wind down my law practice in which I had been overwhelmingly engaged for almost 40 years. As the law practice wound down, other matters started to absorb my time. One of these was to become involved with the Pension Committee of Baker & Daniels including how the firm's pension funds were invested.

Also, I became more involved with the Cole Foundation and the investments there, as well as with the First Presbyterian Church's Investment Committee. These investment committees and learning about all of the factors involved — asset allocation, benchmarking the investments to set indices and setting goals — has become a second hobby for me. In addition, I began to increase my work with the various community organizations with which I was involved.

Also, in this period, new health problems arose for Pat. A heart valve situation arose as well as an arthritic right hip. She spent considerable time trying to determine whether to have a hip replacement. Some doctors advised her to proceed now while she is still healthy and others recommend not rushing and waiting as long as possible. At one point when it began to bother her excessively, she went for an examination and the doctor asked her: "Do you have trouble bending over and tying your shoes?" Pat responded, "I don't believe I do. But I do have trouble buckling my ski boots." The doctor was aghast that she was still able to ski and said if that was the case, he didn't advise a hip operation at all! So Pat held off on getting surgery at this point.

My own knee problems also resurfaced during this time. But overall, we were both able to continue skiing, playing golf, and tennis, and count ourselves very fortunate, particularly as we look at the situation with our friends, including many we have lost over the last number of years. Keeping active, weight under control, exercising and eating properly have helped keep the ravages of advancing age at bay.

Having begun this chapter on a down note by talking about declining health — something older people are prone to do — I will now turn to much more important things. We have been fortunate to have seven grandchildren in eight years. Our first granddaughter, Victoria ("Tori") Parker Johnson was born in October 1994 to Pam and Rodney in Portland, Oregon. After Tori came Haley in 1995, born in Washington, D.C. to Carole and Dan. Then, Christopher was born to Pam and Rodney in 1996. Then Will to Dan and Carole in 1999 on Christmas day! Coming along later, was Sammy and Sasha, respectively in 2001 and 2002, born to Kristi and Frank in Dillon, Colorado.

At this point there were three boys and three girls, with each family having one of each. Finally, a little surprise came along for Carole and Dan. Graham was born in 2003 in a car on the way to the hospital in Burlington, Vermont. Dan and Carole had gone to the hospital the night before but the doctor told Carole she was not ready. They then went home, an hour away, and about four hours later started back to the hospital again. About 20 miles up the road, Dan was forced to pull into a Shell station in Waterbury, Vermont, and delivered the baby with the help of a lady from EMS on his cell phone. By the time the EMS crew got to the Shell station, the baby was delivered and lying on Carole's stomach. Fortunately, it all turned out well, but it was a hairy time, particularly since Carole was 45 at the time. The name 'Sheldon" for the Shell station or "Carson" were passed over for Graham.

One of our joys has been able to get all, or many, of the families together, since they are scattered all over the country. We were able to do this with a trip to Disney World in 2000, and to rent Mark GiaQuinta's cottage at Lake Oliver in 2001, 2002 and 2004. During this decade, the families have made a number of changes and moves. Pam got her CPA license and Rodney attended night school while working full time at Intel to get his law degree. Rodney has had an excellent career at Intel where he has been very involved with the development of the Pentium and other big selling computer chips. Pam worked at two CPA firms, Grant Thorton, LLP. and Geffen Mesher & Co. Once they had two children, she taught accounting at a vocational school.

Dan and Carole moved in D.C. from Capitol Hill to Takoma Park and then on to Chevy Chase where they bought an old house. They spent considerable time and money in fixing it up, later selling it for a considerable sum and moving to Vermont. Carole had worked as an environmental journalist, then as legislative staff in Congress, and at the Pentagon as a

Director of Pollution Prevention. Dan was an environmental attorney for the Natural Resources Defense Council, and then served as Chief of Staff at the Department of Energy and later Assistant Secretary of Energy. Dan then took a new position with Northern Power in Waitsfield, Vermont. After being with them for a period of time, he then moved on to be a partner in New Energy Capital, a venture capital company, and then to California with Google and later Stanford.

For a great number of years, Kristi had been a mediator on environmental matters with Keystone Center in Keystone, Colorado. Later Kristi moved to Lafayette, near Boulder, and started her own business in environmental consulting and mediation.

Pat has kept very active with McMillen Center for Health Education — being not only a founder, but on the board of directors, for 25 years. In addition, she has been active with Boys and Girls Club and Junior League. However, one of her very important endeavors over the last ten years has been learning to use a computer which is both her best friend and worst enemy.

After having bought a condo in Aspen in 1978, and then trading it in 1984 for another place, we finally decided to sell in 2004. There were two or three reasons for this. First, each of the kids have access to skiing close to their own home, although they all still enjoyed coming to Aspen. Second, they were building a great number of new condos near ours and we were concerned as to what this would ultimately do to both rentals and the market price. Third, we had been very fortunate in that we did not have to spend much to remodel our condo at this point, but it appeared that very substantial upgrades would be needed soon if we wanted to continue renting. It now appears that we were a bit premature because the market - after being in the doldrums for three or four years - continued to rise and prices increased. These condos now sell for triple the price at which we sold.

My "supposed" retirement at the law firm was in 1999 at age 70. However, I continued to practice on a part time basis for seven more years. While I cut back on the practice considerably, the daily routine for a number of years was to go to the Cole Foundation in the morning, review the grant applications, finances, handle the checks and other matters, and then head to Baker & Daniels, where I usually had a client or partner lunch, and then work at the firm in the afternoon. Work at the firm included a small amount of corporate work, but was primarily estate planning and estate work. Much of my time involves meeting with clients and letting the smart paralegals handle the procedural matters of the estates. Many of the clients that I worked with for years I have passed along to either Joe Kimmell, Larry Shine or Tim Haffner.

Another organization with which I have been considerably involved is the Allen County War Memorial Coliseum. I was appointed to the five-person Coliseum Board in 1999, and elected President in 2005. The Coliseum has had over a million visitors a year since 2000 and has a direct economic impact of over $100 million on local restaurants, hotels, motels, and retail stores in the Ft Wayne area. Many of the most important events in the community happen at the Coliseum, including major concerts such as Cher, the Eagles, Kiss, Willie Nelson and others; Komet hockey, IPFW basketball; the Shrine Circus; Three Rivers Midway; and almost all high school and university graduations take place here as do any major political rallies. It is truly a community complex. One of the highlights was when the Coliseum expanded in 2003. The existing roof, which was many thousand square feet, was raised on high jacks and the new frame was built under it. This process raised the Coliseum roof by 49 feet, but kept the original roof intact, saving a couple million dollars on the remodeling cost. The expansion increased the seating capacity from 10,000 to over 13,000.

Another non-profit I was involved with for over ten years was the Fort Wayne Sports Corp, with a mission of promoting sports in the Fort Wayne area. After serving on the board for many years, I served as President. At the annual meeting when I was President, our speaker was Peyton Manning, the Colts (and later Denver Broncos) quarterback, and I was privileged to introduce him. We sat at the table and chatted for a short time while the previous speaker talked. He made some notes on the back of a napkin, got up, and spoke for about 20 minutes — a very well-spoken and intelligent young man, which we now see all the time in his many television endorsements.

During my term as President, the Sports Corp launched the Lifetime Sports Academy, offering free instruction to youth 8 to 18 in golf, tennis and swimming at McMillen Park for seven weeks in the summer. While team sports are important, it is also desirable to learn an individual sport that you can play throughout your lifetime. The Academy has grown each year and now about 400 kids attend the program each day in the summer. Instruction is by professional instructors in all three sports.

The Fort Wayne Allen County Economic Development Alliance and the Junior Achievement Business Hall of Fame are other groups which I have been involved in. Also, for over 33 years I have done an annual briefing to a group called Leadership Fort Wayne. This is a group of young leaders in the Fort Wayne community that meet all day once a month to learn about the Fort Wayne community, with the objective that they will get involved in leadership positions with community organizations. It has been my privilege to brief this group annually on the Economic History of Fort Wayne. I have a lecture that has evolved over the years detailing the history of Fort Wayne — from the early battles against the Indians fought by General Anthony Wayne, through the development of the Wabash and Erie Canal, the bringing of International Harvester to Fort Wayne, the founding of Lincoln Life, the depression, the World War II years, the recession of the early '80s and many other factors. I have enjoyed doing this for many years and have received many nice letters from young leaders about how they have enjoyed the presentation. I tell them I am like the Chinese and Russians — I rewrite the history from time to time. I really don't, but I do update the lecture as I come across new material!

For these community involvements, I was nominated in 2000 for an Honorary Doctorate by Purdue University. I received a robe and a gown, and I am now an honorary Doctor of Letters of Purdue University.

Other awards which have fallen my way in recent years are the Sagamore of the Wabash Award, one of the highest Indiana State Awards, and a New Castle High School Distinguished Alumni Award presented in 2005. This was the first year this award was presented, and I was pleased to be included with Robert Allen, the now retired Chairman of AT&T, and Dr. Charles Modlin, a transplant surgeon at Cleveland Clinic, as one of the first three.

One of the great privileges we have had over the past ten years is to maintain a social relationship with Justice Sandra Day O'Connor and her husband, John, and we kept up a correspondence and relationship for a great number of years. They came to Fort Wayne and spoke at the Chamber Annual Dinner in 1991. In 2004, I asked Sandra to come to Fort Wayne to dedicate a windmill in her honor at the Midwest Windmill Museum. She and her brother had written a book about growing up on a ranch in Arizona during the 1930s, where she described how important the windmills were for keeping water available for the cattle in the ranch. If the windmills went down and were not repaired immediately, they were not able to get water to the cattle and the cattle would die.

She described certain types of windmills and in talking with my friend, Russell Baker at the Windmill Museum in Kendallville, he indicated that this particular type of windmill — a "Sampson" — had been made in Southern Illinois up until the 1920s. These were the same type of windmills Sandra had on the Lazy B Ranch in Arizona. The Windmill Museum then located one of these windmills, brought it back to Kendallville, repaired and erected it, and agreed to dedicate it to Justice O'Connor. Sandra agreed to come to Indiana for the dedication and we made arrangements to send a jet to pick her and John up in D.C. and then return them after the weekend. She asked if it might be possible for her brother to join us since he had also been involved with the book. So, we made arrangements to have her brother, Alan Day, to come also. Alan then called me and said he had a young lady friend, Trudy, and would it be possible to invite her? So we invited Trudy. Alan called a few days later, indicating that he and the Justice rarely got together with their cousins who live down in Kentucky, and would it be possible to invite them too? We invited the cousins, who not only came, but brought their two children with them!

While we provided accommodations for Justice O'Connor and her husband at our house and for Alan and Trudy at the hotel, we did not provide accommodations for the rest of the family! The whole event was a very excellent weekend. We had a luncheon on the veranda at the Fort Wayne Country Club, followed by the windmill dedication in Kendallville and then dinner that evening with Justice O'Connor and her husband, Alan Day and Trudy, and the cousins at Joseph Dicuis, a very nice restaurant in nearby Roanoke.

Pat played tennis the next day partnering with John O'Connor against another couple. The Justice, Alan Day, Trudy, and I played a round of golf at the Sycamore. Hills. While the Justice is a reasonably good golfer, she did not have a very good day. Sycamore has a lot of water holes and creeks and so she ended up with a number of balls in the water. However, the game that we played was one in which you pick a new partner for each hole and the game is as much about your strategy in choosing partners for that particular hole as it is about golfing skill. So, while she did not play well, she proved very astute in picking good partners and ended up as the big money winner.

When the Justice visited Ft Wayne earlier, she had no security. This time she was accompanied by five federal marshals, two from local offices and three out of Chicago. The marshals insisted on providing all the transportation and logistics. They proceeded to set up in our driveway for an overnight watch, but the Justice would not hear of it and dismissed them. However, they moved only a short distance away from our house and kept a close watch on the neighborhood during the Justice's visit.

During this 10-year period, Pat and I also went back to a few high school reunions. Pat went back to her high school reunion where she was selected as the outstanding person in her class of over 500 at Bloom High School. We had an arrangement where she did not go to my reunions and I did not go to hers. However, we both returned to our 50th DePauw Reunion in 2001, where we were amazed by the number of classmates coming back. Our total class was around 400, and I think we had 260 people back, plus spouses. Considering that 50 years has passed, and a number of the people were deceased, this was very outstanding.

STILL MOVIN' ALONG

2005-2015

For a number of years, I had no PSA whatsoever which meant that the prostate cancer was in remission. The cancer came back in 2011 and bone scans showed metastasis in a rib and collar bone. After trips to both Sloan-Kettering in New York and Mayo Clinic, I went back to drugs which I had been on previously, but which proved to be no longer effective. Finally, I was put on a new drug called Zytiga in September 2013. For a number of years, this controlled both the PSA and the metastasis, only to stop working again later.

One of the things that I have been able to do — having had prostate cancer for over 25 years — is to counsel other patients similarly diagnosed. Having had the most aggressive type of cancer with a Gleason score of 10 (the highest), I can give newly diagnosed patients some hope that there are many new medications and other types of treatment that will enable them to live with and control the dreaded disease. As I told one person recently diagnosed, prostate cancer is just "another damn thing" that you have to learn to get along with in life, but it is not the death sentence it once was. There have been so many new types of treatment developed over the past several years and from everything I read, we may well be on the horizon of either a complete cure or substantial suppression of getting prostate cancer.

Pat continues to see her cardiologist at Mayo about her tricuspid valve, rapid heartbeat and arrhythmia. She finally made a decision to have her hip replaced in 2011. It was a highly successful operation and she has been back on the tennis courts two or three times weekly. I got a knee replacement in 2012 and we both have progressed quite well. In addition to tennis, Pat plays golf and is out and about every day. We both went skiing in April, 2014, skiing from the top to bottom of Aspen Mountain just like the old days. We were a bit slower, but still able to take most of the same runs we have skied for 60 years. In general, we have been fortunate, very active, and in pretty good health over the last ten years.

In addition to tennis, Pat attends numerous meetings of various community organizations. She was on the History Center Board for a number of years, served as Secretary and could have stayed on to be President, but elected not to do so. She is still very active with The McMillen Center for Health Education, Junior League, and continues to chair the Scholarship Board for Rea Magnet Wire.

One thing I try to do every day is to walk up and down stairs instead of taking the elevator. My assistant, Brenda, is on a different floor than I am at the law office, so I take the stairs a number of times daily. When our offices moved back to the PNC Bank Building (old Fort Wayne National Building), I made sure that Brenda was on a separate floor so I would be forced to continue the daily climbing of stairs to meet with her. I may regret this decision down the road when my knees are not performing as well.

The past ten years has seen a number of changes within our family. Pam and Rodney still live in Portland, Oregon, and Rodney is still involved with Intel. He has a very responsible job with a number of engineers reporting to him in the development of new products. Pam, unfortunately, began having difficulty with her knees and hips and ultimately had both knees and hips replaced.

Dan and Carole have moved various times in the past ten years. From the District of Columbia, they moved twice in Vermont, and then to Piedmont, California. Dan originally went to California with Google and was then offered a position with Stanford where he headed up a "think tank" along with teaching in both the Business School and Law School. Carole, in addition to taking care of all the family (certainly no small job in her family!), has also been involved with a number of projects in the global health area and continued to consult on environmental policy work.

Over the last three years, Kristi has moved from Dillon to Louisville, Colorado, a smaller town adjacent to Boulder where she started her own business in environmental mediation.

We have been fortunate during the last ten years to do a number of trips with the whole family. We took a cruise to Alaska through the Inner Passageway. It was a great trip; all the kids really enjoyed the cruise ship where they could run everywhere on their own and there were enough activities for both young and old. The ship was huge and all the passageways looked the same. The elevator nearest our rooms had a piece of art in a glass case that we dubbed "the purple fart". When we saw this, we knew we were "home."

Also, in the summer of 2014, we took an extensive

trip to China, seeing almost exactly the same cities that we had gone through in 1982 with Pam, Carole and Kristi. The changes that have taken place in the 32 years have been absolutely amazing - it is impossible to believe that any country would change as much as China has since the early 1980s. For example, when we visited Guilin in 1982, there was one riverboat for tourists — now there are hundreds.

Some of our best summers with the family were spent at Culver Military Academy, about 50 miles from Fort Wayne. "Culver Family Camp" was outstanding and included every activity which was available to their 1500 young summer campers — sailing, waterskiing, trap and skeet shooting, riflery, archery, golf, horseback riding (100 horses), zip-lining & rope climbing, swimming, and on and on. It was a wonderful week with everyone signing up for all activities they most wanted to do. Best of all, they offered three excellent meals daily so no one had to worry about shopping for groceries or cooking.

During this 10-year period we have kept in close touch with many of our good friends - the Chapmans, the Christoffs, the Deisters, Earl and Vicki Goode in Indianapolis, Ed and Nancy White and Sandra Day O'Connor in Phoenix. Sandra's husband, John, passed in 2009, but she is still going strong. Unfortunately, when you get north of 80, you find that you lose many of your friends and family each year. In the past ten years, we have lost many — my stepmother, Lora Parker, who died at age 99 in 2007, just eight months short of 100. Other family members lost were Will Parker and his wife, Lois, and my Aunt Lois Parker, also in her 90s. Friends lost included Don and Helen Butler, Joe and Ginne Christoff, Jane Deister, Betsy Chapman, Bob Keesling, Ed Arnold, and my long-time law school friends Jim Buchanan in Colorado and Granger and Joan Cook in Lake Forest, Illinois. While they are still with us, our good friends Jim and Lee Vann moved to Charlotte, North Carolina and then on to Denver. We still keep up with them by phone and internet but it is not the same as them being here in Fort Wayne.

Our law firm merged about three years ago with Faegre & Benson out of Minneapolis. Baker & Daniels had grown to about 400 and Faegre & Benson was slightly larger. Now we have between 800 and 900 attorneys in places as far flung as Beijing and Shanghai, London, Silicon Valley, Denver, as well as in Minneapolis and Indianapolis. I asked the Managing Partner one day whether anyone in the new firm had ever practiced as a solo lawyer. He responded that he didn't think so. "Well, now you do," I replied. I finally retired from the law firm in 2009. The firm merged again in 2019 and is now called Faegre, Drinker with over 1300 attorneys.

Pat and I make an effort to keep up with world events in order for me to be able to converse with the younger lawyers that I have lunch with and for Pat to talk to her younger tennis friends. We read two newspapers, including The Wall Street Journal, and watch at least two television newscasts daily. We each have a computer at home and I also have one at the Cole office and at the law office. We both have iPhones and Pat has recently changed her computer to a Mac, and is really quite proficient. She keeps up with our children, and sometimes grandchildren, and friends with the computer, emailing and occasionally texting and Skyping. Older people who do not wish to try the computer are really missing out on their ability to communicate with family and friends.

Although many of our friends have retired either year-round or spend the winter months in Florida or the Southwest, we have in effect decided to retire "in place." We enjoy our home, and with my job at the Cole Foundation and the other activities we are both involved with, it would be impossible to be gone for four or five months. Being gone for an extended period also means finding new doctors in a vacation area, which our retired or semi-retired friends tell us is no small matter.

From a sports and exercise standpoint, Pat, as indicated earlier, is quite active with tennis two or three times weekly and almost a fanatic about exercising. She has had scoliosis for a number of years but because of extensive exercising has kept it under control. We play golf in the summer sometimes just ourselves, but usually with other couples. My handicap has held up somewhat over the past ten years, going from a 12 to now 16. Each summer I am able to shoot two or three games in the 70s and at least 50 percent of the time, I am able to shoot my age or better. Of course, this gets easier each year as my age goes up. I also do daily exercises with Pat, but I am not as disciplined as she is in keeping a schedule.

The Fort Wayne Fury was sold in 2003 so I was no longer involved as a professional team owner at this time. Nevertheless, I continued to be very involved with the Allen County War Memorial Coliseum — where the Fury played — and was elected President of the Board in 2005. The Coliseum continues to be one of the very outstanding organizations in the region and I feel fortunate to have served on the Board for so many years and even today. Over the years, almost all of the outstanding celebrities have come to the Coliseum at one time or another — including five Presidents, Elvis Presley, Bob Hope and many more. It is really more of a regional civic center, with the hundreds of events that take place each year. I prepared a lecture about the history and importance of the Coliseum to our community and have presented it to the Quest Club and a number of other organizations over the years.

Finally, on sports, I was also fortunate enough to be inducted into the DePauw Athletic Hall of Fame in 2007 based on my college years of playing basketball and running track as a pole vaulter. A photo of me in DePauw basketball attire — short pants and all — has been hung in Spiece Fieldhouse in

Fort Wayne, and I am both surprised and pleased by the number of people who have commented to me about seeing it.

Pat and I have continued to stay involved in many community organizations during this period — Pat with the History Center, McMillen Center for Health Education, Junior League and a scholarship Board. My focus has been largely on economic development organizations — the Fort Wayne-Allen County Economic Alliance, and the Chamber of Commerce. In 2013, both of these organizations merged into what is now called Greater Fort Wayne, Inc.

My involvement with the Allen County Economic Development Alliance led to me writing articles for the newspaper arguing that Fort Wayne had "lost its swagger". I indicated that when I knew people from Fort Wayne in college, they always walked with a bit of a swagger because at the time Fort Wayne had lots of industry and jobs and everyone wanted to live and work here. These articles led to the Alliance hosting the "Swagger Awards" — an annual luncheon and awards ceremony for business leaders that had increased their employment. Because of my long service with economic development, I was the first recipient of a Swagger Award and the award was also named after me. I am quite proud of this award and even prouder to present the "Maclyn Parker Swagger Award" to new recipients at this annual awards event.

Another board I have been on from the very beginning is the Northeast Indiana Regional Partnership which coordinates economic development throughout the 11-county region. I formed a 501(c)(3) called the Northeast Indiana Foundation, which is a primary funder for the Northeast Indiana Partnership. I also served on the board of the Northeast Indiana Innovation Center and helped make significant grants to that organization through the Cole Foundation to help build the Center and several additions.

At this point I had been on the Cole Board for over 55

years, beginning in the 1960s. I was Secretary for many years and have been President for over 30 years. The Foundation has been a big part of my life and I am pleased with all of the good work we have done. We have given scholarships to almost 4,000 students from Noble County as well as a good number in LaGrange county. We have given money to build the school auditorium in Kendallville, YMCA's in three cities, provide Fort Wayne Philharmonic performances at numerous schools and nursing homes, help build hiking trails and many other good projects. We currently grant over $1.2M each year, and over the life of the Foundation we have granted over $50M to all types of causes.

Other organizations that I spend some time with are the Indiana State Museum from Indianapolis and the Howard Arnold Foundation. I set up this foundation for a client who died a number of years ago leaving $350,000 to benefit Fort Wayne area nonprofit organizations. Over the years, this foundation has grown to $1,500,000, and we are currently giving away almost $70,000 each year.

Serving on the Howard Arnold Foundation Board with me is my long-time law partner and friend Larry Shine. Larry has a very interesting story. Larry had one child before his wife died of cancer, another by a surrogate, and then ended up adopting seven children, mostly from Guatemala or Peru. As a single father, he raised all nine kids on his own. Two of the boys are now in military service; a girl graduated from Indiana University and his oldest son from Notre Dame and is now with a major investment firm in Chicago. Oprah Winfrey heard about Larry and brought the entire family — including the family bulldog — on her television show to share their story in a full half-hour program.

Other organizations I am involved with are Visit Fort Wayne which was formerly the Convention and Visitors Bureau, and Questa Foundation, an organization devoted to making loans for kids to go college with a unique system. They loan $5,000 a year for four years, and if the student at graduation has a C+ average, they will forgive $5,000 of the loan; if the student goes to a local university, they will forgive another $5,000, and if the student stays to live in northeast Indiana, they will forgive another $5,000, for a total of $15,000 of the $20,000 borrowed. A very unique loan method, indeed, and it has encouraged many students to keep their talents and grow their families in Fort Wayne and surrounding communities.

Pat and I have been very fortunate to receive community recognition for our work with these various organizations. First, and most importantly, Pat received the Tapestry Award from IPFW, which is an award given to the most outstanding woman in the community involved in volunteer service. This is a whole day event in which they bring in a nationally known speaker — in Pat's case actress Sissy Spacek — with 1700 people attending, breakout sessions on various topics, and sponsor booths. It is billed as a "Day for Women" and has awarded more than $1 million in scholarships for students since it started in 2002. Pat also received a Junior League award and we both were honored by the McMillen Center and received the Janus award, as an outstanding couple supporting community service.

In addition to the Swagger Award, during the past ten years, I received the IPFW Champion Award for community service. Also, I received a community service award from DePauw in addition to the Athletic Hall of Fame Award. From the Better Business Bureau, I received the Torch Award, which is for the "community individual of integrity".

One of the very pleasant things we have done over the last 10 years is to take our grandchildren on a trip with just Pat and I when they turn 13. We took Victoria to Cancun, Mexico; Haley to Costa Rica; Chris to the Dominican Republic; Will to Hawaii, Sam to Cuba, and Sasha to Venice, Italy. Unfortunately, a planned trip down the Mississippi River with Graham was cancelled due to flooding and other problems. It has been a wonderful experience, being able to spend a week or more with each of the grandchildren and getting to know them better, particularly since they all live so many miles away.

INTO OUR NINETIES
2015-2020

Pat and I have had a running joke for many years: "We married for better or worse but not for lunch." In other words, one or both of us would be out exercising, working, seeing friends old and new, and generally staying active — and not be home for lunch.

This credo, however, almost had a very ugly twist. On January 9, 2018, I was at the Cole Foundation in the morning and left as I usually do around 11:00 to drive downtown to my office where I would have lunch with the law partners or others. But while driving downtown, I remembered that Pat played tennis that morning and decided that I should head home and have lunch with her. So, I turned the car around and came home for lunch.

Pat made us soup and sandwiches and as we sat at the

table chatting, I suddenly realized that Pat is talking, but no words are coming out. I run my hand in front of her eyes and see that they are glazed over. I immediately grabbed the phone and called 911.

Looking back, I should have moved Pat off the chair and laid her on the floor because while I was calling, she passed out and slid off the chair to the floor with resultant bruises to her legs, hip and ribs.

EMS came almost immediately, and she was taken to Lutheran Hospital where they quickly decided, as I had concluded myself, that she had had a stroke. I was advised that she was a good candidate for a tPA, or tissue plasminogen activator, which is a procedure to break up the blood clot which was lodged above her left eye. The tPA has to be done within three hours of the stroke in order to be effective. Luckily, we went to the hospital immediately and they were able to do the tPA which avoids many of the unfortunate results which often occur unless the clot is dissolved immediately.

I am so grateful that I decided to come home for lunch that day. If I had gone to my office all afternoon, I would not have been home for Pat's stroke or to get her to the hospital for many hours and well past the time when a tPA could have been performed.

After her stroke, Pat stayed in the hospital for ten days as the doctors were very careful to let the blood clot in her brain and the ensuing pool of blood caused by the tPA dissipate. She then spent two weeks in Lutheran Rehab Hospital and a month at Sage Bluff Nursing Home before coming home.

Upon returning home we employed caregivers, Patti Nichols and Teri Haff, who are with us weekdays while I take over on the weekends. Pat has made significant progress in recovering from the stroke but still requires assistance to do a number of household tasks, pay bills, go to the doctor's office, etc.

Given my advanced case of prostate cancer, Pat's stroke, my fortuitous decision to come home to lunch that day, and finally a tree falling on our house one morning just a few feet away from our bed, we both believe that someone up there is looking out for us, saying: "Hey, your time is not up yet. You have too much to do down there and you better hang around and get it done!"

On the tree, we were awakened suddenly at 5:00 in the morning on May 20, 2019 by a thunderous crash during a rainstorm. I immediately thought that lightning had struck the house. That was not the case, but what happened was equally bad! Luckily, the lights still worked and as we walked from our bedroom to the living room, we discovered that a 30-inch maple tree had broken off about ten feet from the ground and crashed through the roof into our house, leaving two holes in the living room almost four feet in diameter. A green branch with leaves still on it was hanging down in the middle of the living room like a chandelier! The torrential rains continued to fall including into these holes, over our furniture, carpets and all the way through to the basement.

Pat and I tried to put buckets and kettles down to catch the rain but it was overwhelming and a lost cause. I finally said to Pat, "let's go into the family room and sit down. I promise I won't have a heart attack if you don't have another stroke". I then reached the contractor who had worked for us in 2012 when another tree fell close to the bedroom, but also missed us by a few feet. The contractor sent a crew right away to put up a tarp on the roof.

Luckily, the tree fell at an angle onto our living room instead of straight down, which would have been directly into our bedroom where we were asleep. The cleanup was less dramatic but created new problems. The patch on the roof did not hold, even after being redone three times. Every time there was a heavy rain, water would flood through the holes again. This continued for at least three weeks during one of the heaviest May rains anyone could recall. A large crane was brought in to take the log off the roof, over the top of the house to the front drive where it was cut up and carried away. The crane operator told me that the maximum load for his crane was 3,000 pounds. The log weighed 3,600 pounds and he was quite concerned about lifting it and getting it over the house. But thankfully he was able to accomplish this task. It took many months and a great deal of anguish to put the house in order.

Among all the other excitement during the month of May, my cardiologist had me go into the hospital for a cardiac catheterization and have a stent implanted.

As Pat and I roll into our 90s, we are finding that everything is not as easy as it was in our 80s and we are spending considerably more time on health matters — visiting doctors, buying and sorting through prescriptions, and taking care of knees and other aching body parts. Dressing, which used to take almost no time, now goes a lot slower, too.

But, in general, we have both been quite fortunate — health issues have slowed us down but only somewhat. My prostate cancer was a bump in the road, but in general my business and professional life as well as my golf and other recreation held up pretty much into the late 80s. Pat's tennis continued until age 88, and then abruptly ended on the day of her stroke.

We have also both been fortunate to have enough outside interests that occupy our minds and keep us busy, so that every morning there is a reason that we have had to get up and be on deck to get things done. The most important of these for me is my job at Cole Foundation. While Emily Pichon, Kristi Celico and I share the workload, we still have to maintain the investments, review grant applications, prepare for directors' meetings, write checks and the many other administrative tasks involved in running a foundation.

At first glance, it may seem easy to "give away money". However, if one tries to do a reasonably good job at it, it takes a great deal of time and effort, critical thinking and judgment, investigation of facts, review of documents, and meeting with many people — just like running any other business.

In addition to Cole Foundation, there is also the Howard Arnold Foundation, in which Larry Shine and I have been involved with along with PNC Bank for many years. We decided to operate this out of the Cole Foundation offices, retaining PNC as our investment advisor.

I have also spent the last ten years as President of the Downtown Development Trust. The first two years were primarily focused on obtaining options on land in the Fort Wayne downtown area between Berry and Wayne streets and developing the Ash Project, which includes the Ash Brokerage, a bank, restaurant and other businesses as well as a 12-story apartment building. Ash moved all of their employees from a suburban location to downtown, adding a whole new dimension of workers and residents to our Fort Wayne downtown area.

Our other major project is called "The Landing" — where we purchased seven buildings on Columbia Street for rehabilitation. Buying real estate in a downtown location where owners have held property for many years and know a major project is happening is not an easy task. Sellers ask outlandish amounts for their property, even though in most instances, the buildings are almost 150 years old and require extensive rehab.

The matter was further complicated by the fact that the Downtown Development Trust had no funding whatsoever. In the beginning, I made a small gift of $5,000 in order for us to open a bank account and have enough money to pay minimal expenses. From that point on, we have had to rely on the Fort

Wayne Community Foundation, bank loans, grants of City funds, and various other organizations for all of our building purchases. In total we have paid out over $4.7 million for the buildings and we did this without using any of our own funds. I am often reminded of my good friend, Leonard Murphy, who bought a number of buildings in Indianapolis and downtown Fort Wayne without having any equity money involved in the purchase. He did it all by being able to borrow 100 percent of the purchase price. With zero equity or even money for options for our purchases on The Landing, I felt that we were able to do Leonard one better!

After purchasing the majority of the buildings, we advertised for developers to develop the entire street as a commercial and entertainment area, much like "Old Towns" in Chicago, Denver and a number of other places. We received bids from six developers, which we narrowed down to three, and then did extensive interviews. All three developers that we had on our "final cut" list had done projects in other cities rehabbing old buildings into commercial and entertainment venues. We finally settled on The Model Group, which had extensive experience in rehabbing older buildings in the "Over the Rhine" region of Cincinnati and creating the type of building, office, restaurant and entertainment area we were looking for. We then sold the properties to Model Group, who have been remodeling the properties for the last 2 years and very shortly will open the whole street to the public.

One regret I have about the remodeling of The Landing was the removal of the magnificent trees that lined the street. In the 1970s, I was the attorney for Joan White who had purchased a number of these same buildings on Columbia just as the street was undergoing an earlier revitalization. Joan, Pat, and I helped the Fort Wayne Park Department plant small sycamore trees, about 4" in diameter, down both sides of the street. Now almost 50 years later, the trees were small no more but three feet or greater in diameter and towered above the buildings, many more than 50 feet high. Unfortunately, in redoing the road and sidewalks the trees had to be taken down. I spent considerable time lobbying to keep even one or two of the great trees on the street, but to no avail.

The Landing is just a block long area of Columbia Street, but it will have gates at both ends so cars can be blocked off and tables brought out in the evenings from the restaurants. The idea is to create an open-air mall for walking, shopping, dining and entertainment. The new Promenade Park, which opened in August 2019, is only one-half block away from The Landing and a new hotel is also being built close by. Between these three projects, the whole center of gravity for nightlife and entertainment will most likely shift to this area. I am very proud of this project.

I am also particularly happy about my effort to persuade the owner of one three-story building on the Landing still remaining in separate hands to allow a well-known muralist to paint a 40-foot-tall bison and flock of passenger pigeons on an open brick wall facing Harrison street. Painted by Tim Parsley, the mural is intended to bring a vision of the American West to The Landing with the solitary bison and a hint of extinction.

The mural is outstanding, located in a very prominent location, and has received universal acclaim. Even more exciting, this project helped spark an interest in having other murals to be painted all over the city — creating new exposure to public art. Further, the City Council decided to establish a Public Art Commission with funding from the City and other sources.

Another project I have become very involved with is the creation of a bridge across a major highway for students taking classes at both IPFW (now PFW) and the vocational college Ivy Tech. I first learned of the need for a bridge in 2008 from Linda Ruffolo, the Development Director at IPFW, who said there were real safety and time concerns for students traveling from one campus to the other.

Even though the bridge connects two campuses, it will be owned by the State because it's over a state highway. The State Highway required a match of $900,000 from the universities to build a walking bridge across the six lanes of traffic and median. Linda came to the Cole Foundation for the matching funds. Cole Foundation was agreeable to do one-half of the match; the other one-half would have to come from another source. Our family agreed to be the other source.

The bridge is a unique and complex design. A single pylon approximately 100 feet high on the Purdue Ft Wayne side supports the bridge by cables. The pylon is curved and stainless steel which gleams brightly during the day. At night the pylon is lit by hundreds of LED lights which can be seen almost a mile away from the highway and can change color.

Unfortunately, while construction was proceeding on our bridge, a pedestrian bridge fell in Florida shortly after completion. The Indiana State Highway Commission then began requesting many additional safety requirements for the bridge using stricter criteria from a vehicular bridge standard to be applied to this walking bridge. This delayed substantially the completion of the bridge and it is now expected to be done and dedicated in late 2020.

All in all, I am up and out every day. I developed a philosophy about retirement some time ago: A bad day is when I wake up and have nothing to do. I have come to realize that I feel much better and forget my own health problems by being out and about every day and trying to contribute. Being active allows me to stay in touch with old friends and meet new people, particularly younger people who are constantly coming up with new and interesting ideas. This in turn stimulates my own energy and ideas and gives me a reason to get out of bed every day. People constantly ask when I will retire and

I reply — even at age 91 — that is something I should think about, although not very hard. As long as I can continue to make some small contribution and my health permits, I hope to be involved with family, community and life.

As I sit at my desk in 2020 and look out over the city at the projects that are under construction — a new hotel and various remodelings of old buildings on The Landing, I am amazed and pleased at all that has happened to our city of Fort Wayne, particularly in the last 20 years. For a mid-sized city in the Midwest rust-belt, we have made considerable progress. Younger people are returning to the city as a good place to work, live and raise a family.

I believe that Pat and I made the Right Choice in choosing Fort Wayne in 1957. Looking back at our choices of Chicago, San Francisco and Indianapolis, these cities have also grown and prospered. But we have been much better off in Fort Wayne where we have been able to put down roots and get involved, and this has been a better choice for us. Fort Wayne is a right-sized city that embraces newcomers and gives them the opportunity to be involved with the community in significant ways.

For our family, Fort Wayne was not only a good place to earn a living, but a special place to raise a family. We were able to buy a decent home, send our kids to good schools, raise them in a place with strong moral standards, a keen sense of community, and make good, lasting friendships. I am proud to have been involved and contribute in some small way in building this community I love.

LANDING IN THE RIGHT PLACE

*Above. Family in China, 1982, shortly after the Cultural Revolution.
Below. Skiing at Sam's Knob, Snowmass, 1983.*

Above. Loss of four Fort Wayne businessmen and friends in aircraft accident in Lake Huron, 1965. Left. Henry and Cora Blanton in the news after Henry thwart's robbers with a shotgun, 1988.

Above. Fort Wayne Fury games often sold out in early years.
Below. Sportscaster Hilliard Gates interviews Senator Dan
Coats at Fort Wayne Fury opening game, 1991.

Above. With NBA Hall of Famer and Fury coach Rick Barry, 1993. Left. With two Fort Wayne Fury dancers, 1992.

LANDING IN THE RIGHT PLACE

Above Left. Pam & Rodney wedding at Fort Wayne Presbyterian Church, 1984. Above Right. Carole & Dan's wedding in Ashcroft, Colorado, 1989. Below. Kristi & Frank's wedding in Breckenridge, Colorado, 1999.

Left. With Sandra Day O'Connor in Fort Wayne for windmill dedication, 2004. Below. Pat and George H.W. Bush at Fort Wayne political event, 1990. Below Left. Pat with two promising golfing students, one of which is Arnold Palmer.

GOLFER PAT PARKER
AND TWO OF HER PROMISING STUDENTS

Above. The pig that came to Mac's 65th birthday party. Below. Howard and Betsy Chapman and Takaoka businessman Kimio Arai at Sister City celebration in Japan.

Above. The Maclyn Parker Swagger Award for Community Vision and Leadership, an annual award given by Greater Fort Wayne. Below. Pat's headshot for the 2013 Tapestry Award, and with Actress Sissy Spacek, who spoke at the event.

LANDING IN THE RIGHT PLACE

At the Durant condominium in Aspen, 1988.

Above. Mac and granddaughter Tori Johnson in D.C. for the Veteran's Honor Flight, 2018. Below Left. Pat rollerblading into her 80s. Below Right. After a fall at Mayo clinic in 2019, which landed both Mac and Pat in the emergency room.

The tree that fell on the Covington Lake house, 2019, creating a new living room chandelier.

Renewal of the historic "Landing" in downtown Fort Wayne, including a painting of a 40-foot high bison by muralist Tim Parsley, to bring a vision of the American West.

The family at Carole's house in Piedmont, California, Christmas 2019.

EPILOGUE

Pat and I have now lived in Fort Wayne since 1957 — or some two-thirds of our lives. I began writing this memoir on events and incidents which have happened to me and my family personally. Along the way, we have certainly seen a great deal of change to the city of Fort Wayne since moving here 63 years ago.

Fort Wayne came out of World War II with an impressive list of manufacturing industries — International Harvester, General Electric, Central Soya, and many others in what were then known as the East End Industries. I have said many times that people going away to college from Fort Wayne walked with a swagger because the economy was so good and they planned to return to the city. As a result of the great economy, 30,000 new people moved to Fort Wayne in the 1950's and 60's, including our family, of course.

Because Fort Wayne is dependent on its manufacturing economy, the city has had a number of ups and down over these past six decades and each recession in the national economy hit us much harder. Unemployment was 12.7% in the 1970's, but by 1979 it was down to less than 5%. During the strong economy that followed, International Harvester unfortunately became involved in one of its perennial strikes. After the strike went on too long, Harvester opened a bidding war between Fort Wayne and Springfield, Ohio. Although Fort Wayne bid $30 million to try to keep the company, Harvester moved to Springfield, and Fort Wayne lost over 10,000 jobs. After that, things went from bad to worse during the recession of the early 80's, and the city lost 30,000 jobs in 3 years. In fact, Fort Wayne was hit so hard during this recession that the New York Times published a news story called "Death of a Northern City." Bumper stickers began to appear on cars: "Last to leave Fort Wayne — Turn out the Lights." Unemployment rose to 15%.

Still, this was not the worst tragedy to hit Fort Wayne. In my opinion, that ignominy belongs to Fred Zollner taking the Zollner Pistons to Detroit in 1956. Green Bay, a much smaller city than Fort Wayne, has a strong national face because of the Packers. Similarly, Indianapolis did not really shed its old moniker of "Indy-No-Place" until the Colts came to town. The Colts put Indianapolis on the national map and helped the city draw young talent, internet employment, and business conventions. If Fort Wayne had retained the Pistons, it too would have had a national reputation, and consequently would have had a far easier time attracting young people and businesses to stay or return to the city. Increasing the national profile of Fort Wayne was at the top of my mind as I pondered the trade-offs of bringing a CBA team to the city.

After Harvester left Fort Wayne in the early 1980's we got lucky — GM came to town! Once we learned that GM was interested in Fort Wayne, we did everything possible to turn the company's interest into reality. In addition to helping to turn around the economy, the arrival of GM did another crucial thing — it gave the City its confidence back.

Another turning point was the Flood of 1982 in which flood waters unlike any seen in recent history tore through the heart of the city displacing 9000 people from their homes and causing $56 million in damages. Heroic rescue efforts and massive sandbagging by volunteers of the city's rivers saved thousands of properties and brought out the best in Fort Wayne folks. Ronald Reagan, who was President at the time, even came to town to help pass sandbags!

After this, Fort Wayne became known as the City that Saved Itself — not only from the Flood of 1982, but from economic disaster. Fortune and the New York Times both did extensive articles, and the Los Angeles Times published a front page feature story about the tremendous job the city had done to survive the recession of the early 80's.

From 1984, employment in Fort Wayne grew significantly and, although we ran into another downturn in 1991, by 1999, unemployment was the lowest on record for all of northern Indiana until recent years. Manufacturing, of course, led the way and Northeast Indiana still has one of the highest percentages of manufacturing jobs in the country.

The return of the city's confidence began with GM's arrival, but branched out in many new directions. While manufacturing is still highly important to the city and the region, much has been done in recent years to diversify the economy so that it is not wholly dependent upon manufacturing. The expansion of healthcare, particularly Parkview Hospital, IU health, and St. Joseph's Hospital downtown, as well as Sweetwater Sound and other businesses have added to this diversification. Greater Fort Wayne, the successor to the Chamber of Commerce, has led visits to other cities and brought back many new ideas to improve the city's economy including the Downtown Development Trust, a brainchild of Chattanooga, Tennessee. The building of Parkview Field — even though the city had an existing ballpark at the Coliseum — triggered a renaissance in redevelopment of the downtown area including many new buildings, the completion of Promenade Park in 2019, and the rediscovery of our beautiful rivers.

The political leadership of Fort Wayne has also been very interesting during this period. After years of alternating between Democrat and Republican mayors, the Democrats have now held this office for six terms or 24 years, including two terms by Graham Richard, and four by Tom Henry, the current mayor. For much of this time, the City Council has been in Republican hands — proving that at the local level, national politics are often not very important.

The Old Guard of Fort Wayne business leadership — Ian Rolland, Dick Doermer, Paul Shaffer, Dick Inskeep and many others — have all unfortunately passed (all contemporaries of mine), but have been succeeded by Chuck Surack, Mike Packnett, John Sampson, Scott Glaze, and many other talented leaders.

Much housing is being built downtown and young people are starting to return to the city and, just like in the old days, we are getting our swagger back! Also, as in the past — first with the Canal, then the Railroads, and then Manufacturing — Fort Wayne is on the move again, with bold thinking, new directions, and a lot of confidence. In 2020, we are better funded, more diversified, and have strong leadership to thwart a recession. I am very hopeful that the terrible coronavirus pandemic which has struck this year will not derail the momentum we have in our fine city.

In writing this epilogue, I realize that this book — and indeed my life — began in Momentous Times, and will close in equally momentous times! I have every confidence that our bold leadership will successfully tackle the pandemic, that we will grow in new directions from the civil unrest, and our city will flourish for many decades to come.

Fort Wayne has a great history and has been the Right Place for us to settle, raise a family and have a career. We hope to survive the pandemic and be around for many more years to enjoy this wonderful community!

ABOUT THE AUTHOR

Maclyn "Mac" Parker

is a lawyer, foundation president and community volunteer in Fort Wayne, Indiana. He is currently Chairman of the Olive B. Cole Foundation, and serves on the board of other foundations. He was a practicing lawyer for over 50 years, most recently with Baker & Daniels LLP. He is a past President of the Allen County War Memorial Coliseum Board of Trustees and also served two terms as the Chairman of the Greater Fort Wayne Chamber of Commerce. Parker is a U.S. Navy Air veteran and served aboard carriers in the South Pacific. He is a graduate of DePauw University, the University of Michigan Law School, and attended the University of London and the University of California Law School. A life-long athlete, Parker's love of basketball prompted him to become an owner of the Fort Wayne Fury, a professional basketball team, which played in Fort Wayne for 10 years. Parker, and his wife, Pat, have 3 daughters, Pamela, Carole, and Kristi. He continues to reside, work, and be an active community volunteer in Ft Wayne.

Made in the USA
Monee, IL
13 January 2021